THE PRACTICE
OF THE VOWS

THE
PRACTICE
OF THE
VOWS

BY L. COLIN, C.S.S.R.

translated by Suzanne Rickman

HENRY REGNERY COMPANY

CHICAGO, 1955

FOURTH PRINTING,
SEPTEMBER, 1960

Nihil Obstat: Rt. Rev. Msgr. John A. McMahon,
Censor Deputatus.

Imprimatur: ✠ *Samuel Cardinal Stritch, D.D.,*
Archiepiscopus Chicagiensis.

26 November, 1954.

Nihil Obstat: Jacobus Bastible, S.T.D.
Censor Deputatus.

Imprimatur: ✠ *Cornelius,*
Episcopus Corcagiensis.

28 January, 1954.

Published in the United States by special arrangement with the Mercier Press, Cork, Ireland. All rights reserved. Manufactured in the United States of America. Library of Congress Catalog Card Number: 55-5993.

CONTENTS

PART I . . . *INTRODUCTION*

PART II . . . *POVERTY*

PART III . . . *CHASTITY*

CONTENTS—*Continued*

PART IV . . . *OBEDIENCE*

PART V . . . *PERSEVERANCE*

THE PRACTICE
OF THE VOWS

PART I

INTRODUCTION

Chapter I

THE RELIGIOUS STATE

THE RELIGIOUS STATE is one of the most brilliant manifestations of the life of the Trinity, one of the surest ways of imitating Jesus Christ and one of the most authentic and richest forms of Christian spirituality.

It is a stable way of life, in which the faithful, grouped under a rule approved by the Church, not content with keeping the Commandments, strive by the practice of the Evangelical Counsels of Poverty, Chastity and Obedience, to attain the ideal traced by the Saviour. "Be you therefore perfect as also your *Heavenly Father is Perfect."*

Devised by the sovereign Wisdom, from all eternity, proposed by the Master to His disciples, it is one of the exquisite fruits of the Redemption: a vigorous and immortal offshoot growing at the very foot of the Tree of the Cross, watered and nourished by the Blood of Jesus.

The religious state is not a human discovery. Considered, not in the multiplicity and variety of its accidental forms, but in its immutable substance, there can be no doubt as to its divine origin. The Saints, who, under the inspiration of the Holy Ghost, have raised through the centuries so many Orders and Congregations, have merely carried into effect, while defining and adapting it, the fundamental idea of our Lord, that they are the contractors of a work of which Christ was the architect. The Gospels, indeed, do not merely give us a few vague outlines of this way of life, but in definite terms,

1

reveal its essential and characteristic features, i.e., poverty, chastity and obedience. A young man questions Jesus: "Good Master, what good shall I do that I may have life everlasting? . . . But if thou wilt enter into life, keep the commandments—all these have I kept from my youth, what is yet wanting to me?—If thou wilt be perfect, go sell what thou hast and give to the poor, and thou shalt have treasure in heaven." So much for poverty.

Now for chastity. "For there are eunuchs,—who have made themselves eunuchs for the kingdom of heaven. He that can take, let him take it." For it is not granted to all to appreciate and carry out this ideal of purity. It is the privilege of an élite. Saint Paul echoes this teaching of the Master by proclaiming the eminent dignity of virginity. "Now concerning virgins, I have no commandment of the Lord; but I give counsel as having obtained mercy of the Lord, to be faithful."

As for obedience, is it not expressed in the words, "Come follow me"? To follow Jesus is to imitate Him, especially in His total, universal obedience. His whole life was an ecstasy of love in submission to His Father, a fiat of conformity with and surrender to the Divine Will. Obedience was the food of His soul and the quintessence of His whole religion.

A life of poverty, chastity and obedience; let us repeat that this is a nobler ideal, but an optional one offered by Our Lord Himself to generous souls, athirst for sanctity.

Christianity will always be considered a living paradox; folly to some, discouragement to others; while for we believers, it is profound truth and divine reality. And as the religious state is the extension and perfection of Christian life, so it too, takes on the aspect of a paradox; one must sacrifice one's soul in order to save it, one must lose all to gain all. Above all, here poverty becomes enrichment, abjection exaltation, virginity motherhood, servitude liberation, martyrdom bliss, and death life. "For you are dead, and your life is hid, with Christ, in God." With Christ I hang upon the

Cross, and yet I am alive; or rather not I, it is Christ that lives in me.

These contrasts are at first sight extravagant but in truth they are splendid and fruitful, giving to monastic holiness the appearance of a medallion of Christ embossed on the one side, engraved on the other, with this inscription, "Poverty, chastity and obedience."

A holocaust of love in honor of God, which becomes for the soul, a prodigious source of life, such are the obverse and reverse of the religious state.

~

What does the seeker hope to find in religion? Could it be—in addition to peace—the secret of an intensified apostolate, a higher perfection and the assurance of salvation? Excellent motives, doubtless, but tainted with spiritual egotism and somewhat lacking in breadth and disinterestedness. Through ignorance or faulty perspective, those things are placed in the foreground, which should be in the background. One's own personal interests are given first place, and the desire for God's glory comes second, and it would seem that one has entered the religious state for oneself first and foremost and for God only as an afterthought. This state of mind could to a certain degree be laid at the door of more than one contemporary writer, too anxious to extol the personal advantages of the religious state.

The old writers—ascetics and theologians—would appear to have grasped better than we, the deeper, and—to use a fashionable expression—"theocentric" meaning of the religious life. Straight away and, as it were, by instinct, they gave God His place—the first. If one leaves the world, it is indeed less for one's own pleasure and interests—sacred though they be—than for the honor of God.

In the prologue to his Rule, Saint Benedict calls the monastery a "school of the Lord's service" and the monk, a soldier enrolled under the flag of Christ, the King. "Service!"

Word pregnant with meaning. By vocation, the religious is a "servant." The servant of God, like Jesus come down on earth, has entered the monastery, not to be served, but to serve. To serve God, adore Him, bless Him, thank Him, pray to Him, such are the fundamental obligation and the essential object of the religious life. Whence comes the expression, so right and full of meaning, so rich in practical consequences, but in danger of becoming, for the world at least, nothing but a banal and empty formula: "To enter the service of God."

Dom Chautard, one day, recalled this truth to Clemenceau, whom he had approached on behalf of the Trappists: "You must realize Sir, that while we may be pioneers, farmworkers, and cheese-makers, we are first and foremost the worshipers of God. Our Abbeys are not what too often they are credited with being, societies for agricultural development or distilleries; an abbey is the 'Home of God.'"

The word "religious," moreover, clearly indicates this. "Those are called religious, who consecrate themselves entirely to the service of God."[1] This name "religious" is not a freak term or a simple catchword; it is a trademark, clearly expressing the nature and functions of him who bears it.

If every Christian, by reason of his baptism, is already in essence a religious being, he becomes so doubly and preeminently by his entry into religion. As the living personification of the virtue of religion—the first of all the moral virtues—the religious exists from God alone, and lives only for the worship of God. That is his *raison d'être* and the very basis of his vocation.

Now, in Catholicism, one act of worship contains and epitomizes the whole of religion, an act which gives supreme glory to the Trinity, and procures the redemption of humanity: the sacrifice of Jesus Christ. The Church, which was born on the Cross, continues to live on the Altar.

Is it surprising, then, to find sacrifice at the very heart of

[1] Saint Thomas Aquinas.

the religious state? What is a religious? A host. The religious life? A mystic Mass. The greatest service that one can render to God, the greatest honor that one can pay Him, is to follow Jesus' example, and immolate oneself to Him. Of all sacrifices—after the Mass and martyrdom—this is the most perfect, the most pleasing to God, the most fruitful for time and eternity. Indeed, we find in the religious state all the elements that constitute a sacrifice: oblation, consecration, immolation and consummation of a victim. The oblation is the prelude to the sacrifice. At Mass, the priest begins by offering on the paten and in the chalice, the bread and wine. And notice the respect and veneration that the Church displays, in anticipation, for what is soon to become the Body and Blood of Christ: she places it upon the altar, blesses and incenses it. As religious, we are first and foremost this oblation. At our profession, in a gesture of adoration and love, we gave ourselves to God wholly and for ever. In the Benedictine ceremonial, the novice says three times the forty-sixth verse of Psalm CXVIII. "Uphold me, O Lord, according to Thy Word and I shall live and let me not be confounded in my expectation." The gift of oneself is what the Lord expects and exacts of those who hope to enter officially into His service. The religious state is a holocaust, which consists in the first place, in the total gift of oneself to God.

Thus, at the outset of the religious life, and serving as its introduction and foundation, we find a magnanimous act of renouncement and generosity; the total and irrevocable offering of my personality, my being, my powers and my activity. Having received all things from the Creator, I return all things to Him. Definitely, I have surrendered to God the radical ownership of all that I am, and all that I have; I belong no longer to myself but to Him: Totus tuus sum! I have disappropriated myself of myself, to become, in the full force of the term—the inalienable property of God.

His are my body and soul, to be a host of expiation.

His are my spiritual and physical faculties; my intellect to

believe, adore, pray, and praise, my heart to love, my will
to serve; my senses and all the members of my body to become in chastity and through mortification "instruments of
justice unto God . . ."

There is also the offering of all internal or external activity,
physical, intellectual, moral and social; the devoted servant
works for his Master alone. As God owns the trees, so he
owns the fruits. Thoughts, desires, acts of the will, affections,
prayers, works, sufferings, occupations of every kind, even
repose, are so many acts of religion, for all that is done for
the honor of God and in His service belongs to religion.

All is given and sacrificed, so much so that the smallest
reserve would tend to be a sacrilegious theft. I am a religious
for always, as I am man; in everything and everywhere, I
act as a religious, in the same way that I act as man. What
an incomparable life, dedicated to the Trinity, even in its
most insignificant details, and full of the Glory of God! With
and like Jesus, the perfect religious can say at each instant
"I honor my Father." And at the hour of his death, summing
up his whole life, "Father I have glorified thee, on earth."

For God's sake, we have left all, relinquished all. Yet there
still remains the need—if this surrender is to be perfect—that
it should be irrevocable. When one enlists in the service of
God, it is not for a day, but forever, and without any afterthought of a possible withdrawal. One has given oneself,
lock, stock and barrel. In this way, and though it has not
the sacramental character—the religious state participates in
the everlasting fixity of the priesthood. Whoever enters into
religion binds himself to God by perpetual vows. It is our
belief that one can never insist too much upon this total gift
and absolute belonging to God, the Introit and Offertory of
all religious life. Dedicated to God, we no longer belong to
ourselves.

Who are the religious, who have fully performed this fundamental act? With the enthusiasm of youth one gave oneself to God, unreservedly and forever, at least so one said,

and in truth one was sincere. Was one deeply in earnest? That nun was so, who in the evening of the day she made her vows, went back to her cell and wrote in her blood: "Sister Margaret Mary dead to the world. All from God and nothing from me; all for God and nothing for me."

The offering and consecration are entire. This gift of self has a sacred and divine character which is not to be found— to the same degree at least—in other offerings. On waking, at his morning prayer or meditation, the Christian can raise his soul to God and offer Him, along with his heart, his works, his sufferings and his whole life. But this offering, though it be supernatural, has not the same weight as a religious profession. Here the offering is accompanied by a vow which it is a sacrilege to break. The gift becomes a consecration. "Religious profession is a sacred contract, because it is a contract by vow. Now the vow in its substance pertains to the supernatural and even to the divine right . . . I conclude that our contract in religion is of an order superior to all worldly contracts, and consequently, that its breaking constitutes a wrong, different in kind, and graver in quality than all other wrongs. I conclude that with regard to the observance of what we have vowed, we can no longer be unfaithful to Jesus Christ, without that infidelity partaking of the nature of a sacrilege. Why? Because in consequence of the vow, we are specially consecrated to Jesus Christ. This consequence is terrible and would lead me to quote to all those who are honored by bearing this mark of consecration, these words of Saint Augustine 'O faithful soul, remember that you are no longer your own, and that when I exhort you to fulfill the promises you have made to your God, I do it, not so much to invite you to the height of sanctity, as to preserve you from a frightful iniquity.' "[2]

"So it is for the religious. Whatever may be in other respects the form of his religious life, the spirit of his rule and the particular object of his institution, what ranks above all

[2] Bourdaloue. Sixth Sermon on the religious state.

else, what forms the foundation, and gives life to all else, is the fact that he is a religious, i.e., consecrated to God by an authentic act."[3] Does not the Roman Pontifical speak of the "benediction and consecration of virgins"?

After the offering of the bread and wine, the priest consecrates them "This is my Body—this is the Chalice of my Blood." Prodigious words which bring down upon the Altar Christ, the Victim.

"I vow Poverty, Chastity and Obedience." Is not this formula, too, an act of consecration? Such are the creative words which transform the Christian into the Religious, making of him a spiritual victim and a consecrated host.

By giving himself, the religious consecrates himself to the service of God: and God in His turn, ratifies and confirms the consecration to all eternity. It has been rightly said that profession is at once the work of man, and that of God.[4] Taking as it were into his hands this soul which offers itself to Him, God blesses it, and this blessing is more than a mere word; it is an act, a work of sanctification, a consecration. One might well reflect on the fine prayers of the Pontifical on the Benediction and Consecration of Virgins. "Do not wonder that whereas a simple priest can give you the religious habit, your profession, or at least, the imposition of the veil which is its public symbol, remains a pontifical act, i.e., one ordinarily reserved for the bishops. The bishop alone is the perfected priest: therefore, he alone can perform perfected works. The priest prepares: he baptizes, blesses; the bishop perfects; he confirms, ordains, and consecrates. You are, then, consecrated; and all in you is consecrated; your eyes, lips, ears, hands, feet, knees, your whole body; your mind, heart, will, powers, life, strength and time."[5]

And as a temple, an altar or a chalice, by virtue of its consecration, is exclusively reserved for divine worship, so the

---

[3] Mgr. Gay. Rel. Life and Vows.

[4] Dom Marmion. Christ the Ideal of the Monk.

[5] Mgr. Gay, *op. cit.*

religious consecrated to God now exists for Him alone, to adore Him, bless Him, pray to Him, love Him and serve Him. Doubtless, if one judges it by many external aspects, his life remains human; he eats, sleeps, rests, speaks, does manual labor, teaches, nurses the sick; but under all these appearances lies hidden—as Christ is hidden under the sacramental species,—a life which is profound and divine. A religious in all things, everywhere and always, lives religiously for the Father. "In Heaven, the continual occupation is the praise of God; so it is in religion, for all that is accomplished in this state pertains to the praise of God. You praise God when you do your work; you praise God when you take your food and drink; you praise God in your rest and sleep."[6]

But this complete "distraint" of God upon the consecrated soul necessarily implies the idea of separation. "Because Jesus is the great Consecrated, He is also the great Separated."[7] So it is with the Christian who enters religion: he becomes an exclusive property, a private domain, an enclosed garden to which the Godhead alone has right of access. The profession has caused a rift and opened a gulf between the soul and all that is not God or does not lead to God. Chosen out of many, withdrawn from the common herd, the religious must live apart, if not in actual solitude, at least in spiritual isolation, alone with Him who is Alone. So as to unite himself with the Creator, he has renounced the created.

The first renouncement that he must make is that of sin, and this must be total and definitive. By his vocation, the religious is an official candidate for sanctity. Now nothing so impedes the perfect union with God as sin, when it does not completely destroy it.

How could the consecrated soul, who is a living hymn of praise to the Trinity, dare to prove unfaithful, and to dishonor its Father, its Friend, its Heavenly Spouse, and ignominiously to outrage all His Infinite Perfections? and if it be

---

[6] Saint Alphonsus. The True Spouse.

[7] Mgr. Gay, *op. cit.*

true that the religious is a holocaust, has not God made it clear that He will accept only those sacrifices which are holy and unblemished?

This purity of conscience must be protected by withdrawal from the world which all about us "is seated in wickedness."[8] The habit, enclosure and grill are both the reality and the symbol of this separation; the religious, physically set apart, spiritually must be cut off even more.

He must live apart from the world, from its foolish pleasures, its pomps and vanities, its frivolity and its business; above all he must eschew its outlook, its desires and its morals. Nothing is more opposed to the religious spirit than the spirit of the world; that world which was anathematized by Jesus Christ because of its scandals. How fitting, then, is the expression used of those entering religion, "To leave the world." God has called me to the religious state, so that I may live separated from the world, crucified to the world, and absolutely dead to the world.

It would be unfair to attribute this courageous flight to a motive of egotism, or an attack of misanthropy. Those who renounce the world do not act from barrenness of heart, disgust for society, lack of energy in face of the hardships and struggles of life. They have been drawn to solitude, firstly, by a wish to safeguard themselves from the pernicious influences of their environment, secondly, by the desire to rise above themselves to climb towards the heights, to the conquest of God.

Moreover, they will return to this world which they have renounced, but cannot forget, because they have not the right to remain indifferent to the fate of those millions of men who are their brethren in Christ. The religious is not a parasite, but an apostle. He will return to the world in order to minister to all kinds of physical suffering and moral afflictions; he will return through prayer, sacrifice, exhortation and devotion; he will return like a torch advancing through

[8] I Epistle of Saint John V, 19.

the night to scatter the darkness; like salt penetrating the meat and saving it from corruption. Religious in every kind of habit, or without any habit, are to be found everywhere, dedicated to every kind of apostolate, creators and mainsprings of a countless multitude of works of charity; yet, while they mingle with the crowd, they are none the less apart. They live in the world, but are not of it.

The soul is offered and consecrated; it has still to be immolated, for there can be no holocaust without a victim. And is not this, the most austere and splendid aspect of the religious life, its very heart and center?

By his vocation, the religious is a sacrificial being, a host. "My daughters, why do you think God has brought you into the world, unless it is that you may be holocausts, lifelong oblations to His Divine Majesty and victims daily consumed in the flames of His sacred love."[9] On the eve of their profession, Saint Francis of Sales caused his spiritual daughters to meditate upon "The flaying of the victim."

The aim of the religious state is to make as faithful a reproduction as possible of Christ in His circumstances and His life. Now, just as Jesus was formed and developed from the very substance of Mary, from her flesh and blood, so in every religious soul must He be born and grow at the expense of the ego and by the sacrifice of self. The more we die to ourselves, the more Christ will live in us. "He must increase and I must decrease."

The Poor Clares of Bordeaux Talence had written above the gate of their convent "Here, we learn to die." In certain Orders, the ceremonial of profession prescribes that the pall be extended over the prostrated religious—an eloquent symbol of the death awaiting them. In the Benedictine ceremonial, profession is closely bound up with the sacrifice of the Mass, and the novice places on the altar, with his own hand, the text of his promises, as if to unite his own immolation with that of Christ. On All Saints' Day, Saint Gertrude

[9] Saint Francis of Sales.

saw the religious among the immense legion of martyrs.

But what is this immolation and in what does this spiritual death consist?

It must first be stated that the total oblation, absolute renunciation and universal surrender of our being into the Hands of God, already constitutes in itself a sort of destruction and annihilation. To belong to oneself no longer, in all things no longer to act of one's own volition, no longer to live for oneself, but solely for God; at every moment to be in a position to say "I am no longer of any account"—is not this a form of death? "A sacrifice . . . which from the day of profession to the last day of his life, strictly binds the religious to maintain himself perpetually in the state of a victim. Now, what is this state? Few understand it fully, and still fewer are willing to subject themselves to it and to embrace it in all its perfection. For to be a victim, I mean a victim of God, and to be one by profession, one must no longer belong to oneself, no longer dispose of oneself, have no longer any rights over oneself, and no longer aspire to such rights; one must be solely in the hands of God, depend entirely on God, act only according to the commands of God and His adorable Will, through whatever mouthpiece, and in whatever manner, He manifests them to us; one must be in a condition of death, and like a dead body allow oneself to be controlled and disposed of, as it pleases God and those superior powers to whom God has subjected us; and so that every day, we may say with the Apostle, and in the same spirit as he, 'For thy sake . . . we are put to death all day long. We are accounted sheep for the slaughter.'"

Does not this spiritual death consist in the destruction of one's own nature and the effort to kill the "old man," the man of sin, to raise over his corpse the new man, Christ Jesus? The flowering of the celestial man on the ruins of terrestrial man; such is the program of every religious life.

"Every day we must carry on this painful labor of self-demolition, which leads to that great and magnificent construction mentioned by Saint Paul, which we must raise to the skies."[10]

Another form of immolation is the rooting-up, by the faithful keeping of vows, of the three great human concupiscences. How could one practice poverty, chastity and obedience all one's life, with a scrupulousness amounting at times to heroism, without a great spirit of self-denial and sacrifice? The vows are the three nails which rivet us to the Cross. How true are the words of the Imitation: "Verily the life of a good monk is a cross."

The strict, scrupulous and preserving observance of the Rules and Constitutions too, with the practice of those passive virtues called humility, penance, mortification and silence, must also constitute a slow and painful agony. A religious life which is woven of a multitude of daily renunciations, can therefore equal and sometimes surpass, martyrdom.

Thus when he is confronted with a sacrifice, whatever may be its form or its source, the true religious never appears surprised, still less at a loss. Is not suffering his vocation and is he not a victim? However often he finds the cross on his way, even though it be undeserved and crushing, he embraces it with gratitude and love: "O bona Crux!" I am never so much a religious as when, following ever more closely in the tracks of Jesus Crucified, I become with Him and like Him a victim offered to the glory of God. "I found the religious life just what I expected and sacrifice was never a matter of surprise."[11]

Sacrifice, however, is unimaginable without love. Love is its beginning, its middle and its end, its crowning and its consummation. Actually, why should one sacrifice oneself except because one loves, because one wants to love still more, and because it is for the heart of a victim that God has the greatest regard? In olden days, a holocaust was destroyed by fire. The religious is a spiritual victim, and is consumed

[10] Pere Brisson, Founder of the Oblates of Saint Francis of Sales.
[11] Saint Thérèse of Lisieux, Autobiography.

by the flames of love. His offering and immolation only have power to glorify, sanctify and redeem, inasmuch as they are inspired and accompanied by charity. Self-sacrifice can be madness or wisdom, suicide or martyrdom, cowardice or heroism; all depends on the motive that inspires the act.

Christ "loved me, and delivered himself for me." Without Jesus' love for His Father and men, the Passion becomes an enigma or a scandal. Thanks to His love, all is explained and justified. Christ made the Sacrifice so that the world might be convinced of His great love for His Father.

The religious sacrifice, which is nothing but a response to the Saviour's, finds its source in charity. There is no greater proof of love than to yield up one's life. The religious gives this proof every day; he is a victim of love immolated on the altar of the heart. One leaves the world, and renounces all human affections with one sole aim, viz., to devote oneself forever, body and soul, to perfect charity. The religious life, considered either in its interior elements or its exterior activity, is, in fact, nothing but a work of profound and overflowing love. In Christian life, love is the great commandment and the fulfillment of the law; in the religious life it is so, to a far greater degree, for here it is the epitome of the rules, and the very object of the vows.

More than all else, the heart must enter the service of God, must be given, devoted and sacrificed "in an odor of sweetness" because the greatest glory, for the Most High, is but the radiance of charity. Who holds the heart of man, holds all, but who fails to own it, owns nothing.

"At last I have found my vocation, it is love!"[12] Is it not the vocation of every religious soul, called to a holiness of which charity is at once the essence, the measure and the crown?

The sacrifice must also be consummated by God, and this consummation can only be achieved through love. Man crushes the ear of wheat, and kills animals, so that he may

[12] Saint Thérèse of Lisieux.

consume them, nourish himself with bread and meat and
transform them into a superior existence, in his own life; so
the soul immolated by God and for God, in the sacrifice of
his profession, must be consumed by God, drawn into God,
united to God, and be, as it were, deified; a consummation
which can only be brought about by love and in love. After
all, the religious state is but "the perfection of charity in the
perfection of sacrifice." Nevertheless, this sacrifice will only
be perfect at the hour of death. In the life of the religious,
nothing greater can be imagined than his last breath. Lying
on his death bed, he attains his true stature. Many a time, at
meditation or at Mass, he has renewed his vows and his sacrifice. He renews them once more at these last moments, offering himself to God as a total, everlasting oblation, accepting
with complete resignation, in a spirit of piety for the glory of
God and the salvation of the world, the death which he is
facing, more than ever a victim of love, able to say in union
with Christ, his "Consummatum est. It is all over, my sacrifice is consummated."

Shortly before her death, a saintly nun, Mère Marie Thérèse, turning to the nun who watched by her, said "Oh! how
glad I am to be able to complete my sacrifice here."

~

Religion is the first duty of humanity towards its Creator,
but for man, it is also a source of individual and social benefits. The same rule applies to the religious state; God is glorified and the soul enriched. Mystic marriage, spiritual royalty
and priesthood—such are its wonderful prerogatives.

Tradition and the theologians are happy to give to the religious the title of "Spouse of Christ." Saint Paul does not
scruple to say to his disciples: "I have espoused you to one
husband that I may present you as a chaste virgin to Christ."

When rejecting all princely, even royal solicitations, the
Virgins of the first centuries simply used the pretext of con-
jugal fidelity. They were spouses of Christ, what more could

they desire? Was not that enough for their happiness and glory?

When Saint Agnes was urged to accept the hand of the son of the prefect of Rome, she replied: "You offer me a spouse? I have found a better one." How many illustrious virgins renounced royal marriages, in order to become the spouses of Jesus Christ. Joan Infanta of Portugal, refused the hand of Louis XI, King of France; Blessed Agnes of Prague, that of the Emperor Frederick II; Elizabeth, daughter and heiress of the King of Hungary, that of Henry, Archduke of Austria.

There is not a ceremonial of clothing or profession that does not allude to this mystic marriage, and it is symbolized by the ring worn by nuns. "I unite you to Jesus Christ, that He may keep you without spot. Receive then as His spouse the ring of fidelity, if you serve Him faithfully, you shall be crowned for eternity." It is a fact that in the religious state are to be found all the essential elements of Christian marriage, though on a higher plane—a sacred and indissoluble contract, which commits two persons to each other, body and soul, so that their mutual love, blossoming in a life they share, may be perpetuated by the creation of a family. From its origins, the religious state is divinely instituted and the taking of the vows, by its very nature, is an eminently holy action. In one respect, the bonds that bind the soul to Christ are more indissoluble than those which bind earthly spouses, for death, instead of sundering them, makes them eternal. In this way, the religious vocation partakes of the everlastingness of the priesthood. Like the priest, the spouse of Christ remains His spouse forever.

In a generous impulse of pure love, one has given oneself unreservedly to the Spouse, who, in turn has given Himself. "My beloved is mine and I am his." This mutual surrender leads not to carnal union, but to spiritual fusion and a kind of identification "for the contract of this holy marriage is truly spiritual, and I underestimate it, in calling it a con-

tract; it is a true embrace and, as it were, a mutual possession, since the constant unity of will makes the two souls
one."

Thenceforward, there exists between Christ and His Spouse
an intimacy of which the Christian home is but a shadowy
image. A life in which everything is shared: labors, joys, sufferings, prayers. The whole day long, the soul thinks of Jesus,
contemplates, adores and blesses Him, above all, loves Him,
telling Him over and over again, in a thousand different ways,
that He is her all, that she lives for Him alone. The Veronica
of His wounded Heart, she consoles Him for the slights and
insults of sinful humanity. Busy about the duties of her occupation and the observance of her rule, without letting them
distract her, like the bee to the flower, she ever returns to her
Beloved. He has become the faithful companion of her journey; she turns to Him in distress; seeks His aid in temptation,
leans on Him in time of danger. Her life has become a permanent and perfect union with the Spouse.

Again, her love will not be sterile, for the spouse looks
to motherhood. When she became the spouse of Christ, she
adopted his Family. All those souls redeemed by the Blood
of Jesus are her spiritual sons and daughters, and uniting
herself with the Redeemer, she collaborates in their salvation by her prayers, sacrifices, works, her devotedness and
her universal zeal, saying with Saint Paul: "My little children, of whom I am in labor again, until Christ be formed
in you!" This is an admirable motherhood which recalls that
of the Virgin-Mother. Are we not all familiar with the charming words said by Saint Thérèse of Lisieux to one of her
novices: "Is that the way one hurries when one has children
to feed and when one has to earn their bread?" To be the
spouse of Christ is a great honor, a great joy; a privileged
state that bears much fruit. But it calls for great purity, great
fidelity, great love and great devotedness. When Celine,
Saint Thérèse of Lisieux's sister and Monsieur Martin's fourth
daughter, told her father of her decision to enter Carmel, he

joyfully replied: "Come, let us go together before the Blessed Sacrament, and thank the Lord for the graces which He has granted our family, and for the honor he does me, in choosing His spouses from my household. Yes, God does me great honor in asking for my children. If I owned anything better, I should hasten to offer it to Him."

A second prerogative of the religious state, which is the logical consequence of the first, is its character of royalty. How many women, sharing the dignity of their Spouse, have been ennobled by this mystic marriage! The humblest lay sister becomes a princess, and before her rank, all human majesty is eclipsed, or, at the very least, must give way. She has indeed the splendor, the pre-eminence, the independence and the wealth of royalty.

She is the living symbol of that paramount virtue and one of the official ambassadresses of the Kingdom called religion. After the priest, there is none greater than the religious. If it be true that to serve God is to reign, sovereign indeed is a life consecrated exclusively to the service of the Most High.

She is a queen, by the sublimity of her sacrifice, the splendor of her virtues; these are the faultless gems of an immortal crown.

She is a queen by the radiance of her virginity, the grandeur of her poverty and the heroism of her obedience.

She is a queen, by the special place she has in the Church and the mystical Body of Christ, of which she is a chosen member. She has cast off herself and put on Jesus Christ, King of Kings and thus she reflects the dazzling effulgence of the Mind and Heart of Jesus.

She is a queen above all, by her absolute self-mastery. There are no slaves in the cloister, in spite of what is said; whereas they are to be found everywhere in the world, slaves of sin, of their passions, of human respect, of the freaks of fashion: and these are surely the most ignominious forms of slavery. The religious has been freed of these for good.

She has triumphed over sin, dominated her passions, and escaped from the world.

The last royal prerogative belonging to the religious state is that of wealth. To those who follow the path traced by the evangelical counsels, Jesus promises a hundredfold upon earth, and in addition, or rather as reward, eternal life.

The hundredfold is the initial favor of absolute purification. At profession, as at a second baptism, the religious recovers moral virginity and the innocence of a child. She becomes again "the new man, who according to God, is created in justice and holiness of truth."

The hundredfold includes all those countless precious graces of preservation, light, strength, purity, fervor, love and perseverance; graces of environment, encouragement, edification and apostolate. It is a holy land flowing with milk and honey, where joy and peace reign, "where life is purer, falls less frequent, the return to God more prompt, the path smoother, the bestowal of grace more abundant; where peace is deeper, death sweeter; where Purgatory is briefer and Heaven more glorious." Briefly, the religious vocation is a call from God to eminent sanctity and one of the surest signs of predestination.

This is doubtless the cause of the instinctive respect paid even by unbelievers to religious. Vaguely, they feel that here is a person set apart, a superior being, before whom it is right to bow and stand aside. Louis Veuillot wrote to his daughter, a nun, "I assure you that it is a happy and agreeable thought that one is the father of a nun; one is at once humbled and filled with pride. What a great lady this chit of a Lulu has become! What splendor! What majesty! She will be one of the special retinue of the Lamb—and at the same time, she is my daughter, and I have supplied a few of her immense and immortal adornments!"

The religious state is an imitation of, even a participation in, the priesthood itself. By his baptism and his incorporation with Jesus-Priest, every Christian already belongs to the sacerdotal tribe. "You are a chosen generation, a kingly priesthood, a holy nation, a purchased people." How much more so the religious, who, in union with Christ, has offered himself on the day of his profession, as a voluntary, loving and permanent victim to the glory of God, for the salvation of mankind. In its deepest significance, religious life is a spiritual holocaust and the consecrated soul is, like our Lord, at once the priest and the victim.

"The religious, by making profession, fulfills in his own person the role of sacrificer and priest; and this because he binds himself, dedicates himself, gives himself, in short, immolates and sacrifices himself. God is present at this sacrifice to approve it; the minister appointed by the Church attends, to accept it, the faithful take part to bear witness and confirm it; but the religious alone makes it, and none can make it for him."[13] And it is because he makes it of his own free will that his sacrifice assumes a unique character of truth, fecundity, sanctity, stability and permanence.

This is all the more so, because in this holocaust, the victim is no common one. "The religious himself, in the profession of his vows, fulfills the office of host and victim, for in his sacrifice, he offers nothing but himself, and all that is his. And in offering himself, he makes to God an offering which is most precious, most honorable and most universal."[14]

[13] Bourdaloue. De L'état religieux.
[14] Bourdaloue, *op. cit.*

Chapter II

VOCATION

THE RELIGIOUS STATE can be the portion only of an elite: that is to say, of chosen souls. A special vocation is required of those who aspire to walk this narrow and uphill path. One cannot become a religious, just by wanting.

We are now going to study the existence and nature of this vocation; its indications and the moral obligation to follow it.

~

In the etymological sense of the word, vocation means "call." The religious vocation, therefore, might be merely a call to leave the world, to enter a religious Order, and there to consecrate oneself for life to the service of God.

In fact this call, when it concerns the priesthood or the religious state, is twofold—a call of grace and a call of Authority; the latter being merely the official verification and, as it were, the authentic confirmation of the former. The first comes directly from God, the second from God's representatives. Together, they make up a true vocation in every sense of the term.

Considered under its ascetical and mystical aspect—for there is nearly always, in the history of a soul, a share of mystery—the vocation is the echo of a divine choice. From all eternity, God has determined a state of life for man created by Him; marriage, celibacy, ministry, or religion. It is the duty of each one to keep watch for the message.

The spiritual and physical world is composed of a countless number of beings, each of which has its nature, its place, its function and its end. The daisy blooms in the meadows,

21

the bluebell in the woods, and the edelweiss near the snowy summits of the mountains. One flower is grown for its beauty, another for its scent, yet another for its healing properties. In the sky we see an amazing variety of wonders; sun, planets, satellites, stars lying thick as dust. Heaven too, has its hierarchy rising from the Angels to the Seraphim, through the Thrones, Powers, Dominations and Cherubim.

Diversity within unity is found again in the Church. While all baptized souls have a common origin and an identical destiny, none the less, each has its own particular perfection, its special place and its part to play. Pilgrims of eternity, all are making their way to the Father's House, but not along the same road. Every Christian has his special vocation.

This vocation is the natural issue of the act of creation. When He drew us out of nothingness, God traced our life's progress in advance, and it is up to us to carry it out to the best of our ability. He is the Absolute Lord of our being, His is the right to use us, according to the designs of His Providence, for the glory of His Name.

How indeed, could man possibly be entitled to organize his existence to suit himself, according to the whims of his own will and the fantasy of his passions? The Creator has in no wise relinquished His sovereign rights, and He intends to govern His people, mildly, it is true, but none the less strongly, determining for each of His subjects his rank, his position and his work. For a Christian, perfect and loving conformity with the divine plans constitutes the fundamental law and the sole labor of his sanctification: to be where God wants him to be, and to do always what God wants him to do.

What will become of this newborn babe? Will he found another family? Will he become a religious, a priest? None knows, save God who has chosen; and of all possible choices, His is the best, inspired as it is by infinite knowledge, wisdom and goodness.

The vocation is the masterpiece of Providence. God knows His creature through and through, with its qualities and defects, its aspirations and leanings, its aptitudes and failings, and He knows to what use it can be put in the workshop of the world. He knows what we are, better than we do ourselves; He has weighed our physical, intellectual and moral assets, and measured our potentiality of output. The nobleman in the parable did not commit the same number of talents to each of his servants. Taking into account our worth and our ability, God, like a good captain, determines for each his occupation and his task.

This is both sensible and wise. If Providence has care of the sparrow, the lily of the field, and the hair of our heads, how can man, the child of Providence, be abandoned? With greater solicitude than that of a mother bending over the cradle of her babe, the Heavenly Father looks after us, our temporal and eternal destiny, our labors, sufferings and needs. Nothing escapes Him. Not content with showing us our destination and our road, He becomes the faithful companion of our pilgrimage; He is the sun that shines on us, the spring that refreshes us, the bread that nourishes, the arm on which we lean, the smile that cheers our hearts, the grace in a thousand different forms which preserves, forgives, purifies, sanctifies and, at the end, saves.

Happy the man who puts his trust in Providence, and follows its guidance blindly, lovingly, step by step, without evasion or encroachment. Our vocation is the invention of a love that is infinite and eternal. It is a free gift, above price, and comes directly from the heart of God.

However, in certain cases, this choice requires a necessary complement, i.e., the recognition and ratification of legitimate authority.

The religious life and the ministry constitute, in the Church, a public and official state of life, upon which none has the right to enter of his own volition, even though he be personally aware of his vocation. The Bishop and religious Superiors have both the right and the duty to examine candidates, to establish the validity of their aspirations, and finally, to grant or refuse admission. This explains the existence of seminaries, novitiates and scholasticates.

It must be repeated that in its origin the vocation is essentially a call from God, but in order to obviate dangerous illusions, selfish ambition and future scandals, this call needs to be verified and controlled. No enlistment in the army of the priesthood or religion is valid, unless it be countersigned by the commanding officers; none mounts the steps of the altar, nor crosses the threshold of the convent, save by official invitation.

~

No one can enter religion, unless he be called by God. Furthermore, in order to answer this call, he must hear it.

One mistake, on this essential point, can entail grave, sometimes irreparable results; a life that is out of joint, barren if not evil, an eternity that is jeopardized. "The perfection of Christian life is not to rush into a cloister, but to do the will of God; that is our food, according to Our Lord. 'My meat is to do the will of Him who sent me.'"

How can one discover, with certainty, what is this divine Will?

There is nothing simpler or more complicated, more luminous or more obscure, more painful or sweeter, more natural or more astounding than the birth of a vocation. Each one has its own history.

Some appear to have known their undeviating path from the earliest years, and thanks to an extraordinary concomitance of providential circumstances. At the age of six or seven, they were already saying, very seriously: "Mummy, I'm going to be a priest; Daddy, I'm going to be a nun." Their course is like a river flowing from its source to the ocean between flowery banks, through a broad plain, slowly and majestically, without encountering a single obstacle; like a beautiful length of silk or velvet, unrolling without a crease, with its varied and magnificent designs.

Others on the contrary, hesitate for a long time, feel their way, turn back, like travelers lost by night in a trackless moorland, seeking a signpost. At last, day dawns; suddenly the path appears, leading straight toward the sunlit horizon.

Again, a religious vocation may be revealed at the time of some trial, loss, frustration, set-back or illness. The flesh or the heart is bruised; the soul is freed from the futile preoccupations of earth, and suffering, the herald of God, has brought an imperative summons, "Come, follow me." How many, on the battlefield or in the prison camp, have found the way to the Seminary or the cloister! Disgusted with a mad or criminal world, the soul hastens to find a solitude, where it may devote itself exclusively to those things that are eternal.

Sometimes even, a miracle causes and accompanies the sudden birth of a vocation. Some lightning grace breaks a life in half, overwhelms a soul, wrenches it away from a life of profligacy, and finally, sets it towards a career of apostolate and sanctity. How many hardened sinners have become perfect religious and incomparable apostles, such as Père de Foucauld, to take but one example!

In any case, whatever may be its origin and its evolution, the vocation is too grave a matter to be taken lightly, and before coming to any decision, it is imperative that every precaution be taken against error.

It would be most imprudent to set out upon a road that might prove to be a blind alley, or peter out in a quagmire; to take upon oneself today, obligations which tomorrow will prove to be an intolerable burden.

It would appear that in the matter of early vocations insufficient discretion has been exercised, particularly at the present time. By a method of intensive recruitment, quantity may be insured, but rarely quality, and this is prejudical, both to the souls that have been misled, and to the Orders that are cluttered up with mediocre and worthless subjects. A sweet little face, a choir-boy's piety, the wishes of a Christian family, a transitory burst of enthusiasm, a "yes" extracted by pressure from a timid nature, obviously do not constitute sufficient signs of a call to the religious state. "Let Superiors beware of bringing adolescents into their Orders hastily, and in too great numbers, remaining for that very reason unsure of their vocation, and not knowing whether these postulants chose this life of eminent sanctity under the sole inspiration of the Holy Ghost."[1]

Parents, directors and recruiters are responsible only for discovering true vocations, cultivating them and bringing them to a successful issue, without ever presuming to invent them, still less, to impose them. In the long run, it is up to the candidate to convince himself personally of the reality of the divine call, and to respond with complete freedom; to this end, let him pray, ask advice and reflect.

It is rare for a vocation to prove sure from the very first. More often it is revealed to the soul slowly and progressively, like the rising sun. The plans of God are mysterious and in the choice of a state of life, error is always possible, if not frequent. Indeed so many diverse elements, of varying weight, can influence a decision, one way or another; thoughtless enthusiasm, human outlook, dangerous attractions, exaggerated fears, preconceived ideas, interested canvassing, diabolical illusions. In order to disperse the mist of this uncertainty, a rare combination of intellectual qualities and moral dispositions is required: common sense, judgment, prudence, a spirit of faith, honesty in the investigation, and, beforehand, a holy neutrality of mind as to what may be the will of God. It is evident that in the solution of a problem, at once so grave and so difficult, the intervention of grace must be sought and obtained by fervent and assiduous prayer.

If ever supernatural light would appear to be necessary, it is indeed in this case, when a temporal and eternal destiny is at stake. God alone knows thoroughly His own designs

[1] Brief of Pius X to the General of the Dominicans, 4th August, 1913.

upon a soul, and no one is in a better position than He to reveal it.

Prudence demands (and surely the choice of a state of life closely concerns the first of the cardinal virtues) that one should not trust exclusively one's own judgment, and that one should seek around one for additional light. Two guarantees are better than one. Furthermore, one should be careful only to apply to a learned, judicious, supernatural and disinterested adviser. To trust blindly to the first comer may well have disastrous consequences. Not everybody is equally well qualified to direct a soul on its way. There are priests, and pious ones at that, who are steeped in strange prejudices, primarily concerned with reinforcing Catholic Action, with intensifying the Apostolate of Good Works, with safeguarding the recruitment to the secular clergy, and who deliberately dissuade souls from entering religious Institutes, especially the contemplative Orders, which they find guilty of being no longer up-to-date.

Of all advisers, the surest, as a general rule, is the spiritual director. He knows the soul he directs thoroughly; sometimes he has personal experience of religious life; he is, moreover, perfectly disinterested; therefore, in settling this question, he has exceptional competence and authority. In following the decisions of the representative of God, the soul has every chance of not going astray.

In case of doubt, is it wise to take parental advice? As a rule, it seems "children must consult their parents on the state of life that they wish to choose—and they cannot be absolved of rashness, imprudence and want of respect toward their parents, if they presume to choose a state and way of life, without consulting their parents, who are normally more prudent than they are, being older, wiser and more experienced."[2]

But in these days, when so many Christians, no longer understand either the greatness of the religious state, or the

[2] Conference d'Angers.

obligation of responding to God's call, and oppose their children's vocations in every way, it might well be rash to have recourse, in making a decision, to judgments so obviously erroneous and biased. In this matter, how many parents are bad counselors! How many out of selfishness, have "killed their child!" St. Francis of Sales says: "Generally speaking, he must keep his vocation secret from everybody except his spiritual Father. It is especially necessary to keep the vocation secret from parents . . . God, says a grave author, Porrecta, when He calls one to a perfect life wishes one to forget one's father, saying: 'Audi, filia, et vide, et inclina aurem tuam et obliviscere populum tuum et domum patris tui.' By this, he adds, the Lord certainly admonishes us that he, who is called, ought by no means to allow the counsel of parents to intervene . . . Whence Saint Thomas absolutely advises those who are called to religion to abstain from deliberating on their vocation with their relatives. 'For the relatives of the flesh are, in the affair, not our friends, but our enemies, according to the word of Our Lord: A man's enemies are those of his household.' "

To sum up, one should confide in one's parents, only in so far as they can bring light and support.

Finally, there remains the psychological study of inclination, aptitude and intention. Whether natural or supernatural, inclination alone is not the infallible sign of a vocation. It would be wrong, however, to ignore it; in default of proof, it often provides valuable indications. It is an occurrence so common as not to be extraordinary for a soul, called by God, to feel for the religious life repugnance, aversion, even revolt. Might this not be caused by the instinctive reaction of nature to the idea of sacrifice, or the subtle suggestion of the Evil One? It is a simple temptation, which must be overcome.

More usually, a vague attraction or affinity is felt; a sort of pre-established harmony, causing a relaxing and unfolding of the soul at each contact with the religious life. While the agitation and tumult of the world jars and upsets, the peace of the cloister brings calm and delight. This symptom is often enough accompanied by supernatural inclination. At a First Communion, a mission, a retreat, a profession or an ordination, Our Lord's words to the rich young man have been heard deep in the heart. The invitation has been renewed again and again, gentle but insistent, and the soul, amazed at first, finally responds with gladness. Little by little, under the influence of grace, a deep and pious inclination toward the religious state is formed, along with the ardent desire to consecrate oneself to God therein. It is for the director to verify the origin, nature and validity of this attraction.

Without either under—or over—estimating the importance of inclination in the discovery of a vocation, the most vital factor is the study of the general dispositions,[3] that are requisite for one entering religion, and the special aptitudes demanded by different Institutes. Before setting out on the conquest of an ideal, it is surely wise to ask oneself if—considering one's spiritual strength—this ideal is not a mirage and its conquest a dream. Who would undertake to build a palace when he has barely the materials for a shack? Am I made for the religious state? Have I all the qualities I need, if I am to fulfill its obligations worthily? This is a question of the first importance. On the answer depends the direction of a whole life. St. Francis de Sales says, "For it is certain that when God calls a person to a vocation, He is obliged thereby, according to His Divine Providence, to supply him with all the aids necessary for the perfecting of himself in his vocation." The entry into the religious state demands, therefore, a certain fund of qualities and dispositions, the absence of which would be evident proof that there is no vocation. No one can form a serious judgment as to the ex-

[3] We do not mean here the conditions exacted by law for admission to the Novitiate and Profession, which are more the province of canonical vocation.

istence and quality of this fund, unless he knows at least in broad outline, the religious state, its spirit, its duties, its virtues and its demands.

To this general survey, must be added a closer knowledge of the Order, to which one is attracted. Each Order has its own Rule, its characteristic spirit, its apostolic works. It is the duty of the aspirant to ascertain whether he can adapt himself to the mold. Those are few and far between, whose natures are rich enough, and whose temperaments are supple enough, to adapt themselves successfully to every form of religious life, and to wear equally well the habit of a Capuchin or the cassock of a Jesuit, the veil of a Carmelite, or the coif of a Sister of Charity. An excellent foot soldier does not necessarily make a good cavalryman. The religious army, too, has its different weapons, which are in no way interchangeable; one must study them, then make the best choice in accordance with one's physical, intellectual and moral aptitudes.[4] Without being robust, is one's health good enough to stand up to the fatigues of the apostolate and the burden of austerities? A serious, chronic illness or incurable infirmities are incompatible with a life of regular observance, and prove indisputably, that there is no vocation.

"With your letter I received another. I do not know whether it is from a novice or a pupil. She tells me that she cannot partake of oil or vegetables, nor wear woolen garments, nor go to the Office at night, and she asks my advice about her vocation. I have answered her that since she cannot keep the Rule, it is a certain sign that she has no vocation for your monastery. I added that if she desired to be a religious, she would be in danger of losing her soul, and that the religious cannot receive her without committing a grievous fault. It is one thing when infirmity attacks a person that is already

---

[4] This twofold study of the religious state and the Order, begun in the world, is continued and completed during the novitiate and the period of the temporary vows; an experimental knowledge that nothing can equal or replace.

a professed religious, and another, when this occurs before a person has bound herself by vows."[5]

A number of Orders, dedicated to teaching, preaching, or social work, require of their subjects, for the success of their ministry and the fecundity of their apostolate, a certain degree of scientific and professional culture. A person who has very little hope, or none at all, of acquiring a minimum of intellectual equipment, must go and knock at another door. For it is clearly indicated that this particular door must remain closed to them. "Sometimes it has been put forward as justification for adopting a subject of limited intelligence that he is so pious! That is not enough, and one who had great experience of religious life has said of such 'The angel falls, the beast remains.' And remains forever."[6]

Another obstacle which should also bar the way to many a candidate, and against which superiors and directors are not sufficiently on their guard, is lack of sense and judgment. This is an irremediable defect, of itself able gravely to endanger personal sanctity, to give rise to a multitude of difficulties in the Community, and to render sterile, partially, if not totally, a whole life of apostolate. May God preserve the Congregations from these unbalanced minds!

Finally, before entering the service of Christ in one of His chosen bands, one must make a survey of the moral assets at one's disposal; temperament, character, virtues. Not that a candidate should be required to possess a degree of perfection that he can only attain later and progressively, but at least, he must give serious guarantees of fervor and perseverance.

Characters that are irresponsive, hypocritical, uncontrollable, unsociable; temperaments inclined to neurasthenia, flabby or sensual; wills that are spineless, capricious or stubborn; souls that are without ideals, material, eaten-up with egoism, that offer little hope of amendment, are, in general, unsuit-

[5] Saint Alphonsus. Ascetical works.
[6] Father Desens, in a report of the diocesan congress of Paris, 1910.

able for the religious life. Such are barren lands, from which it is vain to hope for a rich harvest. Above all, it is essential to repulse those who are known to have inherited vicious tendencies, particularly concerning chastity and temperance. These passions, which may be dormant in youth, have, later, sudden and terrible awakenings. Poverty, chastity, obedience, humility, self-denial, love of the Cross; these are virtues essential to the religious state. Shall I be able, with God's help, to practice them generously and with perseverance? If the sincere examination of one's aptitudes has led to a firm and favorable conclusion, there is excellent proof of a vocation. In case of doubt, there is no harm in making an experiment, and in letting the novitiate, with added light, provide the definite reply. On the other hand, it would be the height of imprudence to admit to the perpetual vows, those candidates whose vocation has for years been mediocre and unsure.

By its nature and object, the religious life is essentially supernatural; therefore, one should not enter it with an eye to human advantage, such as "solitude, quiet, freedom from the troubles caused by relatives, from strife and other disagreeable matters, and from the cares consequent on being obliged to think of one's lodging, food and clothing," but from higher and disinterested motives, such as the glory of God, love of Jesus Christ, one's personal sanctification, and zeal for souls. The religious state is not a sinecure, a disguise for a comfortable life, in which one may, without worry or danger, work out one's salvation. Are not the words of the Gospel, "If any man will come after me, let him deny himself, and take up his cross," addressed particularly to priests and religious?

Before departing to the convent, then, it is quite unnecessary to have recourse to "ten or a dozen doctors to see if the inspiration was good or bad, if it was to be followed or no." If there be established aptitudes, a right intention, a call from those authorized, and no moral or canonical impediment, the existence of a true vocation can be diagnosed with every assurance.

~

Once the vocation is recognized, it becomes a duty and a right to respond. The right is primordial; no entreaty or menace can prevail against it, for it is founded on the sovereignty of God, and on the liberty of every man to choose and make his own life.

If fidelity to the vocation were merely a right, it would be lawful to reject it, but it is, besides, a moral obligation of conscience. It is a duty of obedience to God, whose providential designs must be respected; a duty of charity to ourselves, for our gravest interests are at stake; a duty of zeal toward a multitude of souls, whose salvation depends, to a greater or lesser degree, on our correspondence with grace. To Our Lord's "Veni, sequere me," let us respond with a spontaneous, prompt and generous "Ecce ego."

God loves a cheerful giver, and to enter His service reluctantly would take from the beauty of the gesture and the value of the gift. Most perfect is the sacrifice which is accomplished with a smile on the lips and a lifting of the heart. If there is in life one action which should not be botched, but performed freely and generously, surely it is this initial action, which is the foundation of and prelude to the total and irrevocable oblation of the soul. Let us not wait to be pushed or dragged on this royal road; let our departure be a noble one. Let there be no regrets, no hesitation, above all, no retreat. The old proverb can well be quoted here "Do not put off till tomorrow what you can do today." Where can one be happier or safer, than where one is meant to be? Moreover, it is neither polite nor prudent to try God's patience and to play fast and loose with His grace. The ticket is bought, the luggage registered and the train in the station; why stay on the platform? Find out what is the first train to leave, and board it.

How many vocations have been endangered or lost through unwarranted delay! "The voice of God must be obeyed without delay. Thus, as soon as the Lord calls a person to a more perfect state, if he does not wish to jeopardize his eternal salvation, he must obey immediately. Otherwise, he will hear Jesus Christ address to him the same reproach that He made to the young man who, when invited by Our Lord to follow Him, asked His permission to go first and put his affairs in order and dispose of his goods. Jesus replied to him that 'no man putting his hand to the plow, and looking back is fit for the Kingdom of God.' "[7]

Do obstacles that are independent of the will, enforce some delay? Then precautions must be taken in order to safeguard the gift of God; one must keep away from the world and from occasions of sin, frequent the Sacraments, make constant use of prayer and meditation, and show perfect obedience to one's spiritual director. Sometimes, the struggle proves arduous and long; one must not take fright, but carry on valiantly, until one overcomes. There is the struggle with ourselves: instinctive repugnance, fear of responsibility, cowardice in face of sacrifice. There is the struggle with the devil; intent on leading souls astray. Lost vocations are counted among his most resounding victories. We must beware of his snares, illusions and obsessions. There is the struggle with the world: its revels may blind us, its pleasures draw us, and its loves makes us captive.

There may also be the struggle with our family; through egoism, ignorance, or lack of faith, they may oppose us with a violence that often amounts to open persecution. It is true that parents have the right of making sure that a vocation is valid; but once it is recognized as such, opposition by every means, fair or foul, would be a criminal abuse of authority, for which they must account at the judgment seat of Jesus Christ. God has greater rights over their children than they! More than one saint has suffered this terrible trial, and has

[7] Luke IX, 62. Saint Alphonsus, *op. cit.*

only triumphed over flesh and blood through prayer, meditation, and even flight. "Do not think that I came to send peace upon the earth; I came not to send peace, but a sword. For I came to set a man at variance against his father, and the daughter against her mother, and the daughter-in-law against her mother-in-law. And a man's enemies shall be they of his own household. He that loveth father or mother more than me, is not worthy of me, and he that loveth son or daughter more than me, is not worthy of me."[8]

Fidelity to one's vocation is, then, a duty; but what is exactly the moral quality of this obligation?

While it is not a commandment or a formal order, the call to the religious life is, at the very least, a gracious invitation and an urgent counsel. Consequently, there is, in itself, no grave sin in closing one's ears and hardening one's heart to the voice of God. We say "in itself" as a matter of principle; but in practice, wilful or motiveless resistance to this immense grace implies the greatest imprudence, which is capable of warping one's whole life, of gravely endangering one's salvation, and, for that very reason, is closely allied to mortal sin.

"In principle, the vocation to the religious state is primarily a matter of generosity. Yet, in practice, it would certainly be a sin to resist a divine command, formally and clearly manifested, for example, by a personal, certain, and indubitable revelation. It would be a grave sin if, while considering one's damnation assured by remaining in the world, because of one's weakness and the danger one runs, one were nevertheless to persist in refusing to enter the religious state to which one believes one is called. Every believer is obviously bound to take the necessary steps to insure his eternal salvation. How many people there may be, for whom a clearly-defined vocation and the well-founded fear of their own weakness in face of the dangers of the world, constitute an absolute duty to enter the religious life! In individual cases, however, it is difficult to establish this obligation with certainty.

[8] Matthew X, 34-37.

At least, the theologians agree in saying, that it is the height of imprudence to resist the divine call, and although the perfection which is the object of religious life, is outside the province of precept, they do not consider that those are innocent of mortal sin, who, while only too aware of their weakness and doubtful of working out their salvation in the world, yet have not the courage to flee from its dangers and tempests into the harbor of religion."[9]

[9] Père Choupin.

Chapter III

NOVITIATE

THE RELIGIOUS STATE is holy ground on which no one has the right to tread, and still less to dwell, unless he be provided with the appropriate permit or pass. Every candidate must appear before the authorities and agree to undergo a period of probation, which is the novitiate.

This is a wise institution, which allows the applicant to examine once again the validity of his vocation, to weigh beforehand the gravity of his future obligations, and to learn progressively his new life. On the other hand, the Order can study the candidate at leisure, form an estimate of his physical, intellectual and moral qualities, and thus make sure that he is suitable. After a year, candidates and superiors may—for the profession is a bilateral contract—bind themselves reciprocally, with full knowledge of the facts.

In order to insure that the novitiate is both serious and efficacious, the Church has carefully defined its nature and object, fixed its length, and specified the conditions of admission, without counting the special arrangements of different Congregations.[1]

It is not the province of this book, to mention and comment

[1] Here we give the main prescriptions of Canon Law:

(*a*) The obligation of a postulancy lasting for six months in all institutes of women in which there are perpetual vows, and in case of the lay members in institutes of men. In institutes with temporary vows the necessity and duration of the postulancy is regulated by the respective Constitutions.

(*b*) The conditions of admission concerning either the validity or licitness of the novitiate and profession:

  I. Conditions of validity: Admission to the novitiate is invalid in the case of: persons who have lapsed from the Catholic faith into a non-Catholic sect; persons who have not attained the required on the many decrees concerning the novitiate. It will suffice if we consider its ascetical aspect, and stress the important part it plays in the present formation and future perseverance of the young religious.

The program of this preparatory school for the service of God can be summed up as a schooling, often a trial, and an apprenticeship.

~

The novitiate is a house of studies, but these are not "literary, scientific or artistic"[2] but ascetical and moral. The candidate, first and finally, must satisfy himself as to the reality and soundness of his vocation. The fact that he has entered the religious state implies a certain desire for perfection, but not necessarily that he has actually received a call from God. He

---

age—viz: their fifteenth year; persons compelled to enter the religious organization by grave fear, or by deceit, or by force, or who are admitted by a superior thus constrained; married persons for the duration of the marriage; persons who are, or have been professed members of another religious organization; persons subject to penalty for grave crimes, of which they have been, or may be accused.

II. Conditions of licitness: The admission of the following is illicit, but valid: clerics in major orders whose admission is unknown to their Bishop, or is opposed by him . . . ; those who have debts to pay and cannot settle the obligations; persons who are under the obligation of giving an account (e.g., for positions of trust) or who are implicated in other secular affairs, which might involve the religious organization in lawsuits and other annoyances; children whose parents (i.e., father, mother, grandfather, grandmother) are in great want and in need of help from the children; and parents whose work is needed for the maintenance and education of their children.

(c) The time of the novitiate is to be spent in the novitiate house itself, for an entire and uninterrupted year, under the direction of a Master, specially appointed for the training of the novices.

c.f., Hoywood. A Practical Commentary on the Code of Canon Law, and Cotel.—Catechism of the vows.

[2] Canon 565.

must make sure that this is so, with the help of a spiritual director, by examining anew his interior dispositions, and by a more thorough study of the religious state. If he discovers that he has no vocation, then he must withdraw at once, for it would be more than imprudent to keep advancing along the wrong road.

Nowadays, when religious instruction, even in the best families, is often very unsatisfactory, most young men and women who leave the world have only a very confused and incomplete idea of the religious life. From the outset they must consider this new and higher life in its true light, and discover its ultimate object, that is, apart from all interested motives, the glorification of God through sanctity and the apostolate, and grasp its essential obligations, i.e., poverty, chastity and obedience. It is imperative also that they get to know the Institute of which they wish to be members; its aim, its Rule,[3] its spirit, its characteristic virtues and its works. It has been said that the most unprincipled act is to insist upon practicing a trade one does not know. The profession, which crowns the novitiate, is an act which is too holy in itself, too grave in its consequences, to be made lightly, without knowing exactly what one is doing, what one wants, what one is undertaking, forever. The provision of asceticism that a religious takes away on leaving the novitiate should not be too light, for it must last a lifetime for some.

Each must make his own ideal of the religious life; and this ideal must be neither blurred nor fanciful, because it is the clear vision of what one must be, and of what God demands; an ideal without which one is condemned almost infallibly to an incurable mediocrity, or even worse, to a lamentable downfall. The artist cannot create a masterpiece unless he has

[3] St. Benedict requires that before a novice be admitted to Profession, the Rule should be read to him on three occasions "that he may know unto what he cometh," and that it should be said to him "Behold the law, under which thou desirest to fight. If thou canst observe it, enter in, if thou canst not, freely depart." (Rule of St. Benedict, ch. LVIII).

borne it, luminous and splendid, in his head. In the moral order, the religious life is a masterpiece that none can produce, unless he first understands its essential beauty. Nihil volitum nisi praecognitum. On the other hand, the clearer the vision, the greater the perfection that is required. Might not this lack of an ideal be at the root of certain monastic careers which, without being bad, are none the less somewhat colorless and almost sterile? "I had never grasped what was meant by a life consecrated to God," is an admission that we have heard more than once from the lips of venerable nuns. A great soul is always a "child of the light." If one leaves the novitiate without an ideal, one is in great danger of suffering from this lack, or defect rather, all one's life.

If the novice gives himself to the Institute with his eyes wide open, the Institute will accept him as a member, only after a careful and satisfactory investigation. It is a matter of the greatest importance to the Order itself. More than ever before, it is vital that only those candidates should be accepted who are serious, if not excellent, steady, virtuous, and full of promise. What is the point of cluttering up a congregation with dead weights, insufferable characters and parasites? Nothing so compromises the vitality and good name of a religious society, nothing is more likely to cause a slackening of observance and to introduce a relaxing of discipline, than the indiscriminate admission to the vows, of all comers, however commonplace. Those in authority should never sacrifice quality to quantity. Saint Alphonsus preferred a handful of fervent and holy religious to a thousand tepid and undistinguished ones. The Rule he has given to the Congregation ordains a strict choice from among the postulants: "Youths who are self-willed, obstinate in maintaining their own views, tepid and lazy, who care little about spiritual progress and self-denial, shall always be sent away, as not only useless, but even harmful, and likely to cause great damage to the Congregation."[4]

4 Saint Alphonsus, Redemptorist Rule.

Either out of mistaken pity for delicate souls, who might be imperiled if they return to the world, or from an over-zealous desire to increase the numbers of the Order, and to come to the aid of numerous good works that are in jeopardy for lack of helpers, there would seem to be a tendency, now-adays, to admit too freely vocations that are doubtful and shaky. Pope Pius XI deemed it necessary to put religious superiors on their guard against this grave and widespread danger.

"This recommendation, for which we assume complete re-sponsibility, must be taken as fatherly advice, given with no other object than the good of all religious houses. And this advice is as follows: Be severe. These are hard words, it is true, but they are full of love; for truth alone can satisfy that true love which is worthy of the friends of our Lord. A cer-tain severity is not out of place when the discipline of the Order, religious communities, and different houses is con-cerned, because discipline preserves religious life; without it, the life may not be completely absent, but it is intermit-tent, weak and slack.

"By these words, it is not our intention only to allude to severity in general discipline, but particularly and above all, to the severity that should be shown when accepting postu-lants. If certain persons were to remark that there is already severity enough, we authorize you to say that it is the wish of the Pope, because in his position, and with his responsibili-ties, he can clearly see the need for it, all the more so, as Providence has granted him a long Pontificate, allowing him so to gain great experience in this matter.

"Indeed, if religious life is to be preserved in all its nobility, we must be severe, especially with regard to vocations, be-cause divine grace assists, but does not destroy human na-ture, and thus the need for effort persists in religious life, where more is at stake. Therefore, these disturbing factors that infiltrate a religious community and put it in danger must be removed, especially as these useless chattels can do it no good, and on the contrary are likely to be an obstacle, a stumbling block and a cause of depreciation.

"It is not exaggeration, but experience which tells us, that wherever there are groups of people, even small, defects become apparent inevitably. This does not mean that a religious community should reduce its numbers; on the contrary, it should always seek to increase them, but it must insure that they are picked souls, tried soldiers. This task may be difficult, but it is necessary. Indeed, when a number of mèn live together, good qualities, particularly the most noble, do not add up, for each keeps his own, while on the other hand, faults and failings are added one to the other, and mingle together."[5]

Might not the absence of this just severity concerning final admission of candidates be the cause of, or at least the opportunity for, certain scandals and too many lost vocations?

~

The religious state is a spiritual holocaust, and cannot be imagined without struggles and sacrifices. Trials begin in the novitiate; trials of every kind, which often threaten the vocation, just as they can also provide opportunities for practicing virtue and strengthening it. For suffering, whatever may be its source, whatever form it takes, has contrasted results; it brings light, or it blinds; it raises up or casts down; it sanctifies or corrupts. All depends on how it is welcomed.

The first trial, a common one, arises from religious life itself, and from its austerity. Obedience, humility, mortification, silence, recollection, and self-denial are virtues of which the novice has little experience, for many young folk, victims of the spirit of the age, have lived to a great extent as their fancy took them, without supervision or restraint, jealous of their independence, and fond of their comfort. Formerly, the education received in the family was thoroughly Christian

[5] Croix—18th June, 1938.

and virile, and was an excellent remote preparation for the privations of the cloister. Unfortunately, this discipline is becoming more and more rare. How many modern children are badly brought up, morally and physically spoiled. For these especially the sudden transition from the world to the convent is like an icy shower. It is not a transplantation but an uprooting; and in their bewilderment and dismay, they wonder if they will ever become used to such a chilly climate. From this, springs the temptation of discouragement and infidelity which is the reaction, more or less violent and lasting, of poor human nature, faced with a new life abounding in sacrifice.

If one must die daily to oneself in a slow agony, at least one has the right to hope for a consoling angel. And indeed, there is no lack of consolations, especially in the first years of religious life. Thabor sometimes precedes Calvary, and God has for these people called novices, the tenderness and indulgence of a father. None the less, it does happen that these sensible graces of fervor and joy come to a sudden end, and give way to spiritual darkness, aridity and interior desolation. The Rule, with its thousand and one regulations, silence and solitude, endless pious exercises, the monotony of a life free from high lights and events, can all combine to engender sadness and disgust for the vocation. One had dreamed of the courts of Heaven, and one wakes within the gates of a prison.

This can be explained by the fact, which so many are tempted to forget, that while the call of God to a greater state of perfection is an absolutely free gift, the response to this call, and the faithful correspondence with this grace, always entail effort and struggle. God wishes to know the measure of our generosity and disinterestedness in His service. One does not become a religious, to please oneself, but for the glory of God and the salvation of souls, to one's own cost. It is good to feel the weight of this fact while still a novice.

Difficulties also arise from a source that is quite unexpected

—from superiors. Although the fashioners of young religious are hand-picked, and in general, possess both the wisdom of a great teacher, and the kindness and devotion of a father, yet one does not always obtain from them light and encouragement. Antipathy, lack of understanding, incompatibility of character, difference of mentality, and want of mutual trust are quite enough to put a novice in a very difficult and painful position. To this must be added the fact, that those in authority have not only the right, but the duty to see that their charges acquire solid virtues, and to try out their powers of resistance. What would be the value of a novitiate without real sacrifice?

Some, after what amounts to an heroic separation from the world, take away with them the insidious memory of a heart-broken or angry family. They have bravely set their hands to the plow, and then begin to look behind them, forgetting that Our Lord said, "Let the dead bury their dead." The thought becomes an obsession and a source of agitation, regrets and temptation.

Others again fear that their health will be affected by the rigors of religious observances. It is true that it is rare for a twenty-year-old to echo Saint Paul, "I desire to be dissolved and to be with Christ." For these, Saint Alphonsus suggests the following reflections, "I have not concealed and do not conceal the state of my health from my Superiors; they have accepted me, they do not dismiss me; it is then, God's good pleasure that I should continue to stay; if it be God's will, although I should suffer and die, what does it matter? How many anchorites have gone to suffer in caverns and forests! How many martyrs have given their lives for Jesus Christ! If it be His will that I should lose health and life for love of Him, enough; I am satisfied. Such should be the language of the fervent novice, who wishes to become a Saint."

A convert joined the Trappists at the age of fifty. He was soon exhausted by the austerity of the Rule, but still refused to leave: "Here I am, and here I stay!" he said, gaily. After ten months in the novitiate, he made his vows on his death-bed, and died. There are not many with his courage.

But of all temptations, the most terrible are those that wear the mask of devotion and the disguise of a greater good. So travestied, their power of seduction is increased. These are truly diabolical temptations, for Satan has every interest in snatching a soul from the cloister, and a lost vocation is one of his greatest triumphs.

The first temptation of this kind is usually the doubt about vocation, which the devil puts into the mind of the novice, telling him: "But who knows whether your vocation has been true or only a caprice? Now, if you are not truly called by God, you will not have grace to persevere, and it may come to pass that after making the vows, you will be sorry and be-come an apostate, so that, whilst you would have saved your-self in the world, here you will damn yourself."

In order to repel this temptation, it suffices to recall the sure signs of a vocation: "A vocation is well founded, when it combines these three conditions: firstly, that one has a right intention, such as to flee the dangers of the world, to increase the hope of one's salvation and to attach oneself more closely to God; secondly, that there is no positive impediment; third-ly, that one is accepted by the Superiors. While these three conditions exist, a novice can have no doubt as to the validity of his vocation."[6]

One last temptation consists in the thought that in the world, free from restrictions, one will be able to give full rein to the surges of one's fervor, and to all the free movements of one's zeal, and thereby sanctify oneself more easily and make one's apostolate more fruitful. This is mere illusion; for it is obvious that the religious state, sheltered from the dan-gers of the world, rich in every kind of grace, is the safest, easiest and shortest road to sanctity. Again it is obvious that

[6] Saint Alphonsus.

a religious life, entirely dedicated, as it should be, to the extension of God's kingdom and the salvation of the world, cannot be other than fruitful, even when that life is strictly contemplative. Pope Pius XI, in a brief, addressed to the Carthusians, recalled that the Orders exclusively dedicated to prayer and penance do far more for the Church and for souls, than the active Congregations.

If the novice would conquer these temptations, with profit to his own soul, and would strengthen his vocation, let him again follow the advice of Saint Alphonsus, and arm himself with one weapon, prayer; draw upon one source of strength —frankness.

Perseverance is a grace that is distinct from the vocation, and which must be earned by prayer. In these dark and troubled hours, it is useless to argue and reason. The best is to fall on one's knees and cry, "My God! I have given myself to Thee, I will not abandon Thee. Permit me, not to be unfaithful to Thee." And repeating this the oftener as the temptation increases, and discovering it at the same time to his Superiors, he will certainly triumph over it. And Saint Alphonsus adds, "In this trial, let him also recommend himself in a special manner to most holy Mary, who is the Mother of perseverance."

"The second remedy, and a principal and necessary one, in such temptations, is to communicate to the Superiors, or to the Spiritual Father of the community, the temptation which affects you, and this at once, before the temptation becomes strong. Saint Philip Neri said that a temptation unmasked is half conquered. On the other hand, there is no greater danger, in these cases, than to hide one's temptations from one's superiors, for then God withdraws His light, because of the lack of fidelity one proves in refusing to be open about one's spiritual sickness; and again the temptation gains in strength, until the source of harm is exposed. It is, therefore, beyond all possible doubt that he who suffers temptations against his vocation and keeps them to himself, cannot fail to lose his vocation."[7]

To look upon the novitiate as nothing but a time of study and trial is, in fact, only to see its secondary and negative side, for it is principally, and in essence, a labor of moral and religious formation, a school of apprenticeship. Before settling down in a higher state of life, with many grave obligations, it is prudent to give it an honest trial.

No one can be unaware that this formation needs to be complete and strong. The novitiate is the immediate preparation for the profession, and the preface to a whole life. The religious profession is an act of major importance which sets a soul irrevocably on the road to the heights of perfection and, of its very nature, it cannot be improvised. One complete year is the minimum period strictly ordained by the Church. The novitiate foreshadows the profession, more often than not, the whole life.

If the profession is intrinsically a sacrifice, the host must be pure, holy and immaculate, worthy in all respects of the majesty of the Most High. If one's novitiate is botched, empty of fervor and generosity, what sort of a religious is one likely to be on the day of one's profession, and later?

A child tainted by hereditary disease, if he does not die of it, will usually remain sickly and delicate. A religious is born on the day of his profession. Is he born deformed, rickety? Then all his life he may suffer from this defect. How many commonplace lives, sterile apostolates, and lamentable fallings-off have been caused, by want of early formation. In both the natural and supernatural orders, it is vitally important to be born with a strong and healthy constitution, offering a guarantee of health and long life. The novitiate is seed-time, and it is well known that one reaps what one has sowed. Later is often too late. Happy the soul who sets off to a flying start.

[7] Saint Alphonsus.

This is all the more important as in many active Congregations, of nuns especially, the formation of their members comes to an end, in practice, with the ceremony of profession.[8] These young nuns are plunged immediately into teaching or works of charity, left to themselves, without control or direction, for the local Superiors have no time, and sometimes no ability to attend to them; and for the most part, they are forced to live upon the modest capital of goodwill, principles and habits, they acquired in the novitiate. On the education of these young religious depend also to a great degree, the maintenance of fervor and strict observance in the Institute. Generations of religious that have been badly or half formed must have a baneful influence on the whole society, and cause weakening, if not a general falling off. For this very cogent reason, the office of Master or Mistress of Novices, which is a most difficult and important one, should be entrusted only to outstanding religious. According to the prescriptions of Canon Law, "The formation of novices shall be entrusted to a Master, who shall be at least thirty-five years old, have been professed for at least ten years (dating from the first profession), and conspicuous for his prudence, charity, piety and religious observance."[9] And the Master of Novices must remember that he is obliged in conscience "to take every care that his novices are thoroughly formed in religious discipline."[10] This formation must not be only exterior, on the surface, but primarily interior and in depth. Its essential elements are again defined by Canon Law: "The year of novitiate, under the guidance of the Master of Novices, is intended to form the character of the novice, by the study of the Rule and Constitutions, by pious meditations and assiduous prayer, by instruction in all matters pertaining to the vows, and the

---

[8] Certain Orders arrange for a sort of second novitiate, lasting for three or six months, before the final vows. It would be a good thing if this practice were made general.

[9] Canon 559.

[10] Canon 562.

cultivation of virtue, and by pious exercises conducive to the complete eradication of faulty habits, the control of the passions, and the acquisition of virtues."[11]

To sum up: the novice receives a twofold formation—a general formation in asceticism, and a formation that is specifically religious.

As faith is the foundation and root of all justification, solid convictions must be acquired, for without these, one builds on the shifting sand, with great risk of collapse.

On these foundations of enlightenment is built an exquisite purity of conscience. "You know that the foundations of all must be a good conscience; you ought to make every effort to free yourself even from venial sin and to do what is most perfect."[12] Saint Alphonsus would have superiors constantly impress on young religious, "the holy fear of God, through a great hatred of sin, rooted in divine love, and by a continual effort to cleanse the soul from its stains, through a spirit of contrition, and a diligent use of the Sacrament of Penance." The novice must strive "to conceive a horror for sin and to avoid, not only all sin, whether mortal or venial, but every fault and imperfection, even the least."[13] But this moral spotlessness can only be acquired progressively, by a generous daily struggle against egoism, and the thousand little passions of pride, self-will, sensuality, defects of character and temperament. It is impossible to lay too much stress on this fundamental element of the spiritual life. A field cannot be sown, until it has been plowed, harrowed and freed from weeds. The novitiate is also a laboratory of virtues. Every novice, guided and encouraged by the Master, must fashion for himself a strong and generous will, and acquire, little by little, humility, mortification, recollection, a spirit of prayer and meditation, and above all, an ardent charity, which is the beginning, middle and end of all sanctity.

[11] Canon 565.
[12] Saint Teresa. The Way of Perfection.
[13] Redemptorist Rule.

This Christian formation is none the less only a necessary prelude to the religious life. With his ideal always before him and becoming clearer every day, with an unshakable determination to sanctify himself, the novice will straightway set to work, and start on the imposing edifice, which will be completed by death alone—scrupulous observance of the Rule and Constitutions, the most careful practice of his future vows of poverty, chastity and obedience, the acquisition of the characteristic virtues and spirit of his Congregation.

If he has given every satisfaction, and if he offers serious guarantees of fervor and perseverance, the candidate is admitted to temporary profession, and, after three years, to the perpetual vows. If the suitability of a novice is in doubt, the novitiate can be prolonged for six months, and the first vows, for three years. After this lapse of time, the religious must make his vows or return to secular life. But—let us repeat it once more—the Superiors must take care to reject, not only candidates who are unfit, but also the mediocre and useless.

Chapter IV

PROFESSION

EVERY HUMAN LIFE is composed of a fine dust of actions, most of them apparently insignificant and forgotten as soon as completed, like a soap bubble that holds its rainbow hues for an instant, and vanishes. But out of this mass emerge, like a chain of mountains in a desert, certain outstanding actions, which form the backbone of our lives, and which we remember till we die.

One of these events is religious profession, "the most heroic and important action of a life." Prepared by a year of novitiate, the first are temporary, so that both the candidate and the Institute may have time to get to know each other better, and be in full possession of all the facts. The profession is defined as "a mutual contract made between the religious and the Order or Congregation, by which the religious gives himself to God and to the Order or Congregation, by making the three substantial vows of poverty, chastity and obedience, under a Superior, who accepts this donation in the name of God, the Church and the Order."[1] It is the official and irrevocable reply of a soul to the call of God. Faithful to his vocation, this man leaves the world to take root forever in the religious state, in the service of God and of souls. Profession is, in some sort, a second baptism. As baptism makes a Christian the child of the Heavenly Father and a member of the Church, so profession makes a religious the servant of God, and incorporates him permanently in His Order.

This action has immense weight, whether it is considered in itself, or in its consequences, immediate or remote, temporal or eternal. From the profession derives a whole series

[1] Père Choupin.

51

of duties to God and the Congregation, and these must now be discussed.

~

In the life of Saint Joan of Arc, we read these admirable words, which are a real summons to heroism and martyrdom: "Go, daughter of God, go!" God repeats these words daily to the soul of a religious: "Go, daughter of God, go!" Indeed, a religious is bound by his profession to a high state of perfection. Christian life itself is of its nature an uninterrupted development from the baptismal innocence. The idea was familiar to Saint Paul. "Not as though I had already attained, or were already perfect, but I follow after, if I may by any means apprehend, wherein I am also apprehended by Christ Jesus. Brethren, I do not count myself to have apprehended. But one thing I do: forgetting the things that are behind, and stretching forth myself to those that are before, I press toward the mark, to the prize of the supernal vocation of God in Christ Jesus."[2] How much more, then, should the religious life mean progress and ascension toward God! "I am going to be a saint," was Saint Gerard Majella's farewell to the world he was leaving. In the private notebook of Saint Bernadette, after she became a nun, we read "I must become a great saint; my Jesus wills it."

With regard to this, a distinction has rightly been made between two types of sanctity: that of "state," and that of "action." Where a religious is concerned, the first consists in the consecration of his life and person to the service of God; a consecration that took effect on the day of his profession. Like the altar or a ciborium, he is, by destination and function, in a state of sanctity. But he must above all be a saint in the sphere of action, i.e., by his personal effort. Sanctity is a profound interior life. It is the duty of each one to act, to grow, to acquire moral strength and virility, and to attain progressively to the plenitude of the spiritual life. We shall now

[2] Epistle to Philippians III, 12-14.

set out the obligation, analyze the nature, and recall the qualities of this striving toward perfection.

A Greek philosopher held that life was naught but a pursuit, and when it is a question of the religious life, a pursuit of moral perfection. The entry into the religious state implies the sacred obligation, not of being a saint, but of striving to become one. The profession exacts, not sanctity acquired, but sanctity ever in process of realization. The result may not be brilliant, but at least, the generous and constant effort will remain. This striving toward perfection is so much an essential of the religious state, that it constitutes its central element, its sine qua non. Without it there remains of course, the habit, outward regularity, apostolic activity; a mere façade masking a ruin. None can live as a religious unless he strives to sanctify himself. In the opinion of the Church, all religious, by their vocation, are aspirants toward evangelical perfection. The ideal was set by Jesus Christ Himself before the young man who came to question Him. "If thou wilt be perfect, go, sell what thou hast and give to the poor, and thou shalt have treasure in heaven; and come, follow me." The only reason for embracing poverty and following the Master, is that one may scale the heights and make of one's life an endless progress in light, purity, strength and charity. Besides, did not the religious make profession of the evangelical counsels, with the aim of perfecting himself? The vows in themselves are not an end, but a means; powerful weapons to be used for the conquest of sanctity; steps to be climbed for a quicker and higher ascension. Doctors, theologians and ascetics, all those who have dealt with the religious state, have insisted most opportunely on this fundamental aim. "The religious state has been instituted, so that it may lead souls to perfection."[3] "The religious state is a stable form of communal life, approved by the Church, which, thanks to the vows of poverty, chastity and obedience, leads the soul to the perfection of divine charity."[4]

[3] Saint Thomas.
[4] Saint Alphonsus.

Thus the religious life is the working out of the program laid down by Saint Paul: "As therefore you have received Jesus Christ the Lord, walk ye in him," in His knowledge and love, in an ever closer union with Him. "That you may walk worthy of God, in all things pleasing; being fruitful in every good work and increasing in the knowledge of God."[5]

The religious state is to the Christian soul as the yeast to the dough, a raising and improving element. And as the yeast permeates the whole mass and prepares it for becoming good bread, so the religious spirit leavens the whole life and turns it into a work of sanctity. This is the great and powerful idea, charged with fruitfulness, which must be laid at the foundations of the novitiate, like the toothing-stone of the building in construction. The great oak comes from the tiny acorn which contains it; so a magnificent life can rise from one word-sanctity. On the first page of the Rules and Constitutions is stated the essential and twofold aim of the religious life, i.e., personal sanctification and apostolate, in all its various forms and innumerable works. The whole legislation of the Institute down to its smallest details, has been devised and issued for the purpose of furthering this end, everything must contribute, directly or indirectly, to the fulfillment of this program.

Should this cornerstone, the striving after perfection, happen to give way, all the rest crumbles, or at least, totters. To what can the decadence of religious Orders be ascribed, if not to the weakening of this pursuit? As long as a Congregation produces saints, as long as its members, as a whole, work generously for their moral perfecting, all is well. But as soon as they relax their effort and quit the uphill path, a laxity sets in, which may lead to the most dire catastrophe. In spite of deceptive appearances of prosperity, the life of the Order and its individual members is stricken at its very core. It is like a tree whose roots are rotting or gnawed by worms; there is nothing more dangerous. "As there are countless numbers of Christians who are not truly Christian, so it can be said that

[5] Epistle to Coloss. I, 10.

there are many religious who are not truly religious. What do these Christians lack, to be real Christians? The spirit of Christ. And what do many religious lack? The religious spirit. And what is this religious spirit? It is a sincere esteem for one's vocation, and an habitual interior disposition to attain that state of perfection, to which one feels that one is called as a religious; in such a way, that this religious perfection, which one knows to be the will of God, becomes the immediate end of all our intentions, all our affections, and all our actions."[6]

This explains why all founders, anxious to safeguard the vitality and continuance of their foundation, never cease to remind their members of this great duty of their sanctification.

Nowadays, when feverish agitation so easily takes the place of ordered and fruitful action, it is well to point out once again, a danger that is both serious and widespread and which threatens more particularly the active Orders; that of unrestrained zeal to the prejudice of the religious spirit. Sanctity and apostolate: these are the two essential aims of the religious state, complementary, but not equal. A religious is a religious first, an apostle next. To concentrate mainly on what is only second in importance, to sacrifice the Work of one's sanctification, to the works of one's apostolate is to commit a major error, which might well jeopardize one's personal sanctity and at the same time cancel a whole life of devoted service. Let us consider the words of the Gospel: "These things you ought to have done, and not to leave those undone."

~

It is perhaps the moment to define the meaning and scope of the formula "to aim at sanctity." Without implying an established state of sanctity, nor a privilege of impeccability, on analysis, the striving for perfection is found to contain a fourfold element, i.e., a desire resulting in a resolution, the

[6] Bourdaloue—Of the religious state.

use of the means of sanctification, accompanied by certain progress. A true religious is one who desires and wills to sanctify himself, who takes the means and progressively succeeds.

First then, comes the desire, which is an essential condition for both effort and success. This desire is to the higher life what the rising sap is to the tree. Fundamentally, what is the religious state, but a great yearning toward an ideal of purity and charity? Candidates for sanctity, those who belong to the race of the seekers of God, alone have the right to enter religion. "Blessed are they that hunger and thirst after justice." The religious is one of these. Never satisfied, always spurred on by fear of sinking into a slough of mediocrity, he is forever asking himself, "What must I do to become a saint?" This desire is the little grain of wheat, cast into the furrow, which germinates, puts forth its green blade and pierces the surface of the earth, because it wants to raise its stem and be transformed into the golden ear.

If the desire is serious, it will naturally be transformed into a resolution; the irrevocable decision of the will which has made a definite choice, never to be rescinded. "I want to sanctify myself, and, with God's help, I will sanctify myself." When his sister, a nun, asked Saint Thomas Aquinas "Brother, what shall I do to become a saint?" he replied laconically "Velle!" Saint Margaret Mary made a similar remark some centuries later: "To become a saint, a fervent 'I want to be one' suffices." Indeed, the whole perfection of a religious life is epitomized in this unalterable, absolute "Yes," with which a soul surrenders to God without reserve, and forever. Unfortunately, many lack, not the grace, which is always within the reach of generous souls, but a firm will. If only all had the courage to say, with a young convert, who became a Trappist: "I have committed every crime, with very few exceptions; at twenty-five, I was already old in sin. Well, through the mercy of God, I will become a saint, a great saint." And he kept his word. But sanctity, with its retinue of renunciations and its prospect of endless acts of self-denial appalls, and too many are content to repeat, until the day of their death "I wish I were," and never say "I will be." This general resolution, made on the day of Profession, must be renewed every day, and become the normal conclusion of every meditation.

Resolution, in turn, leads to action. Where there's a will, there's a way. "It is necessary to have the firm and constant will to employ all the means, by which one may perfect oneself in the vocation to which one has been called." What are these means? There are general and universal ones; the practice of the commandments of God and the Church, frequent recourse to the sacraments, the spirit of prayer and meditation, the accomplishment of the duties of one's state. But what may suffice to foster a Christian life is not enough for a religious, called to a higher sanctity. He must draw upon deeper springs to which he alone has access: the vows, the Rule: "Those who enter the religious state are not bound to use all the existing methods of attaining perfection, but only those that are indicated and imposed by the Rule he has accepted." The legislation of an Order is for the religious the quintessence of the Gospel, and, on the whole, of all his duties, and the great means of his sanctification. No one can keep it scrupulously, faithfully and lovingly, without making immense progress on the road of perfection, and without proving the truth of the words: "But the path of the just is a shining light, goeth forth and increaseth even to perfect day."[7]

~

If the resolution to become a saint makes a religious, only perfect resolution characterizes the perfect religious. For in this matter, as elsewhere, there is a complete scale of moral values. What a difference there can be between two religious, living side by side! They have the same habit, the same rule, the same exercises, the same apostolate: but they are not identical souls. On the road of perfection one may crawl, walk,

[7] Prov. IV, 18.

run or fly. In any case, the essential is safe, since there are effort and progress.

One must not adopt a go-slow policy, and be too ready to trim one's ideal to a span of mediocrity. If, in the world, writers, artists and even simple artisans have respect for work well done and aim at making a masterpiece; if the peasant claims to know his job and takes a pride in the plowing of his field, it would seem strange, not to say scandalous, that in religion one should lightheartedly content oneself with the commonplace and the attitude that "anything is good enough." A tepid life, without great faults or virtues, flat and empty, though not vicious, is none the less blameworthy and a failure. "In the religious state, an ordinary sanctity is not enough; we must have a sanctity that is irreproachable, a sanctity that is proof against all censure, a sanctity in which the critical world can find no spot."[8]

"We must be reasonable!" oh yes! but not too reasonable. After making three attempts to found a Congregation for men, on the lines of the Visitation, Saint Francis of Sales said, with a wry smile, to Mme. de Chantal, who had encouraged him in the enterprise: "And now, do you know how many I have left? One and a half! It is absolutely no use with the people round here, they are too reasonable." A pinch of folly is needed for making a saint, the folly of the Cross which is called the love of suffering and humiliations.

The perfect resolution to become a saint has three characteristics; intensity, continuity and perseverance. Thrusting aside every obstacle in his path, promptly doing penance for each fault and failing—for recovery is one of the most usual forms of virtue—using judiciously, without neglecting any, the many instruments of sanctification, the true religious brings to the work of his Transformation into Christ the best of his mind, heart, will and strength. He is delighted by the motto of Saint John of the Cross: "High and fast!" and he strives to "run rapidly toward his destination . . . and to follow grace

[8] Bourdaloue. Sermon.

in breathless haste." Like any good workman, he does not
spare his pains or waste his time.

He works, a twenty-four day, and in his program there fig-
ures no such thing as the long week-end, days off, or holidays,
still less unemployment or strike. Like the Eternal Father and
Jesus, he must work always, without interruption. Time is a
precious grace which must not be wasted, even though it be
but a minute. After enumerating the seventy-two instruments
of the spiritual art, Saint Benedict recommends that they be
used untiringly, night and day. To enclose oneself within
the framework of God's will, as it is expressed by the Rule,
the Superiors, the duties of one's state, the inspirations of the
Holy Spirit, and by purity of intention, to direct toward the
glory of the Trinity and the redemption of souls all the manifestations of outer and inner activity, is not this, really, a constant work of sanctification? Thus, whether he is at Office or
at work, at recreation or in the refectory, at his desk or in the
garden, in the puplit, in class, or at the bedside of the sick,
whether he prays, works or suffers, the religious does but one
thing; he sanctifies himself. What beauty, unity and fruitfulness there is in a life so marvelously full, in which nothing is
spoiled nor barren! He is like a cornfield, stretching as far as
the eye can see, with every head straight, full and golden.

This generous and constant effort toward sanctification,
which was started on entering the religious state, continues
through maturity to extreme old age; for to quote Saint Francis of Sales, in the monastery of the devout life, one is always
a novice and never professed. Retirement starts in the tomb,
and rest in Heaven. As eternity gets nearer, while illusions
fade and solitude and indifference gather around those who
are about to go, it would seem that the soul, detached from
earthly things, must grow closer to God, and by a recrudes-
cence of purity, trust, recollection, prayer, abandonment and
love, get ready to make a holy death and a noble end. A fervent religious never advances his sanctification more, than in
the evening of his life. He will be happy if at the hour of his

death and about to appear before the judgment seat of Jesus Christ, he can bear himself the same testimony as Monsignor Hulst. "On looking at them carefully, I do not find, in the past thirty years of my sacerdotal life, one instant that I have not consecrated to God. I hope He will take this into consideration."[9]

~

What precisely is the gravity, from the moral point of view, of this obligation to strive towards perfection, and what are the principal ways of failing to fulfill it?

It must first be stated, that even on his deathbed, the religious is not bound to be a saint. For him, sanctity will ever remain an ideal to be attained progressively. Actually the result is of less importance than the effort, the actual arrival, less than the purposeful advance.

Neither does the religious state impose, on pain of sin, the use of all the means—and they are countless—of spiritual improvement, but only of those that are proved to be essential, or which are bound up with the Profession, such as the vows and observance of the Rule. Nor do the seeking out of what is most perfect, the actual continuous practice of virtue, nor absence of all sin, form part of the duty of self-sanctification. Faults, even serious ones, provided that they are accidental and immediately expiated by penance, can quite well be reconciled with a true religious life, by giving the fervent soul the opportunity of strengthening his humility and trust, and in a spirit of reparation, of redoubling his generosity and love. All things considered, this may be a happy fault. O felix culpa! Through the mercy of God, the momentary check has been changed into a leap forward.

All the same, to tend toward perfection is a grave matter of conscience, and any disposition of the soul, any interior or exterior act that would destroy—destroy, not weaken—this habitual progress would, we think, constitute a mortal sin.

[9] Memoirs.

Such would be the case, albeit a very rare one of a religious despising the means of progress toward perfection; transgressing his vows and the Constitutions with the object of halting his sanctification, or out of contempt, forming a resolution to make no effort to work at his perfection, or by frequent grave infractions of the commandments of God and the Church, living in an habitual state of mortal sin.

As for the religious, who is the victim of general and incurable tepidity, whose sole preoccupation is to keep in a state of grace, who has made up his mind to yield to all his little passions and to every opportunity of committing venial sins, he can scarcely be said to be free from grave sin; for such conduct "would put him in imminent danger of committing mortal sins, and from contempt of venial sin, would lead him to contempt of mortal sin and of perfection itself, in as much as it is the aim of the religious state."[10] And what are we to think of a religious, who, to the scandal of his brethren and at the risk of bringing decay into his Community, and of being expelled from his Order, scorns all disciplinary rule, and, uncontrolled by authority, only acts according to his whim and fancy? Such a life, though not in direct and flagrant opposition to the striving after perfection, would none the less be fraught with danger, and often blameworthy in the extreme. The profession is a bilateral contract between the religious and the Order, and binds both contracting parties to a number of mutual obligations.

With regard to each of its members, the Congregation undertakes to look upon him and treat him as its son, to provide both body and soul with their daily bread, in sickness to give him all the treatment compatible with poverty; to use to the best advantage, for the glory of God, the good of the Order and the salvation of souls, his intellectual powers and moral virtues, never to cast him out, unless he prove unworthy and incorrigible; in short, to be a true Mother to him. On his side, and as a result of his profession, the new religious takes upon

[10] Choupin.

himself duties toward his Institute, the disregard of which would form a grave injustice.

Of its nature, by its spirit and its aim, every Congregation is a society, a family and an apostolic army. Now a society cannot be imagined without a twofold authority, static and dynamic, written and living, its laws and its leaders. The Institutes, which are spiritual societies, also possess this structure and organization, and they, too, have a legislation: the Rule and Constitutions, and Customary—a personal authority, the Superiors. Every member of a religious Order is bound absolutely and universally by the Rule. "All religious, in general and in particular, Superiors and subjects alike, are bound not only to keep faithfully and integrally, the vows they have taken, but must also live according to the Rules and Constitutions proper to the individual organizations, and in this manner strive for religious perfection."[11] These Rules and Constitutions are true ecclesiastical laws, from which none has the right to consider himself exempt, and whoever transgresses them without a legitimate reason deserves a penalty. On their observance depend, to a great extent, the vitality and fecundity of an Institute.

It follows from the above, that the worst enemies of religious Societies, are the habitual transgressors of the Rule. In one of his conversations with his Sisters of Charity, Saint Vincent of Paul asked one of them: "What do *you* think, Sister, could ruin the Company?" "The Company would be ruined, Father, if the Sisters were not faithful to their Rules." "Well spoken, daughter." This respect for exterior discipline does not, however, exhaust the sum of a religious' duties toward his Congregation. He must also absorb its spirit, and see that his spiritual life is steeped in it, and that it animates all his apostolic activities. "The spirit of a religious order is a characteristic and permanent outlook, a disposition of the will and feelings." The definition is excellent, all its words are worthy of consideration. "Characteristic": it is not a monopoly—a fact

[11] Canon 593.

too often forgotten. "Permanent": a spirit is a thing that cannot be altered; matter evolves, the spirit remains. "Outlook": the thought that directs the intelligence, the central idea. "A disposition of the will": or the nuances of love. "A disposition of the feelings": i.e., of rejoicing and suffering.

"For besides the written documents in which the distinguishing marks of different religious Orders are laid down with regard to their end, vows, ministerial labors, offices and other obligations, there is impressed on each separate order a certain intrinsic seal or characteristic mark, resulting from the peculiar spirit of the founder, and especially from the ends which, by the inspiration of the Holy Ghost, he has striven to attain, a mark in its ultimate course emanating from the will of God, Who has decreed, from all eternity, that such a kind of tree, and no other, should be planted in the garden of His Church. This mark does not consist in anything distinct from the Rule, and far less in anything opposed to it, but is precisely that which animates and vivifies the letter of the Rule, and is so very properly called 'the spirit of the Institute.' "[12] This spirit consists in one virtue or another, which, while it is common to all religious Institutes, must none the less be cultivated and practiced, in a preferential manner, in a particular Institute; consequently, it must illumine and dominate the life and all the sentiments of its subjects, as in the manner of arranging all business, both exterior and interior. Without this spirit, the religious still belongs to the body of his Congregation, but not to its soul: he is a branch still attached to the trunk, but in which the sap no longer circulates. A close participation in the spirit of the Order constitutes for each subject, one of the best guarantees of sanctification, apostolate and perseverance. On the contrary, there is nothing more dangerous for the individual religious and harmful to the Institute, than the absence or loss of this spirit.

Our profession, which surrenders us body and soul to the Order, implies thereby the abdication of the will into the

[12] Novices Rule, C.S.S.R.

hands of the Superiors, who, thenceforward, have the power and the right—within the limits of the Rule—to make free use of our person and our strength. It is a contract of servitude; the foundation of an obedience that is prompt, blind and total. Whoever refuses to submit to legitimate orders, commits, in truth, an injustice. He takes back what he has given. When he makes his promises, the newly-professed religious signs a blank sheet, that the authorities will undertake to fill in the future.

~

The Congregations are more than Societies, they form real spiritual Families, the members of which are brothers or sisters. When the Institute accepted us, it introduced us to a new and higher form of life, the religious life. It has become, as it were, our Mother. Having given us this new life, it does all in its power to protect and develop it. Through the Rule, the voice of Superiors, general edification, the Institute is wholly bent on the sanctification of its sons and daughters. "The religious Orders are the incomparable benefactors of their associates. You are adopted by Saint Benedict, Saint Bernard, Saint Francis, Saint Dominic, Saint Ignatius, Saint Vincent of Paul, Saint Alphonsus of Liguori, Saint Teresa, Saint Jane of Chantal, or others like them, and you rise to heights which you used to think inaccessible. You are distinguished by superiority of knowledge, virtue and action. You, the sons of illiterate parents, of sceptical bourgeois, of hardened sinners, to whom do you owe your halo of doctor, apostle or saint? You owe it to the Order which, after educating your intelligence, forming your will and cultivating your talents, allows you to wear its livery before the whole world!"[13]

After this, how can one refuse to pay to such a Mother the respect, gratitude, affection and devotion of a son?

First, respect, amounting to veneration. If we venerate our

[13] Janvier. Lent 1918.

Congregation, we shall never presume to judge, underrate, criticize, or disparage it. When did a child have the right to censure and deride his mother, especially in front of strangers? Doubtless, imperfections, failings, even scandals can creep into the most fervent Orders. Are they not found in the Holy Church of God?

What does a perfect religious do when he is faced with laxity and departure from fervor? He suffers in silence, finds excuses or at least extenuating circumstances, prays for the preservation or recovery of the primitive spirit, and tries to cure the evil by good example, and, if he is a Superior, by the exercise of his authority. "If she sees that her Order is declining in any way, let her try to be a stone so firmly laid that she may serve to strengthen the edifice," says St. Teresa, "The Lord will give her aid to do so."

What is the use of setting up as a merciless critic and unauthorized reformer? Of moaning about laxity and decadence? This is untimely, sometimes pharisaical zeal, which usually has the effect of poisoning the wound, instead of healing it, and of compromising the reputation of the Order, which, in any case, is not always responsible for the mediocrity of wrongdoing of some of its members. The graver the sickness of a mother, the greater should be the compassion with which she should be treated, and the care with which she should be nursed. Moreover, this would be an excellent way of showing her the gratitude she has deserved, by her many boons and her devotedness. We have received so much from our Congregation! It is only just that we should keep until death that deep, ineradicable feeling of gratitude which will manifest itself in our affection and devotion. We owe to our Institute "the assurance of our salvation, the fecundity of our apostolate, the consolations of piety, the pledge of God's love, the dignity of an ordered existence, the joys of common life, the paternal solicitude of our Superiors, the brotherly affection of our co-members, family life and countless other benefits, which all combined must arouse in us the most filial love for our Mother in God."[14] Certain religious are more prone to complain of what they lack, than to be thankful for what they receive. They seem to expect their Institute to give them everything, without stint and without return. Even in the religious world, selfishness and ingratitude are not, alas, completely unknown.

But of all the feelings one should foster with regard to one's Congregation, the deepest and most sacred is love. Each of its members should love it with predilection. Can a son be exempt from cherishing his mother? Other Orders may be more powerful than ours, more famous, but they are not our Mother. "The daughters of the Visitation will always speak very humbly of their little Congregation, and set all others above it, when it is a matter of honor or esteem; but they shall prefer it to all others, when it is a question of their affection."

"Thus wives must prefer their husbands to all other men, not in esteem, but in affection; so every man prefers his own country to others, in affection, if not in esteem; every seaman loves the ship in which he sails better than the others, though they may be richer and better equipped. Let us admit frankly that other Congregations are better, richer and more excellent, but not for that more pleasant or desirable, as far as we are concerned, since Our Lord wished it to be our motherland and our ship, and since our hearts were espoused to this Order."[15] We must love our Congregation, its Rule, its spirit and its works. Nothing that goes on in the Institute should leave us indifferent, but produce in our souls a joyous or sorrowful reaction. For our Superiors, we must have filial, respectful and trusting affection; for our brethren, union of mind and heart. Each should take his share in furthering the family spirit, and this is the flower of charity, composed of simplicity, cordiality, tolerance, intimacy, understanding and affability.

[14] Desurmont, Spiritual Testament.
[15] Saint Francis of Sales.

Far from being platonically selfish, the disinterested love of the Order calls on our devotedness. "To be a member is to have neither life, nor being nor movement, save according to the spirit of the body and for the body."[16] If the religious lives by his Institute, how could he not live for it? Each, being a member of the same family, must forget himself, work and sacrifice himself for the benefit of all. In a perfect being, the part exists only for the whole, and each element should contribute to the general good. The spiritual faculties and physical senses contribute, naturally and necessarily to the good of the complete man. So it is of that moral body, that is called a Congregation. Profession is not a government bond, but a contract of employment. There can be no drones in the Communities, only working bees. Besides being a deadly sin, in a religious, sloth would be a shame and a scandal. Did not Jesus toil and earn His bread by the sweat of His brow? One does not enter religion to be served, but, like Saint Paul, to make oneself everybody's slave. He is a true religious who leaves behind him the reputation of a great worker, and who, never shirking any responsibility, task or mission, has slaved all his life, until he is worn out, in the interests, whether temporal or spiritual, of his Institute.

In one of his fine prayers, after giving and dedicating himself completely, without reserve and forever to God, to Jesus Christ, and to the Church, Père de Condren added: "I dedicate myself also with all my heart for the Congregation of the Oratory, which I wish ever to regard as my mother and my mistress, desiring to obey her, serve her, and devote myself to her interests, with all my strength, without ever being in a position to free myself from this absolute dependence."

Yet another form of charity, less obvious, maybe, but no less effective, is mutual edification. To edify means to build up, not to pull down; to raise, not to lower; to develop, not to stunt. It is, by the encouraging sight of a perfect life, to collaborate with one's brethren in the work of their sanctifica-

[16] Pascal, Pensées.

tion, and thereby to maintain the vitality and fecundity of the whole Order; and it is yet another sacred duty that a religious must never forget. On the other hand, what a responsibility lies upon those faint-hearted religious who, by the mediocrity and tepidity of their lives, lower the standard of observance and fervor, and who, if their numbers increase, can bring a whole Order to a state of laxity and decadence. These are unworthy children, who maltreat their mother, and cause her to die of exhaustion. Happy are those, who at the judgment seat of Jesus Christ, and in the presence of their founder, can testify that they have always reacted against any tendency opposed to regular observance, and have always done their best to maintain the Institute in its pristine fervor. Yet, if it be of the first importance to safeguard the inner vitality of the Order, it is also right, always from the same motive of love, not to neglect its recruitment. It is the duty of each one, by prayer, sacrifice, exhortation, and most of all by the example of a noble life to raise up around one good vocations, to draw after one excellent recruits, and by this means, to maintain, if not to increase, the numbers of God's army.

~

For every Congregation, by its essential object, is a picked army, in the service of Christ the King, mobilized for the extension of His Kingdom and the triumph of His love. As soon as one has enlisted in one of these shock troops, one is faced with the duty of living thenceforward as an apostle and of fighting like a soldier, of bringing to this labor of redemption, absolute devotedness, esprit de corps, and loyalty to the flag. Every vocation or profession includes many obligations—some of them grave—that are a matter of conscience. When it is a question of the glory of God, and the salvation of souls, devotedness is indispensable for a religious. This devotedness will prove itself in the first place, and in the early years, by constant attention to a serious and complete training in the apostolate, intellectual, moral and practical. For on the quality of this training, depends the success and fecundity of a whole life. Whether one is dedicated to teaching, preaching or works of charity, one does not become an apostle extempore, and one only harvests what one has sown.

It is, therefore, a duty of their state for all future apostles, that they should sow good seed, i.e., put their youth to the best possible use, acquire, by intensive work, knowledge, virtue, professional skill, and thereby insure that, in the future, their apostolate shall bear the maximum of fruit. It is with intent that we say the maximum! A religious or cleric who loves Christ, and is aware of the nobility of his vocation, and acquainted with the dire needs of our contemporary society, will never be content with an education that is commonplace and merely adequate. "Always better; always more!" will be his watchword. What a responsibility will be his and from what regrets he must suffer if, for lack of a good training, unworthiness or simple incapacity, he should be instrumental in the falling away or eternal loss of a soul. The harvest stretches as far as the eye can see. The harvesters are few, they must at least be excellent.

Once the religious is launched on his career, let him go ahead gladly and conscientiously, under the orders and guidance of his Superiors. Whatever may be the district assigned to him, even if it be the remotest corner of China, whatever the task allotted to him, be it the most thankless and obscure, the religious will obey. For discipline is the mainspring of an army, and by definition, the apostle is a messenger, "missus." Combining military obedience with successful and fruitful initiative, this champion of souls will spare no pains, no sweat, not even his blood, after the example of his Leader. Far from him be the thought of tucking himself away in a peaceful and inglorious little post. With his fighting temperament, nothing frightens or discourages him, not fatigue, nor opposition, nor failure, nor persecution. At the disposition of one and all, he gives himself to all, without thought of himself. It is better to be worn out than to rust, and if his life is to be a short one, at least it will have been full.

When one of his friends reproached him for his excessive zeal, saying, "But my dear abbé, you are not reasonable, you will kill yourself!" Abbé Perreyve, already mortally stricken, replied with a faint smile: "Well! What's the good of a priest who doesn't kill himself?" Completely disregarding the premature retirement of old fighters, the true apostle works until he drops. He only stops when ordered to do so, or when his strength deserts him. Like certain crack regiments, the Institutes have their own esprit de corps, a very different thing from snobbery, which is a kind of collective pride, jealous, distant and peevish. One can have a particular esteem and love for one's own Congregation, without presuming to despise, envy and denigrate other religious societies. Corporate pride has always been opposed to true humility, and Our Lord snubbed the Jews, who despised the Gentiles, and preened themselves on being the sons of Abraham.

Esprit de corps is a principle of homogeneity, cohesion, solidarity, and, for that very reason, of success, and is a virtue that everyone should try to acquire. It is a form of supernatural team spirit used in the service of the Order, and consequently of the Church and souls. Thanks to this spirit, all the members of an Institute, initiated in the same methods, experienced in the same exercises, orientated towards a common ideal and animated by the same zeal, give one another the closest support, and in both defense and attack, stand shoulder to shoulder, Cor unum et anima una; unity is strength. Finally, for every religious there remains the sacred duty of fidelity. The perpetual vows form a lifelong engagement, made before God and countersigned by the Authority. No one has the right to break it without grave cause. To ask to be dispensed from one's vows and to abandon one's post through inconstancy, cowardice, tepidity, or moral unworthiness, must surely be a camouflaged desertion, if not a betrayal.

Perseverance in one's vocation can be put to long and painful trials. Yet a soldier keeps his parole; far from breaking the bonds that tie him to his Order, sacrifice only draws them closer. Fidelity unto death; such is the object of his resolution and his daily prayer. "I ask but one thing of God; to live and die amid my brothers in arms, fighting for my flag and the greater glory of Our Lord Jesus Christ, and to suffer much for His love."[17]

[17] P. C. Clair, Pierre Olivint.

Chapter V

THE THREE VOWS

PROFESSION, which establishes a novice in the religious state and incorporates him definitely in the Institute, finds its official manifestation in the three vows of poverty, chastity and obedience. The vow is a deliberate promise made to God of a good thing that is better than its opposite, and comes under the virtue of religion, which is the first of the moral virtues. Unlike simple retreat resolutions, which are inspired by fervor, the vow binds the conscience directly, and cannot be broken without sin, grievous or slight. Three vows are essential to the religious state; poverty, chastity and obedience, and they are temporary or perpetual. The latter, again are of two kinds: solemn in the Orders proper, simple in the Congregations or religious Institutes.

The solemn vows are made "in a manner which is absolute and are accepted as such by the Church, or by the Order in the name of the Church, so that they do not admit of absolute dispensation: only the Head of the Church in exceptional and very rare cases, can declare that they no longer exist; or partially suspend their effects, or grant an extraordinary dispensation from them in the name of Jesus Christ whose Vicar he is."[1] One of the properties of the solemn vow, is as we shall see further on, to render acts contrary to the vow, not only illicit, but invalid.

Before analyzing the nature of each of the religious vows and establishing their numerous obligations, we must first make a preliminary and general study of the extent of their influence. The Congregations, like the whole order of creation, both natural and supernatural—exist only for the glory

[1] Cotel. Catechism of the Vows.

of God. Subordinate to this supreme end are two immediate aims: the sanctity of their members and their apostolate. The aim of every religious life is to glorify God, by personal sanctification and dedication to the apostolate.

Precisely what part is played by the vows in the achievement of this program?

~

"The first of all the fruits of the religious life, is indubitably the particular and excellent glory given to God by every soul that undertakes it."[2] In His Incarnation, Death and Resurrection, in the founding of His Church and the Salvation of mankind, Jesus, "the first of God's religious" had no aim but the glory of His Father. This glory was His great passion; it inspired His labors and His sacrifices, it was the constant subject of His prayer and predication "Father, hallowed be Thy name, Thy Kingdom come." "But I seek not my own glory. If I glorify myself, my glory is nothing." On the eve of His death, looking back over His thirty-three years of life, the Redeemer summed up the whole of His work, saying "I have glorified Thee upon earth."

The religious seeks to imitate Jesus, so he too makes the glory of God the one aim of his existence. "God first!" and the first service he owes his Master is to honor Him in all the actions of his life. This is what he does. Wherever he may be, and in all that he does, the consecrated soul is a host of praise "hostia laudis," the purest and most radiant reflection here below of the sanctity of the Trinity. The religious state draws this power of glorification, principally from the three vows of poverty, chastity and obedience. Like the virtue of religion from which they derive their essential object is to give special homage to the sovereignity of God. "When we cut ourselves off from the world in order to consecrate ourselves to God by the solemn vow of religion, we accomplish in fact and in spirit what the carnal Israelites only did in figure, when they en-

[2] Mgr. Gay. Of Christian Life and Virtues.

tered the Promised Land. Not only do we choose the Lord, but we choose Him so that He may be particularly our God. . . . This choice gives glory to God. . . . For by virtue of this choice, we bear authentic testimony to God that He is God, and perfectly our God, to the exclusion of all else, our sole and unique God, since He deserves that we should leave all for Him, and that for Him we should renounce ourselves. For God alone can deserve this total surrender, and to Him alone may we renounce ourselves to the point of sacrifice (a sacrifice, a holocaust can only be offered to God . . . and by making the vows, we become the victim offered to God by ourselves). Also, the religious soul alone can render to God this honor to the fullest extent possible on this earth . . . and that is why the choice we make of God, gives him so much glory."[3]

It is by the painful daily practice of detachment, obedience and chastity that the religious becomes a holocaust; the most perfect spiritual sacrifice of all, second only to the Mass and martyrdom, and therefore, best able to give glory to God. Poverty bears magnificent testimony to the abundance of God. He who, of his own free will renounces all things created, and contents himself with the One, proclaims before the materialistic and sensual world, that God is the only Being Who is of consequence and Who is worthy to be sought after, that He is the pearl of great price, for the acquisition of which, one should be prepared to sacrifice all one's worldly goods, that nothing can equal the splendor and joy of poverty "Blessed are the poor in spirit; for theirs is the Kingdom of Heaven."

Another testimony to the Sanctity and Goodness of God is the vow of chastity. It is the revelation of an Infinite Purity whose predilection is for the innocent and the immaculate. To those who have ears to hear, the complete renunciation of all carnal pleasures, even the healthy joys of home life, recalls that nothing on earth can equal the immense and virginal

[3] Bourdaloue. Sermon.

happiness of loving the sovereign God, and Him alone. The human heart is a gulf that can only be filled by Beauty Itself, and Eternal Love.

Finally, by his vow of obedience, the religious pays homage to the universal dominion and supreme authority of the Creator. Amidst our modern materialistic and atheistic society, impatient of all control, revolutionary minded, admitting neither God nor master, it is well that there are believers to rise up and protest against such blasphemous heresies, and to assert by a whole life of voluntary servitude, the imprescriptible rights of God over humanity. Along the centuries, what else have those millions of soldiers done, those volunteers in the service of the Conqueror of nations, all that army of slaves, chained by love, save acclaim the Kingship of Christ, which has now been solemnly proclaimed by the Church? By his vocation, the religious is the herald of God.

~

There exists however, a danger that the primary preoccupation with the honor of God may put into the shade, the duty of personal sanctification. May one not have underestimated with more or less awareness, the part played by the vows in this work of perfection, whereas they are the essential conditions, the distinctive mark and the primary source of all religious sanctity. Without any doubt, the ideal of the spiritual life is identical for all, and in all ways of life, and it consists in a perfect union with God by love. Doubtless Christians and priests can be found, and indeed there are those who without having made the Evangelical Counsels a matter of vow, transcend the "professionals" of perfection; but for all that, the fact remains that the sanctity of a consecrated soul cannot be imagined and is never effected without the vows. It is necessary for any person seeking after religious perfection, to bind himself by perpetual vows to obedience, chastity and poverty. These are princely virtues which, from the first, count among the most characteristic and best known traits of every monastic character, and their unfolding in a life always bears witness to a great religious spirit.

Without mutilating or impoverishing nature, the vows of religion are a safeguard and an enrichment of the moral life. They are to the soul what dikes are to a river, rails to the steam engine, and pruning to the tree. "Ah! if only serious souls in the world knew how the human being has his powers concentrated, his vital energy condensed, and his soul impelled toward heaven, by the effect of the compression exercized upon him by the vows, how many lives would be less frittered away, how many resources less wasted. No, the religious does not bind himself, so as to stifle or empty himself, not to weigh himself down with a heavy burden, but so as to force himself to rise; not to vegetate within four walls but to go forth and breathe the air of heaven. Blessed are the souls who are called to the understanding and experience of the power of the vows!"[4] According to Saint Thomas they form an excellent preparation of the spiritual field and count among the best of the tools that fashion sanctity. For those who keep them, they become a permanent source of purity, fervor, and above all of charity. Whence do most of our faults and imperfections come, if not from egoism? Pride, sensuality and cupidity, these are the plague spots that engender sin. "But every man is tempted by his own concupiscence, being drawn away and allured. Then when concupiscence hath conceived, it bringeth forth sin. But sin when it is completed begetteth death."[5]

Now the vows attack those three great concupiscences, and therefore tend to nip the evil in the bud. Chastity tames the flesh, obedience bridles pride, and poverty roots out the possessive instinct. The happy result of this triple renunciation is the progressive diminution of our moral faults and failings. How many sins are committed by those who give free rein to their passions, particularly those of sensuality and love of

[4] The Contemplative Life, by a Carthusian.
[5] Epistle of St. James I, 14-15.

riches! Moreover, it is an established fact that an exquisite purity of conscience was ever the privilege of those religious who are perfectly poor, obedient and chaste. The influence of the vows is no less potent in the acquisition and development of fervor, which consists firstly, in the complete surrender of one's person to God, and finally, in the intense and universal activity of the virtues. That soul can be deemed fervent, whose virtue is robust, and who lives for God alone.

This should be the case of the religious. On the day of his profession, he gave himself body and soul, without any reserve and consecrated himself irrevocably to the service of God. His profession, therefore, places him in a fundamental state of oblation and fervor, and in fact, he would only have to avoid taking back piecemeal, what he had offered outright, in order to preserve until his dying day, this initial fervor.

"The act of profession itself only lasts a few moments but its effects are permanent and its fruits eternal. As Baptism is the starting point of Christian holiness, so is Profession that of our monastic perfection. It should appear to us like the gradual development of an initial act of immense weight. 'The property of the vows' says Saint Thomas, 'is to immobilize the will in good. And the acts which proceed from a will thus fixed in good, appertain to perfect virtue."[6]

Poverty, chastity and obedience, because they are the objects of a vow by which the will is rooted in what is good, acquire a strength and perfection that are out of the ordinary. All the other virtues benefit from this perfection. It would indeed be odd, if not abnormal, that a religious, who is generously faithful to his essential duties, should prove mediocre in all the rest. The practice of the vows demands the exercise of all the virtues. There can be no poverty without humility, love of sacrifice and trust in Providence. How could there be perfect obedience without deep faith and total self-sacrifice? And a virginal chastity entails great prudence, austerity and daily prayer. Furthermore, the moral virtues are interde-

[6] Marmion—Christ the Ideal of the Monk.

pendent. They are born together, live and die together. All
the powers of our moral organism, like the members of the
human body, grow simultaneously and in harmony. Advance
or recession in the observance of the vows must, therefore,
strengthen or weaken the whole spiritual life.

This situation is intensified by the fact that all the prescriptions of the religious state relate to the three vows, in
particular the Rules and Constitutions, in which "are contained and specified all the evangelical counsels, all the
virtues, the purest love of God, the most unselfish charity
toward one's neighbor, continual mortification, both interior
and exterior, humility, self-contempt, patience, submission,
recollection, retreat, silence, modesty, fasting, abstinence,
perseverance in meditation, divine office, spiritual reading,
examination of conscience, frequent confession and communion, fidelity to work and the duties of one's state; in brief,
all that can help to perfect and sanctify the religious soul."[7]
We must count the vows among the most effective means of
attaining perfection of charity, which is the object of the religious state. They clear the ground, remove obstacles, and
thus greatly ease the climb to the peaks of love. "They cure
the ill that kills it, break the bonds that trammel it, and by
protecting its integrity and assisting its progress, they insure
its final triumph. As soon as love is free, it is master; simply
remove the obstacles, and it will overflow of its own accord
and fill the world."[8] The role of the vows is precisely this:
to do away with everything that can be an obstacle to charity.

When the love of riches dulls and contaminates the heart,
a thousand material cares assail and shackle the soul, poverty
applies the remedy. It frees, purifies, and lends wings to the
soul, and thus becomes the first essential element of perfect
charity. It is easy for a soul who has no ties on earth, and
who has broken all his chains, to soar in contemplation and
love of God. What else did Our Lord require of the young

[7] Bourdaloue.
[8] Mgr. Gay, *op. cit.*

man who wished to follow Him, save that he divest himself of his property? "If thou wilt be perfect, go sell what thou hast and give to the poor—and come follow Me." Again, chastity delivers from the tyranny of the flesh and senses. Blessed are the pure for they shall see God, and in this divine light, they will love much. Vice withers and dries up, but innocence preserves the freshness and youth of the soul. A virginal heart does not grow old, and never wearies of loving. Who can tell the strength of a love, which instead of being dissipated, is completely and immovably concentrated on one Being alone?

As for obedience, it is but the living expression and the delicious fruit of charity. One gives up one's own will to subject oneself totally to the will of God, and this subjection is love. "If you love me, keep my commandments." The motto of the religious who is the voluntary slave of his Rule and Superiors should be "My God, I want what You want, as You want it, because You want it." And such perfect conformity to the will of God can but lead him to perfect charity.

If the religious life is a slow martyrdom, it is made so, chiefly by the practice of the vows, and is not martyrdom an incomparable act of love? Poverty, chastity and obedience "are the three branches of the cross. The three great means of acquiring perfect devotion." When they have been vowed they place a man "in a state of perfection." When they are practiced, they place him "in perfection itself."[9] So that it would suffice to keep one's vows scrupulously and lovingly, in order to become a perfect and saintly religious.

~

In the Church of God, the Orders without exception, count as picked forces and shock troops. While personal sanctification is the primary aim of the religious, there is a secondary one, no less important, and this is the apostolate under every form, with its many varied works, which are all fruitful and always adapted to the present needs of contemporary society.

[9] St. Francis of Sales.

This sacred obligation takes an important place in the Rules and Constitutions. The religious, like the priest, has a special vocation to be an apostle of Jesus Christ.

The part played by the vows in this many-sided apostolate —preaching, teaching, nursing, foreign missions, succor for every physical and moral distress—has not, perhaps, been sufficiently appreciated. They are the tools with which we fashion our sanctity; why should they not also be weapons? Doubtless their main object is to free, purify and elevate souls; but they also possess considerable power for the apostolate. They form at the same time, the saint and the apostle. And one may speak of the "apostolate of the vows" just as one says "the apostolate of the word, of prayer, of sacrifice, or of works." "The aim of the vows of religion is twofold: first, to raise those persons who make them to a higher degree of perfection; secondly, to prepare them by purifying them and fortifying their souls, for an external ministry that they exercise for the eternal salvation of their neighbor and for the alleviation of the many sufferings of humanity."[10]

By its nature, the observance of the vows is already a whole apostolate. Firstly, an apostolate of sanctity, for the practice of the vows leads to perfection. Wherever he may be and whatever he does, even if he be cloistered like a Trappist, or solitary like a hermit, the religious, just because he is a saint, mysteriously shines forth in the world of souls. The blood carries life to the human organism, and charity carries life to the Mystical Body of Christ. How many souls have been saved by the thousands of unknown saints who people the monasteries! Humble lay brothers, gardeners, cooks, porters, who, on the day of judgment, thanks to their poverty, chastity and obedience, will prove to have been incomparable apostles. Such was, and still is, the amazing posthumous apostolate of St. Thérèse of Lisieux. "My sword is love, and with it I will drive the invader from the Kingdom, I will have Jesus

[10] Pope Leo XIII.

proclaimed King of all hearts."[11] The vows also have power to redeem, because they cannot be practiced without sacrifice. To keep them faithfully, one needs a constant spirit of self-sacrifice, and one's life becomes a holocaust. Nailed to the cross by his three vows, the religious collaborates with Jesus crucified in the redemption of humanity. Who can tell the profound and widespread influence of all those contemplative Orders vowed to penance, fasting, silence and nocturnal prayer? Who will ever calculate the innumerable graces of conversion and salvation, obtained by these voluntary and anonymous victims?

Then, the religious state is a living predication of the Gospel; a silent and extremely efficacious predication, for a man will influence souls far more by what he is, than by what he says. Through his devotedness, humility, mortification, detachment, chastity, and virtue the religious is a living vindication of Christianity. He proclaims God, confesses Jesus Christ, affirms the existence of the immortal soul, and of eternity. Even his habit, though it may be a little archaic and unfashionable, is always worn as a lesson and a flag. His is the victorious apostolate of joy. The cloister is the refuge of the evangelical beatitudes, and in these oases, the turbulent and anguished world can contemplate the spectacle of peace and joy. At the sight of these monastic faces, shining and almost haloed with faith and love, how many sinners and unbelievers have recovered, along with the forgiveness of their sins, the God they knew in their childhood and at their first communion.

In each of his vows, the religious finds a special combat weapon and a store of apostolic strength. It has always been one of the problems of the military strategist to lighten the foot-soldier's pack. If a troop is weighed down and heavy laden, it loses some of its attacking power. Poverty frees the soldier of Christ from the burden of material cares. Free in

[11] Spirit of Saint Thérèse of Lisieux.

his time, movements and activity, he can, without anything impeding his progress and zeal, at the North Pole or on the Equator, dedicate himself body and soul, until death, to the salvation of his brethren. Saint Jerome held that nothing equals the sanctifying and apostolic power of poverty. "The summit of the apostolate and the peak of perfection is to sell all one's goods, give them to the poor, then light and free, to soar toward Christ." In a world where the golden calf has more adorers than ever, the poverty of the apostle is at once an eloquent protest against selfish and sensual luxury, and an assertion of the superiority of the spiritual over the material. "Woe unto you that are rich." "For what doth it profit a man, if he gain the whole world, and suffer the loss of his own soul?"

How persuasive are the words of a man who brings all and demands nothing! When truth comes in the company of unselfishness, it is far better received by mind and heart. So as to be in the debt of no man and to keep his freedom, Saint Paul became a leatherworker. Showing his hands calloused by work, he could proudly say, "For such things as were needful for me, and them that are with me, these hands have furnished." When Jesus sends forth his apostles to conquer the world, He specially recommends to them absolute poverty: they must set out without staff or scrip, bread or money, and they must give as they have received, without payment. And He preaches by example, Who has not a stone whereon to lay His head. The very fact of his poverty makes the poor man an apostle, because he provides the rich with the opportunity of giving alms, of serving Christ in the person of His suffering members, and thereby expiating their sins, and saving their souls. "For I was hungry and you gave me to eat, I was thirsty and you gave me to drink; I was a stranger and you took me in."

The great founders of the Apostolic Orders, Francis of Assisi, Dominic, Ignatius of Loyola, Alphonsus of Liguori, were all remarkable for their love of poverty. That fiery soul Saint

Teresa of Avila, never wearied of encouraging her daughters in the practice of perfect renouncement, because she considered that ardent zeal is only to be found in hearts that are quite detached. The love of riches and the pursuit of ease quench the thirst for the glory of God and the salvation of souls. "The means of saving France, Europe, the world, is simplicity, charity and evangelical poverty."[12]

The vow of chastity strengthens the apostolate and makes it ten times more fruitful. In the church of God, virginity was never the synonym of sterility. Beyond and above human parenthood, there exists another, which is infinitely superior to it, and divine. When we gave up the idea of founding a family, we adopted as our children all the souls redeemed by Jesus. "My little children of whom I am in labor again, until Christ be formed in you!"[13] How admirable is this participation in the spiritual Fatherhood of God, and in the virgin Motherhood of Our Lady! How multitudinous is the posterity of the chaste! Ecclesiastical and religious celibacy is more than an honor; it is an apostolic force that Protestantism has always envied to Catholicism. How can one care properly for two families at once? What one gives to one is taken from the other. Like the priest, the religious only exists for the salvation of souls. All his prayers, sufferings, labors; all his daily, hidden and often painful acts of devotedness belong exclusively to the souls that must be saved. The whole life of these heroic solitaries goes to achieve the redemption of mankind.

Moreover, their incorruptible chastity is in itself a safeguard and a remedy against the corruption of the age. It is the salt that prevents the earth from becoming sheer putrefaction. It is thanks to the pure that the level of morality has fallen no lower than it has, and that the world is not utterly depraved. Their virtue shines forth as a condemnation of the vicious, an encouragement to the weak, and an example to

[12] Trochu. The Soul of the Curé d'Ars.
[13] Epistle to Galatians VI, 19.

all generous souls. Where should we be, without the reaction and influence of their blameless lives? But of the three vows, surely it is that of obedience which has the greatest influence on the active life of the religious. An apostolate which is subject in its orientation, its works, means and methods, to the orders of a Superior and the guidance of a Rule cannot, indeed, be other than blessed and fruitful. For the apostle as for the soldier, discipline is a virtue, a force and an essential condition for success.

The apostolate is at once, a power, a right and a duty; but none, be he religious or priest, can exercise the power, make use of the right, and fulfill the duty, outside certain conditions, and of these, the first and essential one is a legitimate mission. Whether it be a matter of predication, teaching or nursing the first place belongs to grace. Man is, in fact, but an instrument in the hands of God. All ministry concerned with souls entails collaboration and a subordination. The apostle works with God, but under the stimulus and control of God. The closer the collaboration, the more complete the subordination, the better the results he may expect. Now this is the outcome of religious obedience. None may, at will, wander into the golden harvest, choose his field and reap as he pleases. It is the right of the Master of the harvest to hire His laborers, and to allot to each his task. A free-lance apostolate is usually at war, the decisive victories have always been gained by the regular troops. By working only under orders and according to the Rule, one can always be sure of doing God's work, and of doing it with His support and as He wills. What better guarantee of success can be imagined? The right tool, well suited to the hand that uses it, always does good work. Such is the case of the religious who is blindly obedient to the authorities. Far from shackling his zeal, or hampering his initiative, his perfect dependence acts as a safeguard, a source of strength and of exceptional graces. In fact, obedience legitimizes his apostolate and renders it fruitful. "The obedient shall sing of victory."

Of all the virtues that Saint Alphonsus exacted of his missionaries, the first was obedience, as being the essential condition of a fruitful apostolate; "If during a mission, one does not obey the Superior with exactness, all will be disorder, confusion and trouble, and success will not be attained. How can such a mission redound to the greater glory of God? A vessel directed by a different pilot cannot but make a disastrous passage." The Redemption was first and foremost a work of obedience. The world was lost by the disobedience of one man, it could only be redeemed by the obedience of Jesus. The disciple is not greater than His Master, and it is only through obedience that he can successfully collaborate in the extension of the Kingdom.

PART II

POVERTY

Chapter VI

THE NOBILITY OF POVERTY

WHO HAS NOT HEARD of the marriage of Saint Francis with the Lady Poverty, of which Dante wrote in the "Para-
diso," and which Giotto painted in the basilica at Assisi? On
an Umbrian road, the Poverello one day encountered Poverty,
who was on her way back to Heaven, for none would welcome her on earth. She looked so beautiful in spite of her rags,
that Saint Francis took her to his heart and wed her. The
religious, too, weds poverty when he makes his profession.
She is an excellent match, and her dowry is the Kingdom of
Heaven. He must live happily with her ever after and never
allow his love to weaken; never look at her askance, never
maltreat her; never, never divorce her!

Among all the virtues, both lowly and glorious, poverty
holds a place apart. She is of noble birth, and it would be
most unjust, because her name smacks of the commonality,
to relegate her among the "servants." The Lady Poverty is a
great lady, and as maid-of-honor, she holds first rank in the
royal retinue of Charity. "Poverty of spirit is a good, which
contains in itself all the goods of this world; it is a high sovereignty . . . it confers a dignity recognized by all."[1]

Poverty derives this moral splendor from the choice that

[1] Saint Teresa, The Way of Perfection.

86

Our Lord made of it, from its rarity, from its deifying power, for it makes of man the image of God.

~

How Jesus loved poverty! with what tenderness and fidelity! From the manger to the tomb she was, to quote Saint Magdalen of Pazzi, "His chosen spouse."

"For you know the grace of Our Lord Jesus Christ, that being rich, he became poor, for your sakes; that through his poverty you might be rich."[2] Our Saviour adopted poverty freely and with love. Able to choose between riches and poverty, without hesitation, He chose the latter. He became poor, even indigent, choosing to be born in a stable, and to lie upon straw; to earn his bread as a laborer, by the sweat of his brow. Our Lord was neither a capitalist, nor a bourgeois, nor a man of means, but a workman with calloused hands and weary limbs. He was so poor that He had not a stone whereon to lay His Head, whereas the birds of the air have their resting places and the foxes their holes. He was poor to the point of beggary. Saint Bernard has three words to express his poverty: "Pauper in nativitate, pauperior in vita, pauperrimus in cruce." Poor at His birth, poorer in His life, poorest on His Cross. And because Jesus loved poverty, His nearest and dearest were poor. His mother was a humble woman who had to mend and do the housework; His father was a carpenter, a fact of which the haughty Pharisees did not fail to remind Him: "Is not this the carpenter's son? Is not his mother called Mary?"[3] He picks His disciples from among humble folk such as fishermen, and if one of the bourgeois class expresses a wish to follow Him, he is first told that he must become a poor man. The shepherds were called to His cradle before the princes and kings. Jesus' first care is for the lowly, the workers, those who toil and those who suffer. These He blesses. The poor have the gospel preached to them;

[2] II Corinthians, VIII, 9.
[3] Matthew, XIII, 55.

this is the sign that the Kingdom of Heaven is at hand and that the Messiah has come.

Thus evangelical poverty is none other than a "participation in the spirit of Jesus Christ, whereby the Christian, thinking like his Master, living by Him and moved by His grace, shares, with regard to earthly goods, His views, His tastes, all His divine dispositions, according to His word: 'They are not of the world, as I, also, am not of the world.' "[4]

Why did Jesus choose to be poor, if not to teach us to esteem and practice this virtue? Whether He were rich or poor, Our Saviour could equally well have glorified His Father and saved the world; but, by His example, He had to reveal to mankind the splendor of poverty: "Poverty did not exist in Heaven; it was widespread upon earth, but man was ignorant of its worth. Then the Son of God came here below so as to choose it for Himself and make it dear to us."[5] Thus, since Our Lord rehabilitated it and made it honorable, the poor have been persons of distinction in the Church. None, then, can be the friend of Jesus poor, unless he become poor like Him, for there cannot "be a perfect friendship between a rich man and a poor one." The disciple of the Master must do as Saint Jerome suggests—Christum nudum nudus sequere. Stripped, follow Christ stripped. And this rule should apply all the more to the religious. When he bound himself to Christ on the day of his profession, did he not espouse poverty?

~

A second characteristic of poverty, one that lends it greater beauty and increases its worth, is its rarity. In our days, especially, it amounts to a phenomenon. It may well be the most unappreciated of all the Christian virtues, the one that is least put into practice. The really poor are the exception, and are hard to find. The world teems with the indigent, with vagabonds and starvelings. If proof is needed, one only has to

[4] Desurmont.
[5] Saint Bernard.

visit the slums of our great cities, to climb to the attics in the industrial areas, to make the round of the caravans and disused coaches that litter every acre of waste ground. But nearly all are the enemies of a poverty which, as far as they are concerned, is not a virtue, but simply a misfortune or an injustice. "I meet a poor man, yet I seek a poor man," said Saint Augustine. This arises from the fact that evangelical poverty does not consist in the dispossession, but in loving the dispossession. Our Lord gave His blessing only to the voluntary poor. Enforced poverty only creates bitterness and revolt. Communism was born of the destitution of the masses. Poverty is not the same thing as pauperism, which is the plague of modern society. To be numbered among the poor by virtue, it is yet not enough to love poverty and embrace it freely. Certain philosophers, indeed, gloried in their rags. It must be practiced with a spiritual intention, for the good pleasure of God and the salvation of souls. It must be repeated that material destitution is not necessarily, and indeed is rarely, a Christian virtue.

Since poverty cannot be found in the hovel, does it exist among the well-to-do? For the spirit of poverty is not irreconcilable with riches and magnificence. How many saintly kings have been admirable for their poverty! Virtue is essentially, and above all, an affair of the soul. One may be well endowed with worldly goods, yet remain poor through one's detachment of mind and heart. On certain days, Saint Elizabeth of Hungary would put off her royal dress, don a wretched cloak of a gray color that was only worn by the poor and lowly, cover her head with a torn veil, and walk before her companions like a pauper, pretending to beg her bread. Then, as if forewarned by some heavenly inspiration of the future God reserved for her, she spoke these prophetic words: "This is how I shall walk when I am poor and in want, for the love of my God."[6] But here again, here above all, where are the rich who are not slaves, who have as if they had not, use as

[6] Montalambert, Life.

if they used not; whose hearts do not cling to their money, and whose purses lie open to succor all forms of want? Theirs is the passion for lucre, which can provide them with luxuries and pleasure and the passion is ruthless, savage and universal. They will tread underfoot the most elementary laws of charity and justice, in order to build their fortunes, as scandalous as they are colossal. The power of money has created in our age the most tyrannical form of feudalism. Blessed are the rich, woe to the poor! At the basis of all the social and political strife, which over the last fifty years has shaken the world and turned it upside down, there lies an antagonism of pride and greed: the struggle of those at the bottom against those at the top, of those who have not enough against those who have too much. If only peoples and individuals had hearkened to the voice of the Prince of Peace crying "Beati mites . . . Beati pauperes!" how much hatred and bloodshed, how many tears we should have been spared! Even in the convents, poverty is not as common as might be believed. The sign is over the door, but the virtue is not always in the hearts.

The religious has made a vow of poverty, and whether he thinks of it or not, he practices it to a certain degree at least. His habitat does not in any way lend itself to worldly luxury, and allows of very little bourgeois comfort. By its nature the religious state enforces privations, and involves a system of restrictions that is more or less austere. But what is the precise value of this "official" poverty in the eyes of God? Do we esteem and love this "command" poverty? Do we desire it? Do we keep it joyfully? Have we a lively regret for our most insignificant transgressions? Does it pain us when we see that it is not observed around us? If we keep to the prescriptions of the vow with sufficient fidelity, have we care for the finer points of the virtue? Do we ever think of the spirit of poverty, the total detachment from all things created? Alas! our poverty is only too often a half-poverty, a matter of routine, unconscious, unmeaning. It is a mere deprivation that one puts

up with as best one may, with which one makes shift un-
graciously.

Mother Veronica, the foundress of the Victims of the Sacred
Heart said that "the vow of poverty is the one about which
the Sisters delude themselves most, whereas it is a source of
constant merit, as its practice is universal. Our Lord will have
many faults against the vow and virtue of poverty to reproach
us with on the Day of Judgment."[7]

~

Poverty makes us akin to Jesus Christ, the King of the poor.
"If there is any inequality in this world, the poor are at the
top and the rich at the bottom of the hierarchy. The poor rep-
resents perpetual sacrifice, the suffering God of the Redemption, the pain imposed on human nature for its good and its
salvation."[8] It brings us closer to God, too, Pater pauperum,
and enables us to participate in some of His adorable attrib-
utes. It is the partial accomplishment of the ideal set by the
Saviour: "Be perfect as your Heavenly Father is perfect."
God, indeed, reveals Himself as the richest and poorest of
beings; and as poor, precisely because He is rich. The richness consists in the possession and eternal enjoyment of Himself. Infinite by His nature, perfections and glory, God has
need of nothing and nobody. He suffices unto Himself. The
universe adds nothing to His essential fullness, and if the
world were to crumble to nothing, He would be in no way
diminished nor impoverished. The Divinity is itself its own
richness. This is why the whole of creation is as nothing before the Creator; why God desires nothing and needs nothing. While He is rich because He is and has all, God is poor
"in spiritu" because He prizes nothing outside Himself.

Is it possible for man to be at once rich and poor, like God?
Of course. If our poverty is firstly, as we have already stated,
a splendid homage paid to the divine plenitude even more

[7] Prévot, Life.
[8] Therive. The Curé d'Ars.

than a testimony, it is obviously a participation in this plenitude. Rich is the soul filled to the brim with God. Does not
only true richness consist in loving, desiring, seeking God
alone, and once He is found, in being content with Him,
clutching Him closely as a miser his gold, taking complete
possession of Him, filling one's mind, heart and will with Him,
to capacity; sinking into His Infinity, finding in Him one's delight, crying "Deus meus et omnia!" Such a man can be rich
as God, for he is rich in God. Now, therefore, we are poor,
totally, universally, admirably poor, after the example of the
Heavenly Father poor "in spiritu," i.e., detached from everything. I own God; what need have I of creatures? Filled with
God, why should I beg? Does the fish, lost in the ocean
depths, sigh for the brackish pools? Those who possess God
can do without many things, if not all.

Divine poverty is the mother of true liberty. To be tied is
to be a prisoner. So those who tie themselves to riches become the slaves of them. The chains may be made of gold,
but they are none the less chains. On the other hand, if one
breaks every tie, one must be free. After God, there is nobody
on earth so absolutely free as a poor man; nothing clings to
him, and he to nothing. Avidly to pursue worldly goods is to
debase oneself, to stoop, to admit one's dependence and indigence. To despise them and cast them aside is to rise and
dignify oneself, to assert one's independence and abundance;
it is to proclaim that one is greater than the whole world;
that there is one being only, who overtops us, and whom we
need: God. Jesus stated this reversal of values in the Gospel.
After promising a hundredfold reward and life eternal to
such as would leave all because of Him, He added: "But many
that are first shall be last, and the last, first." The poor man
resembles the Heavenly Father yet more closely by his interior peace, by that immutable serenity which is the reflection, in his soul, of the serenity and immutability of God. The
heart is untroubled and unafraid, when its Treasure is in
Heaven and its desire is God. Riches are hedged about by

so many thorns: such as desire for gain, fear of business failure; despair after a bankruptcy, a financial ruin. The poor man can lose all: fortune, reputation, health, position, human friendships; but he still has his great treasure, God, the one thing necessary. Besides, is not poverty a beatitude? The poorer one is the happier one is, like God. "Amen, I say unto you, there is no man who hath left house, or brethren, or sisters, or father, or mother, or children, or lands for my sake and for the gospel, who shall not receive, a hundred times as much, now in this time, houses and brethren, and sisters, and mothers, and children and lands, with persecutions; and in the world to come, life everlasting."[9] Further, by an extraordinary privilege, God has determined to ally poverty with the exercise of His justice. The poor of Jesus Christ will judge the world with Jesus Christ. "Behold, we have left all things and have followed thee, what therefore shall we have? And Jesus said to them, 'Amen, I say to you, to you that have followed me, in the regeneration, when the Son of Man shall sit on the seat of His Majesty, you also shall sit on twelve seats, judging the twelve tribes of Israel.'"[10] On the solemn day of general judgment, the religious will occupy a "rank of distinction, superiority and power," they will be members of the High Court, as assistant judges. And "this glory will be granted them, not only to honor in their persons the state of evangelical poverty in which they have lived, but because, having been the disciples and imitators of Jesus Christ in the profession of evangelical poverty, they will have a special grace to be His assessors and even a kind of authority to judge the world."[11]

[9] Mark X, 29-30.
[10] Matthew XIX, 27-28.
[11] Bourdaloue. Sermon.

Chapter VII

THE TREASURE OF THE POOR

IF POVERTY were nothing more than admirable, it might be considered a luxury, and consequently optional, and reserved for the few. This is far from being the case. It is of vital importance and everyday utility, and all, whether lay folk, religious or priests, must practice it to a certain degree. It is a tool, rather than an ornament.

In chapter four, we have briefly outlined the part played by the three vows in the development of the spiritual life; they are the sources of purification, fervor, charity, and holiness. Nevertheless, we feel it opportune now to define more precisely and stress the special influence—which is considerable—of evangelical poverty. "Sanctity is easier in poverty . . . it is, so to speak, more complete, more vigorous. We see such noble deeds in this condition, and we see that they are so common, that even in this modern world, where the bulk of the poor have been deprived of hope, and have returned to paganism, we have reason to believe that it is precisely those destitute Christians who are responsible for the supernatural growth of the Mystical Body."[1] As it is a virtue at once individual anad collective, personal and social, poverty affects both the vitality of the Order and the sanctification of its members. Souls and convents must be poor, if religious spirit is not to weaken, and laxity to set in.

~

Detachment has its fixed and compulsory place in every Christian, and especially religious life; it is one of the mainsprings of our moral organism. By emptying and freeing the

[1] Regamey.

94

soul, poverty attracts grace, while enabling us to rise toward God. An incident in the life of Père Chevrier is a telling illustration of this fundamental, preparatory function. On January 17, 1872, Mlle. Tamisier, the foundress of the Eucharistic Congresses, went to confession to Père Chevrier. She told him about her life, which seemed so barren, her failures, her disappointments, her attempts at the religious life, and particularly her great desire to spend her life in the service of Our Lord in the Eucharist. Père Chevrier listened to her in silence for a long time. Then, suddenly, he said: "You want to serve God, and you don't know the first thing about Christian life. You don't even know the A.B.C. of sanctity. Now, you must be a saint to go to Heaven. You must do what the saints do, and obey the Gospel literally. 'Go, sell what thou hast, give it to the poor and follow me.' When you have nothing, become a beggar . . . Stop the first poor woman you meet, ask her to change clothes with you; put on her rags and start serving Our Lord. . . . When you feel up to coping with such a life, come back to me, and I'll see to your soul. For your penance, and as a preparation for this new life, go into five churches, kneel where the poor kneel, as near the door as possible, like the publican in the Gospel, and there very humbly and in shame, say five Our Fathers and five Hail Marys. When you feel strong enough to dress in rags, come back to me, and I'll deal with your soul." It took her six months to bring herself to make the sacrifice.

Poverty is a sacrifice most of all in the cloister. With obedience and chastity, it makes up the religious state, which is a spiritual holocaust, and is the distinguishing mark of monastic perfection. Without it there can be no religious, certainly no perfect religious. Its presence in a soul is a source of light; it shines out, giving strength and joy. The constant and generous practice of poverty is nearly always accompanied by a reaction against the passions and vices, while stimulating, sustaining, and strengthening our spiritual powers. Those who practice poverty exercise all the virtues, and

in particular, certain virtues which seem more closely implicated than others. "Poverty is justly styled by the holy Fathers
the guardian of virtues, since in religious it preserves mortification, humility, detachment from creatures, and above all
interior recollection."[2]

Poverty and humility are twin sisters, who are often found
together. It might almost be said that one is the finer expression of the other. Many doctors, indeed, understand the first
beatitude to mean, "Blessed are the humble." The humble
are the true poor in spirit. In the opinion of Saint Thomas,
the man who is voluntarily poor, the imitator of Jesus Christ,
by his very poverty, gives proof of the greatest humility. Just
as the rich man is likely to be proud, the poor man is likely
to be self-effacing and simple. Too often, among those blessed
by fortune, especially the new rich, one remarks a way of exacting service, of giving orders, of showing off in public, a
whole mode of life that reeks of arrogance, domination, and
contempt for the less fortunate. Those who know them, flatter them, even while being exploited by them. In our day,
money establishes a claim for consideration; you have only to
watch in a train how differently a ticket-collector behaves
and speaks, according as to whether he comes to a first-class
or a third-class compartment. The powerful are always respected, and money is one of the great modern powers, taking the place of nobility and virtue. This attitude of pride is
difficult to throw off, even in the presence of God. The rich
of whom the Gospels speak—whether it be Dives or the Phari-
see in the temple—were not conspicuous for their humility.
The rich man is always tempted to rise above other men. A
rich man may be humble and good, since his heart can be
detached from riches—but it rarely happens! "Pride," said
blessed Angela de Foligno, "can be found only in those who
have possessions, or who think they have. Man and the angels
fell, through pride, because they thought they had possessions. Neither man nor angel possesses any thing. All things

2 Saint Alphonsus, *op. cit.*

belong to God. Humility can dwell only in those who believe that they have nothing. Poverty is the supreme good."

As for the poor man; he has every facility and a thousand opportunities of practicing humility and meekness. Because he has no possessions, or very few, because he is detached from himself, and emptied of all creatures, he feels more strongly than anyone, that he is nothing, and is worth nothing, since he possesses nothing. And this consciousness of his obscurity will become the foundation and motive of a deep humility, of adoration, self-effacement and abasement. The poor man has nothing to glory in, either to God or himself or the public. He knows it, and were he to forget it, the world would undertake to remind him. Men in rags get more rebuffs than compliments; and the bare-foot Capuchins, the little Sister begging from door to door, know by experience, that it is sometimes dangerous to exhibit one's poverty. That is one of the main reasons, in Saint Thomas' opinion, that justify the existence of the Mendicant Orders; the begging they do gives them the daily opportunity to practice one of the noblest forms of abject humility.

Another virtue closely allied to poverty is interior and exterior mortification. How can one divest oneself without self-sacrifice? The poor man has not always what he would like. He often lacks what would be useful, and even what is necessary. The Rule, with its numerous prescriptions and prohibitions concerning furnishing, clothing and food, provides a complete program of austerity. In virtue of the vow of poverty, the religious is forbidden to appropriate anything, use anything, accept or give anything without permission. This obligation to have constant recourse to one's superiors, simply and humbly, is an excellent reaction against self-esteem and the spirit of independence. The detachment from all things created must involve the death of all human and natural desires. To practice poverty is to deprive oneself and to deprive oneself is to mortify oneself. And it is a fact proved by experience that mitigations of poverty, introduced into religious Communities and Congregations, have always been brought about by a desire for an easier, more pleasant, freer life, and have finally resulted in a weakening of the original austerity. If there is less poverty, there is less mortification.

Who can tell the importance of poverty in the life of prayer? Its function is preparatory, doubtless, but necessary and most efficacious. Why are so many meditations badly made, while all our faculties gad about? Why are so few religious really recollected and united to God? Why, in the cloisters, among all those professional contemplatives, are there so few real ones? Because of a lack of humility, mortification and above all, of poverty. Too many desires intrude, too much preoccupation with self-interest or self-love, too much worry about one's position, health, labors and success. One is trapped, torn between conflicting interests, caught in the toils. Freedom and interior peace have fled. Then how can one rise and fix oneself in God? Saint Teresa admitted that she could not meditate or turn her thoughts to God, if she had kept a superfluous object in her cell. But to a soul that is quite empty and detached, meditation is a joy, habitual recollection a need, and contemplation a hope, until such time—and it will not be long—as the hope becomes a reality. Nothing stops a poor man in his flight toward God—"For where thy treasure is, there is thy heart also"—and all his treasure is in God. And might not this be one of the most precious advantages of the religious state: by depriving us of our goods or at least of their administration, by freeing us from every material preoccupation, to give us all the time to devote ourselves in peace to a life of prayer and meditation.

Finally, poverty maintains and develops the cult of Providence. When we have given all to God for love, we have the right to expect to receive all from His goodness, for He never lets Himself be outdone in generosity. One has given all for all. When, with a solemn gesture, Saint Francis of Assisi had thrown at the Bishop's feet the last of his garments, thus separating himself from all things created, and even from his father, he cried in rapture, "Listen to what I have to say; up to now, I have called Peter de Bernadone my father, but now I return to him his gold and all the garments that I have from him; so that henceforth I shall no longer say: My father Peter de Bernadone, but 'Our Father, who art in Heaven.'"

"Our Father, who art in Heaven." The poor man has the right to repeat this prayer every day, more than any other, with faith, trust, love and complete abandon. Is He not doubly his Father, who is called the "Father of the Poor." Who can ever tell the delicate attentions, the amazing kindnesses of this Father for all His little ones, those who are destitute from choice, who have kept nothing save their heart to love with, and their voice, with which to pray. The poor man knows that he will receive his daily bread, he is sure of it, and has no anxiety. If the Heavenly Father has care of the sparrow, and the grass of the fields, if He gives to one its grain of corn and to the other its drop of dew, how could He forget him, since His ear ever harkens to the cry of the poor?

The prayers of the poor, steeped in trust and humility, is always answered. At the gates of divine mercy, the favored clients, who are never repulsed, are the destitute. Trust! The true poor never lack it; their need is a draft which enables them to draw on the funds of Providence. God is the treasurer of the poor, so they need have no care for supplies. Mère de Rodat, a foundress, wrote to one of her Superiors. "Our purse is at your disposal. It is empty, but when some need arises, God always sends us money." Witness the permanent miracle of the "Cottolengo" in Turin, where thousands of poor, sick, orphans, workers, and nuns have lived for a hundred years from day to day on voluntary alms, without capital, regular income, or reserves for the rainy day; without accounts, simply in the hands of Providence! What must be the joy of the religious who lives on his destitution, as others live on their wealth! He has found the treasure mentioned by Our Lord, that no moth or rust consumes, that no thieves break in and steal. His poverty, if loved and generously practiced, will be all his life, an ever-gushing spring of light, strength, charity, joy and intimacy with Our Lord. On the contrary, how much to be pitied is the religious who has lost, altogether or to a great extent, the "feeling" for poverty; who does not understand or love it, and strives to remove it from his life, as far as he may. Too often he becomes a proud and unmortified religious, without real piety or spirit of recollection, worldly. A religious who is not poor can only be a poor religious. To quote Saint Francis of Sales, "A nun who has a groat is not worth a groat!"

~

What would be the worth of a Community in which poverty had lost its place of honor? For if poverty is an individual perfection, it is also a collective virtue, and the Congregations, in their quality of Societies or Families, are not exempted from practicing it. For Institutes as for Monasteries, poverty is one of the strongest ramparts of the religious spirit, besides being a source of interior vitality, and success in the apostolate. "The founders of every religious Order endeavored to establish in all the Communities of their Institute a perfect spirit of poverty as the basis of common good. Saint Ignatius of Loyola called religious poverty the fortification by which the spirit of fervor is preserved. Indeed, in the Communities in which poverty is maintained, fervor flourishes, and in which poverty is violated, irregularities soon prevail. Hence the powers of Hell labor so hard to introduce a relaxation of poverty into the observant Orders. Speaking of her own religious, Saint Teresa once said from Heaven: 'Let them endeavor to have a great esteem for poverty; for while it lasts, fervor will be maintained.' "[3] Indeed, the vigorous growth and wonderful blossoming of sanctity, which is to be found at the origin of most of the great religious Orders, may well be attributed to the heroic poverty, that accompanied their beginnings. Poverty is the best earth for new planta-

[3] Saint Alphonsus.

THE TREASURE OF THE POOR

tions. But from the moment that this austere virtue falls into oblivion, or is scorned, that abuses creep in, openly or sub rosa, contrary to the prescriptions or prohibitions of the rule, that the pursuit of comfort, show and grandeur replaces the love of what is lowly, unassuming and simple, it soon becomes evident that there ensues a cooling of fervor and an adulteration of the religious spirit. "Without poverty there remains nothing of religion in the spirit or the virtue." Absence of poverty means worldliness in the convent, and then it is goodby to recollection, humility, mortification, obedience and charity; good-by to the spirit of the cloisters; to zeal, temperance, solitude and innocence itself. The words "Woe to you who are rich, for you have your consolation!" apply most particularly to those religious who are rich in spirit and in fact.[4] Woe to those Communities in which poverty is on the way out; the door is wide open to laxity. The crumbling of this cornerstone must endanger the whole edifice. How many famous abbeys, in days gone by, have found their ruin in the excess of their riches! God cannot bless decadent and degenerate Institutes. He abandons them, when He does not visibly afflict them.

While all the Congregations are bound to practice poverty, the rule does not apply equally to all. The poverty of a Cistercian is not that of a Jesuit, and the destitution of a Poor Clare, not that of a Sister of the Visitation, or a Sister of Charity. The rule laid down by Saint Thomas is excellent; since poverty is only a means or instrument, it must only be practiced in the different religious Orders to that extent which will insure, considering their nature and particular aim, that it will contribute efficaciously to the sanctification of their members, and the force of their apostolate. In this, above all things, the law of the happy medium applies; not too much, not too little.

Let the Institutes, which are made up of men, not angels, have enough possessions to secure, on a modest scale, the sustenance of the members, the upkeep of the houses and good

[4] Desurmont. Rapports de la Règle.

works; let the authorities, by a wise administration and investments that are neither too cautious nor too rash, see that their capital is laid out to advantage and increases reasonably; let certain Orders even possess considerable wealth, so as to be in a position to practice generous hospitality, to provide for the poor and the many needs of the Church; such as the founding of new parishes, Church schools, good press, foreign missions, etc.; all that, in reality, is only prudence, justice and charity, and all that—since it is consistent with poverty—can in no way compromise religious perfection. Abuse, however, remains possible, and is a danger that cannot always be avoided: lack of trust in Providence, over-eagerness to acquire possessions, doubtful financial negotiations, attachment to money, a tendency to hoard; and where the members are concerned, with regard to food and clothing, a parsimony bordering on stinginess, a vice more opposed to the spirit of poverty than prodigality, and which often only has the effect of making, not true religious, but malcontents and rebels. The régime of extreme restrictions has never contributed much to the fervor of convents. Strictly to exact one's due, to be forgetful of charity and alms, are regretable defects, quite contrary to the spirit of the Gospel and the liberality of Our Saviour. It would be strange, almost scandalous, to come across a religious who has made a vow binding him to poverty and self-sacrifice, and who would none the less deserve to be called a money-grubber. Howbeit, each religious house must practice both affective and effective detachment, as it is imposed by the Rule, traditions and spirit of the Order.

This fidelity to corporate poverty is dependent, to a great extent, on the vigilance, firmness and good example of those in authority, for whom it is a grave matter of conscience. Most abuses and modifications only creep in to the Institutes, thanks to the weakness and ignorance—one dare not say connivance—of superiors. If one of these, worldly-minded, a lover of pomp and ease, were to ignore the vital importance of poverty, and through his fault, suffer it to wither and die, he would become a public menace to his Community, and possibly to his whole Congregation.

Each and every member of a Convent must maintain the pristine purity and integrity of poverty; must observe standards of simplicity, humility and austerity with regard to furnishings, clothes and food; must make an inflexible stand against all dangerous innovations that arise solely from vanity, sensuality, love of comfort, the desire for a free and easy existence.

Nowadays one rarely, if ever, finds Communities to whom Bossuet's vehement apostrophe might apply: "Families that are accustomed to poverty are careful about everything; they subsist on very little, but the Communities cannot do without abundance. How many hundreds of families could live comfortably on what is barely enough for the expenses of a simple Community, which has made profession of renouncing worldly goods in order to embrace poverty! What a mockery! What a topsy-turvy state of affairs! In these Communities, the expenses of the infirm often exceed those of the sick of a whole town. One has leisure to coddle oneself in one's slightest indispositions; leisure to anticipate them, always to be busy with one's self and one's delicacy; one is not living a simple, poor, active and courageous life. This causes, in houses that should be poor, a scandalous eagerness for profit . . . I am ashamed to say so, I do so only in secret and with anguish, privately, so that the spouses of Christ may be made aware; but it must be said, since, unfortunately, it is true. Base hearts, narrow hearts, can you have been formed in the school of Christ? Is this what you have learned of Jesus, who had not where to rest his head."[5]

Still more carefully should we avoid, even in our houses, anything approaching worldly luxury. When Saint Bernard made his first visit to the abbey of Haute-Combe, which had been built by the Dukes of Savoy, with a magnificence and

[5] Bossuet, Sermon.

luxury that was the very contrary of Cistercian poverty, he began to weep, and raising his hands towards heaven, he cried: "Haute-Combe! Haute-Combe the arrogant! You are too proud and cannot last!" These words were taken to be a curse, for shortly afterward, the abbey collapsed. Thus is explained and justified the insistence with which the holy Founders recommended to their sons the practice of poverty. "If I were at the hour of my death," said Saint Paul of the Cross, "I would make three recommendations: to preserve the spirit of prayer, the spirit of reclusion and the spirit of poverty."[6] On his deathbed, Saint Dominic threatened with the curse of God, those who should tarnish the brilliance of the poverty of his Order; and the gentle Saint Vincent de Paul one day cursed, three times over, those of his Company, who should give way to sentiments of self-interest.

Poverty is a grace for which religious should pray daily, not for themselves alone, but, like Saint Grignon de Montfort, for each of their brethren and their Congregation: "My God, what do I ask of Thee? Liberos! Priests free as Thou are free, completely detached, without father, mother, brothers, sisters, or relations in the flesh, without friends as the world understands them, without goods and encumbrances, without cares, and even without self-will."[7]

[6] Strambi, Life.
[7] Laveille, Blessed L.—M. Grignon de Montfort.

Chapter VIII

THE ENEMIES OF POVERTY

We are all familiar with the scene in the Gospel, where the young man knelt before Jesus and asked Him for the secret of salvation. "Good Master, what shall I do that I may receive life everlasting?" Jesus said to him, "Why callest thou me good? None is good, but one, that is God. Thou knowest the commandments; do not commit adultery; do not kill; do not steal, bear not false witness; do no fraud; honor thy father and mother." But he answering, said to him: "Master, all these things I have observed from my youth." And Jesus looking on him, loved him, and said to him: "One thing is wanting unto thee; go, sell whatsoever thou hast, and give to the poor, and thou shalt have treasure in heaven; and come, follow me"; who, being struck sad at the saying, went away sorrowful; for he had great possessions. And from his withdrawal, Our Lord drew the conclusion: "How hardly shall they that have riches enter into the Kingdom of God!" The disciples were amazed, but Jesus insisted: "Children, how hard it is for them that trust in riches to enter into the Kingdom of God! It is easier for a camel to pass through the eye of a needle, than for a rich man to enter into the Kingdom of God." Who wondered the more, saying among themselves: "Who then can be saved?" And Jesus looking upon them, saith, "With men it is impossible; but not with God. For all things are possible with God."[1]

Since poverty proves to be so necessary for salvation, and, where we religious are concerned, for our sanctification, it would appear that it must be a common state. Nothing of the kind! How many, when faced with the unpalatable prospect

[1] Mark X, 17-27.

of a humble life of poverty, follow the example of the young man in the Gospel, and withdraw, sad and discouraged. This austere virtue, which is one of the least attractive forms of the cross, with its exterior deprivations and interior renouncements, does not appeal to them. Nature can find that it pays to undertake certain acts of heroism that have a flourish to them, but that little is to be gained by courting this lowly maid in rags. Poverty is no royal road, along which one rolls, coach-borne, at ease; it is a narrow, steep, stony track, overgrown with thorns, with stumbling blocks at every step. Reacting as it does against tendencies to egotism, and combating the influence of the world, it calls for courage and perseverance, far more than do other virtues.

What are the enemies of religious poverty? We are now about to examine the chief ones: enemies private and intimate, enemies exterior and public.

~

The first adversary of poverty, from which none escapes, and at the same time the most dangerous, is the enemy within the stronghold, ourselves, our egotism. Since the sin of Adam, everything in our nature is violently or latently opposed to the demands of evangelical renouncement; within us are the passions of ownership, materialism, pride, sensuality, the effects of a warped education.

Saint John warned the Christians of his own day against what he called "the concupiscence of the eyes," "concupiscentia oculorum"; the innate and universal desire to possess, to acquire, to enjoy. At the bottom of our hearts, we all bear the indestructible instinct of cupidity, a growth which, says Saint Benedict, "must be cut off from the Monastery by the roots." Even in the religious, there is always, on a small scale, a dormant man of property, a capitalist, even, maybe, a miser, and sometimes he awakes. It is as if one never has enough, and is always afraid of being without, and from this condition is born the passion for riches, or at least, the pursuit of plenty. To be poor means to restrict oneself; to do without, to suffer, and the idea is repugnant. Whence arise the host of these ideas that make of the human heart a veritable ant hill? From our intractable tendency to procure for ourselves what we lack. "Now the role of poverty is to repel all these. Think of the attacks it must sustain, since it must always choose what is least convenient, what is humiliating, small, shabby, and sometimes even to do without what is necessary. It is hard for our human nature, and therefore, there is reason to fear, all the more so as the motives in support of poverty are mysterious."[2]

Certain virtues arouse our admiration at first sight, because of their beauty or splendor; such as fortitude, generosity, devotedness and charity. It is not so with poverty. At first sight, it seems unnatural, gloomy, even shocking; a relic of barbarian antiquity, that has strayed into our age of progress. For unbelievers, it spells wretchedness and shame. To love it, one must be mad. Did not Virgil put into his Hades "shameful indigence"? Without going quite so far, may it not be that we, too, have to a greater or lesser degree, been affected by this pagan way of thinking? In itself, wealth is neither a vice nor a sin, so it would appear that poverty, its opposite, must be a neutral thing. How many religious are without firm convictions about this point of the spiritual life! A certain worthy nun, a fervent soul, and, what is more, a mistress of novices, admitted that she had never been struck by the primordial importance of the vow of poverty. Now, the absence of a lively faith is fatally attended by a falling off in the practice of this virtue. Poverty is no longer properly understood; so we have a host of objections inspired solely by human reasoning, and which have no other aim, but to excuse all frailties, and to justify any abuse. "One must be conventional and avoid ridicule." What is the point of attracting attention and making oneself conspicuous? What of the honor of the Institute? And the dignity of the priesthood? One must move with

2 Desurmont, *op. cit.*

the times: the modern world does not care for the poor, and
if one were to approach the world in the guise of a pauper,
one would run the risk of antagonizing it, and compromising
one's apostolate. Then there is the question of health. One is
under the obligation of taking care of it, of taking precautions.
It is a fact that a religious who had trouble with his throat,
and who lived in an inclement climate had the grandiose idea
of building a magnificent convent on the Riviera! These maxims are all the more dangerous, because they are ambiguous,
and true, up to a point. All depends on the way in which they
are interpreted and put into practice. To use them as a justification for treating lightly the poverty that is regular or
traditional in the Institute would be to practice a strange de-
ception upon oneself.

Another enemy of poverty is the second concupiscence, the
pride of life, superbia vitae. Humility and poverty are in-
separables, as we have already said, but pride loathes anything that savors of destitution. Now, pride has us by the
throat, and self-love is the very marrow of our bones. Even
though we are religious, unless we have exceptional virtue
we remain susceptible to respect, consideration, attentions,
compliments: the special preserve of the rich. One may not
be one of them, but at least one will do one's best to have
dealings with them. Who would not rather speak of one's
relations with high society, than one's association with the
common people? The counsel of the Imitation is always up
to date: "Be not a flatterer with the rich, nor willingly appear
in the presence of the great. Associate thyself with the humble and simple." "Nature rejoices in a multitude of friends and
kindred; . . . she fawns on those in power, flatters the rich . . . ;
grace favors the poor rather than the rich; her sympathy is
with the innocent rather than the powerful." This can give
rise, in Institutes dedicated at their origin to the apostolate
of the lowly, the outcasts and the needy, to a tendency to
deviate, to depart from the original end, for which they have
been founded, and to launch forth in new works, which may

not be more necessary and fruitful, but are at least more interesting and ostentatious, from the human point of view. The poor have been sacrificed to the rich, and the lowly to the great.

In the eyes of the world, the poor are at the foot of the social ladder, and it may seem hard to our pride to find ourselves in their company, on their level, we, the sons or daughters of the well-to-do, born, maybe, in good or even high society. Because one practices poverty, one seems to have come down in the world. When traveling, one would be so comfortable in second class, with polite conventional people, instead of rubbing shoulders in third class with rough workmen, drunken soldiers, and women going off to market to sell their cheese. It would certainly be pleasanter to go and have lunch in the dining car, than to pull one's sandwiches out of a bag and to eat there, simply, like everybody else. It can be humiliating, for young vanity especially, to appear in public, amid a crowd of impeccably and fashionably dressed people, with a patched cassock and a battered hat. Without a well-founded humility and sincere self-contempt, the religious will always be tempted to depart from evangelical simplicity, to push himself, and to become in some measure "a man of the world," instead of remaining one of Jesus Christ's poor.

No less a threat to poverty is that third form of egotism, which Saint John calls "the concupiscence of the flesh." Not the shameless sensuality of the age, but a lesser, modified sensuality, "monasticized," that branches out in a double tendency: love and pursuit of ease, fear of and flight from discomfort and austerity. With a spice of mischief, Saint Teresa pokes fun at those mollycoddles who use the slightest indisposition for obtaining dispensations, and who seem "to have entered the convent for the sole purpose of warding off death, so zealously does each go about it." How can one look after oneself, coddle oneself, be perpetually on the lookout for one's ease, without transgressing the virtue, and even the vow of poverty? The Rule has many prescriptions and prohibitions concerning furniture, food, clothing and common life, and some of these are severe. Can one call oneself truly poor if one complains, recriminates, and criticizes these austerities? Can a grudging, whining poverty be called evangelical? If one is ill, or merely unwell, one makes demands, concerning treatment, medicines and doctors that would be surprising enough in the world, and that are quite incompatible with the spirit of simplicity and detachment. In spite of the Constitutions, and without the knowledge of one's superiors, one is tempted—and more than one has succumbed—to give oneself sub rosa little treats—were it only a smoke—to procure for oneself little extras, to accept very welcome, and sometimes sumptuous gifts. Perfect poverty can never thrive in a feather-bed type of life, from which sacrifice and mortification have been banished.

The wrong kind of early education—and this is a frequent occurrence nowadays—can also prove to be an obstacle to religious poverty, and give rise to many failings and abuses. It is hard to acquire in maturity, virtues that have not been practiced in youth. The soul is like a field. The sap flows sluggishly in the autumn, and the yield is poor. For many, poverty is a virtue of late growth. At home, one has been trained in obedience, humility, industry, piety and modesty; but who has ever made even the slightest allusion to poverty? One has always heard the rich spoken of with envy, and the poor with pity. One has been brought up, not in luxury, perhaps, but in comfort and plenty. Throughout one's youth, one has had everything one could wish for, and one has never been in want; moreover one's parents have taken care that one should suffer no privation. Now, at twenty or twenty-five, one enters religion, and must change one's mentality, and throw off the habits acquired in a comfortable, easy life. This reversal is not the work of a day. "What's bred in the bone will come out in the flesh." For many a novice, poverty has been a none too pleasant revelation with its niceties and its delicate nuances. And many religious has kept all his life a soupçon of the easy circumstances of his young days. A young religious, who saw someone, on a journey, take the trouble to save fifty centimes, publicly made the tactless remark, "What cheese paring!" Maybe. The saints used to save match sticks. And what of Saint Thérèse of Lisieux who used to gather carefully her pencil shavings? Is she to be accused of narrow-mindedness and over-fussiness?

~

To these enemies of poverty, which are interior and personal ones, must be added others, these being exterior and public: worldliness, contact with the world, the contagion of bad example, carelessness on the part of superiors, and the material prosperity of religious houses.

It is a historical law, and a fact proved by experience, that the secular and regular clergy never completely escapes from the moral and intellectual influences of its own century. Surreptitiously its spirit, whether for good or for ill, creeps into the sanctuary, and into the convents too, in spite of any enclosure. Now the manners and mentality of contemporary society are in flagrant opposition to evangelical poverty. More than ever before, this virtue is misunderstood, rejected, treated as an outcast, it is the leprosy of our modern materialistic civilization. From the top of the social ladder to the bottom, there is a mad rush for money and the host of pleasures that money can buy: "Nowadays, there remains nothing to remind us of the one-time simplicity of the Gospel. Everywhere, we see unbridled luxury, an astonishing taste for and cult of ease, a refinement of pretension and elegance, and a never-ending accumulation of the superfluous. The atmosphere about town is brought into the convent: we cannot shut it out; the age, with its trappings of vanity, lays siege to our doors, and willy-nilly, some part of it always finds its way inside."[3]

A poor religious, who advertises poverty and preaches its beatitude, must inevitably appear to the public eye in the

[3] Desurmont, *op. cit.*

guise of an anachronism and a scandal. If one would immunize oneself against this harmful influence, it is necessary to react continually and powerfully. Without this reaction, one follows one's century, and adopts something of its ideas, tastes, and way of life, one brings one's poverty up to date, that is to say, one suppresses it as far as possible. This danger of contamination is increased when one finds oneself in frequent and prolonged contact with the world, as is the case of the active, hospitaler, teaching, preaching and charitable Congregations. From this point of view, the cloistered Orders are fortunate. How is one to free oneself from the sort of fascination, often quite unconscious, which is exerted upon the senses, imagination and heart? How many opportunities there are of breaking one's vow, forgetting the virtue and forming an attachment to creatures! When one is removed from the vigilance of authority for weeks and months, away from community life, it is very easy to make oneself comfortable, to slacken the reins, to procure certain pleasures and fit oneself out with various articles, briefly, to lead a life that in no way conforms to conventual poverty and the religious spirit! It would be a different matter if one took the trouble to obtain the necessary permission. But it is so convenient to adopt the mistaken tactics of tacit or assumed permission. There is also the temptation, for those who are often in and out of the presbyteries, to shape one's life on the same lines as the clergy. It must be remembered that the secular priest has made no vow of poverty, and is consequently not obliged to practice it in the same degree as the religious. "One goes out on a mission; one finds that one's belongings compare unfavorably with those around one. One feels humiliated; one begins to covet, one fabricates imaginary needs, one accepts presents, and one increases the stock of one's possessions. One returns to one's house; there, one should be as well equipped as in a well-furnished presbytery."[4]

Without going into the world, stumbling blocks can be

[4] Desurmont, *op. cit.*

found even in the most fervent convents: the bad example of certain colleagues who treat lightly the multiple points of the Rule, who "make demands, grumble, set the fashion and lay down laws." From the moment that superiors do not acquiesce to their claims, they are branded as direct descendants of Harpagon, the miser. This example is all the more pernicious, when it comes from religious, whose age renders them venerable, or whose talents give them influence.

Those who have firm convictions and a solid virtue will not allow themselves to be swayed. But the weak, and the young, are always in danger of chorusing their agreement, and following where they are led, even if they can only justify themselves by distorting the meaning of "common life." Equality for all! Why should *he* have such and such, and not the others? Are there two kinds of poverty in the Congregation?

But the gravest, and perhaps the most widespread of all the dangers, may come from those in authority.[5] They may have their large share of responsibility in the falling away from regular poverty, whether they sin from ignorance, weakness, harshness or—though God forbid!—by their bad example. One of the first duties of a superior is to watch over the perfect observance of the Rule, especially in what concerns the practice of the vows, and this task implies that he has two kinds of knowledge.

Firstly, the knowledge of his powers: as he holds a delegated, and therefore a limited authority, he is not free to administer it according to his whim, or to grant dispensations and permissions as he thinks fit. Poverty has limits beyond which nobody may go. "In the administration and dispensation of the community's goods, they cannot act as proprietors and masters, but only as instruments of superior authority, and conformably to the Rule. Their infractions have this spe-

---

[5] We do not refer here to the general chapters whose influence, with regard to the maintenance of primitive poverty, is not always very felicitous. How many mitigations can be traced to them!

cially, that besides their personal sin against the vow, there will also be a sin of scandal."[6]

Secondly, the knowledge of Canon Law, of the Constitutions and traditions of the Order: the prescriptions of the vow are many and varied, and so are the demands and nuances of the spirit of poverty. How can one remind others of them and see that they are respected, if one does not know them oneself? Unenlightened government can only lead to despotism and abuses. For instance, a certain Superior General allowed the peculium, saying that she had forgotten that it was strictly forbidden by the Rule. Had she ever known it? Once the duty is known, it must be fulfilled with gentleness and firmness, without weakness or human respect. The authorities must set themselves against dangerous tendencies, wherever they may come from, within or without; they must cure the negligence of some, and the obstinacy of others; in a word, they must safeguard the integrity of primitive poverty. How heavy is the responsibility of a superior who, from fear, good nature, or desire for popularity, closes his eyes and allows unfortunate customs and laxity to be introduced into the Community! "With regard to their subjects, Superiors would themselves violate the vow of poverty if they permitted or granted what they have not the right of permitting or granting and their authorization would be null. It would also be a culpable connivance on the part of Superiors, to tolerate in inferiors the infraction of a vow, which they can prevent."[7]

Yet firmness does not mean narrow-mindedness, hardness of heart, or niggling parsimony. To make a virtue of refusing one's subjects what is allowed by the Rule, concerning food, clothing, and chattels; to dole out in thimblefuls to the sick, the old and infirm those medicaments and treatments which are compatible with the religious spirit; to add supplementary restrictions to the austerities prescribed by the Rule—all this is bad policy, which not only shows a lack of prudence

[6] Cotel. Catechism of the Vows.
[7] Cotel. Catechism of the Vows.

and kindliness, but compromises albeit unwittingly, the observance of perfect poverty. Such a regime will produce more malcontents than saints, and means will be found of procuring surreptitiously, even from outside—to the detriment of common life and personal conscience—those things that the superiors have refused to grant.

What if the superior adds bad example to these other faults? He publicly violates the law of poverty, how does he propose either to recommend or exact it from others? "There are superiors who have but little personal knowledge of the mysteries of poverty, and have for this virtue neither the esteem nor the concern that it deserves. What happens? They coddle themselves: their person, their room, their chattels are all arranged so that nothing is lacking; their office, indeed, is a source of profit. As they are soft with themselves, they cannot deal too hardly with their subjects. Gradually, the standard of austerity is lowered, possessions are accumulated; a few years suffice for the former austerity to be replaced by modern comfort."[8] We are now in a position to understand the remark of Saint Alphonsus "Oh! how many superiors we shall see damned on the day of judgment, because they have transgressed the law of poverty themselves, and helped to weaken in others the love of the simple life!"

Finally, among the dangers that threaten poverty we must include the material prosperity of the convents. It is difficult for a Community to be rich without its members being affected in some degree. "As long as we are poor," Père Passerat used to say to his religious, "we shall be able to hope and pray, and so obtain all things from God. But if we were to grow rich, we should play the noble Lord, and then we must bid farewell to trust in Providence, to prayer, and above all to the desire to serve the poor and destitute."[9]

True poverty, holding the balance between want and superfluity, suppresses many human desires, and cuts short many

[8] Desurmont, *op. cit.*
[9] Gautron. L'Ame du Père Passerat.

abuses. But how can one feel oneself to be in the midst of abundance, and not be tempted to turn it to account and enjoy it? While avoiding scandalous excess, one yields more readily to the caprices of nature, and the desire for an easy life, when it is a question of journeys, holidays, seasons, feasts and purchases. One is not too particular; one adopts a comfortable style of poverty, which is, indeed, correct, but allows one to live like a fighting cock.

The holy founders, then, feared lest their Congregations should grow rich. "The less there is in a convent the easier is my mind, and Our Lord knows full well that I am more distressed when we have appreciably more than we need, than when we lack something."[10]

[10] Saint Thérèsa. The Way of Perfection.

Chapter IX

THE VOW

POVERTY BELONGS to the essence of the religious state; it is the foundation of perfect charity, and therefore, of holiness. Like all the other virtues it is subject to the law of progress, and comprises many degrees, which are commonly reduced to the three most important: the vow, the virtue and the spirit of poverty. We shall make a special study of each of these.

It will surprise no one, if we state that, of the three vows of religion, poverty is certainly the least known, the most easily forgotten, and therefore, the most frequently infringed. This is due, we think, to a certain lack of understanding, and to a certain distortiton of conscience and conduct. The vow of poverty is infringed through ignorance, which is more or less culpable. Before making profession, one should have acquired an exact knowledge of the new moral obligations about to be undertaken. Now the prescriptions and prohibitions of the vow of poverty are many, varied, and subtle. Has one taken the trouble to make a serious and detailed study of them? The novitiate should have enlightened us on all these points. Unfortunately, the doctrine explained has not always been grasped; and who can say whether the teaching, which may have been over-brief and inexplicit, has been altogether satisfactory? Be that as it may, for many, the novitiate is already long past; the truth has grown a little dimmed, and few have thought of brushing it up; save at the occasion of the annual retreat. Whence arise many an oversight, and sometimes, even in the case of priests, grave errors.

With regard to poverty, is a certain action permissible? Perhaps so, perhaps not. Without more ado, one forms, or rather deforms, one's conscience, and one goes ahead. Such conduct is risky, when it is not culpable. No one has the right to lay himself open, without good reason, to the danger of infringing his vows. Where there is doubt, there must be further investigation, made either by oneself, or with the help of one's superiors or confessor. Some are the victims of a certain fecklessness and of dangerous settled habits. These are religious, who play fast and loose with what they call the minutiae of poverty, who act with complete independence in their duties and occupations, free from direction or control, who readily forget to ask the requisite sanctions, or make an extensive use of tacit or presumed permissions. By degrees, their conscience dulls, shrivels and warps; and in this way, they may end by committing, almost without being aware of it, grave sins against the vow itself.

It is also dangerous to set one's standard by certain wrong and scandalous customs, which are nothing else than a decline of primitive poverty and a corruption of the vow. Not every custom is legitimate, especially at its origin, and when it is practiced by a single community. To quote it as an authority would be a culpable illusion.[1]

In order to obviate these manifold dangers we have deemed it useful, first to study the nature and obligations of the vow of poverty, and then to compose, as it were, a repertory of the most usual and frequent violations.

~

The vow of poverty is a promise made to God to renounce

---

[1] "Custom in general is an unwritten practice, which has been introduced by degrees into a Community, either to interpret or modify some point of the rule. Lawfully established, custom has the force of a true law, as well for prohibitions as for permissions; if it be not lawfully established, it has no value . . .

"A custom is lawful only on three conditions: first, that it be reasonable; second, that it exists really in the major part of the Community, and not be the act and custom of only a few; third, that it be sufficiently established by the prescription of time, without any competent authority having protested against it." Cotel. Catechism of the Vows.

material goods of monetary value.[2] Goods of an intellectual and moral order do not come under the vow. The renunciation, which is more or less absolute, according to whether the vow be simple or solemn, has the object of bridling, if not of destroying, the fierce passion of cupidity, and consists in a total abstention from any independent act of ownership. Mark the word "independent," for if it be duly authorized by the Rule or superiors, it becomes legitimate and is in no way contrary to the essential obligations of the religious state.

Herein lies the importance of asking and obtaining the requisite permissions in order to safeguard the conscience and to preserve one's quality of "poor" religious.

Substantially, this permission may be express, tacit or presumed.

It is express, when the superior, by a formal act, verbally or in writing, sanctions the commission of an act of ownership, such as to acquire, administer, give away, buy, sell, lend, exchange, employ, use up. From the point of view of validity, it is the most reliable.

The same cannot be said of the tacit or presumed permission, which easily lends itself to illusion and abuse. That permission is tacit which is implicitly contained in an explicit and general permission, and which proceeds from it as the normal result of a principle, or which offers itself as a necessary means to an end. Thus, for example: If the superior gives me, or allows me to accept objects, for which he knows I have no use, and which obviously are intended for distribution, such as packets of holy pictures, medals, or pamphlets, he tacitly gives me permission to make the distribution; . . . if he allows me to accept money, and it is the custom of the house that it be used for a certain purpose, he tacitly gives me permission to use it for the same purpose; . . . if I am allowed to make a journey, I can spend, accept and give what

[2] Exceptionally, ecclesiastical honors, offices and benefits can be prohibited in virtue of the vow of Poverty—such is the case for Redemptorists.

good religious do spend, accept and give on such occasions, and I do not need a special permission to do so . . . ; if the superior allows me to accept and keep in my room eatables for my own use, he tacitly permits me to use them when I think fit . . . ; this same permission is also included in the silence of a superior, who after witnessing an action of one of his subjects, makes no objection, though he could easily do so. All these tacit permissions are valid, unless "the custom of the Community or the particular Rules of the Institute demand an express or formal permission."[3]

Presumed permissions are also legitimate under certain conditions. Actually, the subject has been given no sanction; but he supposes that it would be granted if the superior were there, and so he acts, as if he had, in fact, obtained it. The grave and numerous abuses to which such a practice can give rise, if it becomes a habit, must be clearly perceptible. To obviate this, three conditions are necessary to make it valid:

(1) one must be pressed for time and forced to come to an urgent decision;

(2) it must be impossible to have immediate recourse to the absent superior;

(3) one must have good reason to believe—in view of the usual attitude of the superior—that if permission could be asked, it would be granted.

Without such guarantees, one is in danger of infringing the vow. Howbeit, fervent religious, who have a care for poverty, only make use of such permissions with great prudence and moderation. Furthermore, if one is to avoid breaking the vow of poverty, all these permissions, whatever may be their nature and source—must be valid, granted by a competent authority for proper motives.

Superiors, general, provincial and local, have not unlimited powers where poverty is concerned. They are merely the delegates of the Institute, and in the ordering and administration of its property, the range of their jurisdiction is de-

[3] Choupin, *op. cit.*

termined by Canon Law and the Constitutions. They must restrict themselves to it carefully under pain of making a misuse of their authority, of granting permissions that are invalid, and of themselves breaking the vow of poverty, while their subjects do the same.

Any permission obtained by fraud, surprise, or under false pretexts is equally null and void. There is nothing finer or safer than always to act with simplicity, straightness and sincerity. To attain one's end by ruse, dissimulation and tortuous and deceitful means is conduct unworthy of a religious, and necessarily bring in its train sin and remorse. When a permission is valid, but wrongful, because it has been granted without sufficient reason, or because it is not in conformity with the religious spirit, one cannot make use of it without committing faults against the virtue of poverty at least.

Now, since the vow lays an obligation on the conscience one may wonder what is exactly the gravity of this obligation. It is difficult to give a precise answer to this question—one that can serve as an absolute and universal rule. Obviously, not every fault against poverty is a mortal sin. In order to assess the morality of an infraction of the vow and to determine the degree of guilt, one must take into account the nature and circumstances of the act, how far it is opposed to poverty, the extent of the harm done to the convent, or to other persons, the financial position of the Community, and the relative severity of the different religious Orders. Each case must be examined in detail in the light of the following general principle: "The grave matter required for the commission of a grave fault against the vow is the same as that which is required for the commission of a grave fault against justice."[4]

~

The least known and most exposed of the religious vows is without any doubt that of poverty. So as to remedy this

[4] Choupin, *op. cit.*

ignorance and take precautions against the dangers, we now offer a list—perforce incomplete—of its chief prescriptions and most common infringements.

All independent acts of ownership are forbidden, whatever be their nature, whether they affect one's personal fortune, the property of the monastery, or that of a third party, unless such acts are rendered legitimate by the Rule or Constitutions.

With regard to what belongs to the religious in his own right, a distinction must be made, between the solemn vow and the simple vow of poverty.

In the Orders, where solemn profession is in force, the novice, before binding himself finally, must make absolute and irrevocable surrender, in favor of whom he pleases, of the ownership of his property, personal and real estate.[5] He renders himself radically incapable of acquiring anything in the future, by legacy, inheritance or gift; everything that comes to him, from whatever source, belongs by right to the monastery, the province or the Order, according to the Constitutions.[6] As for those acts of ownership that a monk may venture to commit, without permission they are not only illicit, but null.

The legislation of Congregations using simple vows is quite different.

During his novitiate, the candidate to the religious state cannot lawfully or validly surrender his rights to benefices or goods, or assume any obligation concerning them.[7]

Before his first vows, the novice must freely make his will, disposing of the use and revenue of all the property he possesses or may acquire in the future.[8] In doing this he must not fail to respect the law of justice or charity toward his kin or his Institute. Once the will has been made, it cannot be modified without the permission of the Holy See, or in

[5] Canon 581.   [7] Canon 568.
[6] Canon 582.   [8] Canon 569.

case of urgency, of the Superior general, or, where this is impossible, of the local Superior.[9]

The professed religious must retain the ownership of all his goods, and cannot surrender them by free deed of gift. This is a wise provision of the Church, leaving to those religious who return to the world the means of subsistence, so that they are no destitute. Further, the religious may acquire more property and add it to his capital.[10]

Though he may own a fortune, the religious may not administer it himself. For this, he must choose a prudent and reliable person, from whom he may, so many times a year, receive an account of his management. The best course would probably be to entrust this function to the Institute, in the person of the local or provincial bursar.

There remains the use or usufruct of all these goods, revenue, interest, income of all kinds. Before his profession, the religious must freely determine the use of it "either in favor of a third party, or even of the Institute, or in his own favor, in the sense that he can decide that the income from the capital shall return to swell the capital."[11] None the less, if the Rule and Constitutions contain special arrangements on this point, the religious must abide by them.[12]

But it is especially in respect of the Community's property that the religious is the most exposed to infringe his vow of poverty. He would do so, indeed, in the following cases, supposing, of course, that he acts without permission.

(1) To appropriate any object whatever with a view to keeping and using it: clothes, books, pictures, medals, office stationery, etc.

(2) To give alms, unless the Rule and traditions allow it; to give presents to one's colleagues, relatives, friends, strangers.

[9] Canon 583.
[10] Canon 580.
[11] Dr. Bastien. Directoire Canonique.
[12] Canon 569.

(3) To sell or exchange books, pictures, needlework or paintings, various products of farm or factory. "The same must be said of the religious who, having re-received a general permission to sell on behalf of the Community, raises or lowers the price named by his superiors, and in this respect is no longer dependent upon his superiors, and leaves the path they have bidden him follow. This can easily happen in hospitals where pharmaceutical objects are sold, and in other religious Communities, where the house turns to account the work of its members, in boarding schools, for the needs of the pupils."[13]

(4) When on holiday or a journey, to buy a suitcase, dressing case, small articles, and to indulge in extraordinary expenses such as an ascent in a funicular, a boatting trip, a pilgrimage that is not included in the fixed itinerary.

(5) To make use of linen, supplies, medicines, and books, to eat and drink between meals, to pick fruit in the garden.

(6) Through his fault and by culpable negligence, to break, damage, or lose objects of which he has the use, at least if he has knowingly disposed of the object, as if it were his own.

"Unquestionably, to damage or destory an object belonging to another or to the Community, is to sin against justice."[14] "But to destroy or damage an object in a fit of temper, does not make a fault against the vow of poverty. In this case, indeed, the idea that one was disposing of an object as if one were the owner simply does not exist."[15]

(7) "One would also sin against justice, by allowing objects that have been entrusted to one, to be damaged

[13] Choupin, *op. cit.*
[14] Choupin, *op. cit.*
[15] Creusen. Religieux.

or lost, through one's own fault; and likewise, there would be a sin against the vow of poverty, if one disposed of the object, as if it were one's own. Thus a cook, or storekeeper might allow his stores to deteriorate; a cellarer might let the wine turn sour; a bursar might, through negligence, find himself obliged to buy articles of inferior quality, or to pay much more, because he has not taken the trouble to buy at a favorable time; a buyer might let himself be tricked over the price, through his fault; a wardrobe keeper might let the clothes in his charge become moth-eaten, etc. Such religious could sin gravely against justice, and even against the vow of poverty. The same thing could be said of most offices."[16]

(8) To lend anything to one's brethren or to seculars; and, still more serious, to advance money to strangers.

(9) To keep an object for a longer period than that allowed, or to keep out of sight, by hiding or locking away, certain objects that one wishes to reserve for one's exclusive use. Saint Benedict recommends that "the beds must be frequently inspected by the Abbot." A palliasse can become the last refuge that the spirit of ownership at bay has been known to transform into a secret library or an annex to the larder.

(10) When one moves from one house to another, to take away to another house—over and above one's personal trousseau and the small amount allowed by the Rule or traditions—linen, books, tools and various instruments.

(11) To refuse to surrender or lend to a confrere, armed with the necessary permission, an object of which one has the use.

(12) In the various offices, to dispose of the articles one is in charge of, contrary to the prescriptions of the Rule, or the directions of the superiors.

[16] Choupin, *op. cit.*

On the other hand, personal notes, sermons, manuscripts, not intended for publication, relics (provided that the reliquary is not valuable) and waste of time, do not come under the vow of poverty.

It should be noted, that if one has, at one and the same time, sinned against the vow of poverty and justice, with respect to the Community, one is obliged in conscience to make restitution. "He must compensate for the harm he has done the House, either with his personal goods, or by extra labor, if he is capable of it, or else he must obtain remission from his superiors."[17]

We have indicated a third category of material goods—not belonging to the Community—and with regard to these all independent acts of ownership are also forbidden to the religious in virtue of his vow. In particular:

(1) To accept presents, sweets, medicines from outsiders; or if one has judged it permissible to accept them—making use of a supposed permission—to keep them afterwards and make use of them without an express permission.

(2) To borrow anything from relatives or friends, whether in kind or in money.

(3) To refuse the reward of one's labors or the honorarium offered for preaching, for "everything that the religious earns by his work for the good of religion must be devoted to religion."[18]

(4) When one has been offered a sum of money, with the request that it be devoted to good works, to use it as one thinks fit, without the advice or control of one's superiors.

(5) To surrender an income or pension, which by right should revert to the convent.

But there would be no infringement of the vow in the following cases: to refuse to accept a gift or an alms for the

[17] Cotel. Catechism of the Vows.
[18] Canon 580.

House, even though this refusal may be contrary to charity, and obedience; to receive money for a specified work and to use it for that work; to accept a deposit, even though this is dangerous and often forbidden by the Constitutions.

It can be seen, from this simple enumeration that the chances of sinning against the vow of poverty are multifarious. Therefore, the fervent religious will always be on the qui vive to keep his vow faithfully and scrupulously. Contempt for little faults, in this point above all others, could have grave consequences, and passing from illusion to indifference, lead to mortal sin.

Chapter X

POVERTY OF SPIRIT

THE VOW OF POVERTY is not an ideal; it is a minimum program with which a fervent religious cannot and may not be content. Here, as elsewhere, he aims at perfection.

Faithful to his vow, he will now strive to attain a higher level; the virtue of poverty. Indeed this is the object of the vow, by which it is protected and sustained. The vow is like a flying base, which one uses in order to take off more safely and rise to greater heights, as the soul leaves created things behind, and soars toward God. If the vow is the root of the tree, the virtue is the trunk and the branches, and the spirit of poverty is the exquisite fruit.

With its demands and its finer points, the virtue extends far beyond the limits of the vow, so that one can offend against the latter without infringing the former. Otherwise, the virtue is but an extension and an intensification of the vow.

But what exactly is it? "This true divestment is effected in three steps; the first is a love of poverty, which is created in us by the consideration of the beauty of this poverty; the second step is the resolution, which follows upon the affection, for we easily resolve upon a good for which we entertain an affection; the third is the practice, and is the most difficult."[1]

Thus, the virtue of poverty comprises a twofold element, one interior and spiritual; the other exterior and material. The first would be the soul and the second the body. This capital distinction is sometimes, in practice, rather over-

[1] Saint Francis de Sales. Spiritual Conferences.

looked: and the result is a poverty of routine, almost forced, and is only the shadow of true evangelical poverty.

The present chapter is consecrated to affective poverty; the next will deal with real or effective poverty.

~

Poverty, like all Christian virtues, is first and foremost an interior quality, an affair of the soul. Our Lord did not bless all the poor indiscriminately, but a certain category of poor, not a "social class" but a group of chosen souls. "Blessed are the poor in spirit." Indigence, as we have already said, is not a synonym of poverty. The world is full of beggars, but where are the poor? Sometimes alongside, or rather above, the material destitution, is found a spiritual poverty, which is loved and desired, which is held to be not an evil but a good, not a misfortune but a joy, which is not a misadventure, but a virtue.

This poverty does not necessarily consist in the effective loss of earthly goods—certain rich men have been admirable for their poverty—but in a certain attitude of the soul toward these goods; i.e., an habitual, stable, interior disposition of the mind, heart and will. Faith, which is the root and foundation of justification in general, is particularly that of poverty, a strange mysterious virtue that human reason has difficulty in understanding; the Gospel alone revealed to the world its greatness, fecundity and importance.

The virtue of poverty is based on a clear and solid conviction: the conviction that poverty is a most noble virtue, that it makes us like God "the Father of the Poor," and like Jesus Christ "King of the Poor," the conviction that the poor man is one of the chosen members of the Mystical Body of Christ, and one of the most priceless jewels of Christianity.

We are poor, if we are convinced that riches are a terrible danger for all, and for many, an irreparable misfortune; that poverty, on the other hand, is a safeguard and a blessing, the condition of all sanctity, the breeding ground of those great virtues called: humility, mortification, spirit of prayer, abandonment to Providence, love of Jesus Christ; if we are convinced that poverty is for the Congregations and the monastic Orders a principle of internal vitality, of apostolic fecundity and of long life. We are poor, when we really believe that the only treasure of a religious is his poverty, that the poorer he grows, the richer he becomes; and that his poverty is the pledge of his perseverance and eternal salvation. Complete renunciation does not spell ruin—it is good business. Briefly, we shall have acquired the virtue of poverty when we have meditated, studied and appreciated the words of Our Lord, "Blessed are the poor," and "Woe to you that are rich, for you have your consolation!"[2]

Too often, the power of money is a source of evil, mammona iniquitatis, and though they are rarely used in the pulpit, the invectives of Saint James are easily understood. "Go to now, ye rich men, weep and howl in your miseries, which shall come upon you, your riches are corrupted; and your garments are moth-eaten, your gold and silver is cankered; and the rust of them shall be for a testimony against you, shall eat your flesh like fire. You have stored up to yourselves wrath against the last days. Behold the hire of the laborers, who have reaped down your fields, which by fraud has been kept back by you, crieth; and the cry of them hath entered into the ears of the Lord of Sabaoth. You have feasted upon earth; and in riotousness you have nourished your hearts, in the day of slaughter. You have condemned and put to death the Just one, and he resisted you not. Be patient, therefore, brethren, until the coming of the Lord."[3] Briefly "How hardly shall they that have riches, enter into the Kingdom of God."[4]

Faith in the pre-eminence of poverty over riches, such is the first element of the virtue of poverty. "Blessed is he that

[2] Luke VI.
[3] Saint James V, 1-7.
[4] Mark X, 23.

understandeth concerning the needy and poor; the Lord will deliver him in the evil day."[5]

~

The second is the love of poverty, a genuine supernatural love. How can one understand the splendor and richness of this virtue, and not love it as Jesus Himself did? "Poverty of spirit consists not only in being poor, but in loving poverty—— It is not poverty, but the love of poverty, that is reputed virtue."[6] The heart, above all, must be poor, and Saint Francis of Sales wished his nuns on the Visitation "to have their feet shod, but their hearts discalced and bare." Saint Angela of Foligno, speaking of the seven gifts that will transform the soul into Christ, says "The first is the love of poverty, by which the soul strips itself of the love of all things created, so that she now desires no possession save Jesus Christ Our Lord, and expects the aid of no creature in this life, and proves it by her works." Without this love, it is impossible to practice perfect poverty. Despoilment implies sacrifice, and how is one to sacrifice oneself generously, unless one loves? "For God loveth a cheerful giver."[7] And a smile is nothing else than the outward blossoming of love. Poverty is a sorry business, when the heart is not in it. If we are to believe Saint Mary Magdalen of Pazzi, a liberal poverty, that is cherished, is better than a rigid poverty that is endured with ill grace; the former is a source of sanctification, the latter of perversion and damnation. "We can rest assured as to the salvation of a religious who has everything in abundance, provided that the abundance comes to him through his superiors, and that he desires nothing more. On the other hand, there is no hope of salvation for the religious, who is ill-fed, ill-clothed, but who longs for prosperity, and strives to stifle the remorse of his conscience by this outward appearance of

[5] Ps. XL, 1.
[6] Saint Alphonsus, *op. cit.*
[7] II Corinth. IX, 7.

poverty. Unless he strip himself of all he possesses by desire, he expects heaven in vain; there is no such thing for him."

Love of poverty means love of what is modest, humble, unpretentious, old, worn, of all that spells destitution; and, therefore, a great love of the poor who are the privileged ones of the Heart of Jesus; for, while no one may despise or hate the rich, it is none the less praiseworthy to be attentive to, and shower kindnesses upon the poor. If Providence has led us into an Institute specially devoted to the evangelization, instruction or physical care of outcasts, or paupers, let us be happy and proud of our priceless vocation, and be faithful to it. Love of poverty means love of the privations, self-denial and restrictions attached to the practice of this virtue. "I will also add this," wrote Saint Ignatius to the Fathers of Padua, "those who love poverty, must love its consequences, as far as they can; such as poor food, poor clothes, hard beds, and contempt. He who would love poverty, without being willing to suffer, is too finicky a pauper; without any doubt, he would prove that he loves the name of poverty more than the reality, he loves it with the lips, not with the heart."[8]

Love of poverty means love of one's vow, and of its many laws and prohibitions; love of all the practices and details of poverty imposed by the Rule, or recommended by tradition.

Love of poverty includes as a natural consequence supernatural hatred of comfort, abundance and superfluity; of what is showy or valuable, of worldly luxury, of all that weakens or corrupts the spirit of poverty in the soul or the Community.

Is this love as common as might appear? The virtue should be loved "like a mother." How many grant it barely the love afforded a stepmother. They put up with it, rather than embrace it. Without emulating the Poverello, whom Bossuet called, "the most desperate lover" of poverty, could we not be numbered among its greatest, most faithful friends?

We find the passionate note of this love in a prayer of Saint Francis of Assisi: "Have pity on me, O Jesus, and on my lady

[8] Dudon, Saint Ignatius of Loyola.

Poverty, for I love her so ardently that I can find no rest without her, and Thou knowest, O God, that Thou Thyself did kindle this love within me. O most poor Jesus! The grace that I ask of Thee, is to grant me the privilege of poverty; I ardently desire to be enriched with this treasure. It is Thy Will that it should mark the elect with the sign of Redemption: Oh! who would not love Lady Poverty above all others!"

~

Is it possible to believe in poverty, love it tenderly and still not finally decide to practice it? Resolution is the third and most important element of evangelical poverty. All moral virtues are, indeed, essentially perfections, stemming from the free will, and none can become virtuous, unless he will it. "A compulsory virtue," is a meaningless term. Poverty is no exception to the rule, a fact that cannot be stated too often. When speaking of obedience, humility, chastity, no one thinks it necessary to add the word "voluntary." What would be the point? Who could be mistaken and confuse virtue with instinct? But when it is a question of poverty, it is at once coupled with the word "voluntary." "Voluntary poverty" is an expression often found even in the concise style of Saint Thomas. "Voluntary poverty is necessary to the perfection of charity—its foundation is voluntary poverty."

This is explained by the presence of a danger, met both in the world, and in convents, which is the error of making shift with an outward poverty, material rather than spiritual, from which the soul is often divorced. One lives in a state of poverty, but as it were, unconsciously, without directing to it one's thoughts or will. It is a low standard of living, that one accepted long ago, once and for all. However, it must be repeated that there is no virtue, without the exercise of free will. To be poor willy-nilly or with reluctance, is not a virtue, but simply a state of necessity or want. To become one of the poor of Jesus, one must know how to choose, make up one's mind, form a resolution.

Thus it is clear that the religious practices poverty, not from necessity, routine, or force of environment, but deliberately, from choice, with a generous, unshakeable and effectual act of the will. In his novitiate, he acquires a true and precise knowledge of the poverty he must practice in his Congregation. He knows what it means to be poor and to live a life of poverty. He knows exactly the meaning and scope of the vow. The reading and careful meditation of the Rule, Constitutions and Directory, have revealed to him the many prescriptions and finer nuances of the virtue and spirit of poverty; and it is this same poverty, thoroughly grasped and daily loved more and more, which he has vowed, in his profession, before God, to keep intact, in all its traditional purity and austerity. And he will be faithful to his vow. He will encounter enemies of poverty on his way; but he will vanquish them, armed as he is with his invincible resolution that nothing can weaken, not the suggestions of greed, nor the persuasions of the world, nor bad example around him. If sometimes—and it may happen—poverty does appear to him in the shape of a cross, the sacrifice to be made will make him neither swerve nor recoil. His resolution stands firm, and at need, with all the force of his will, he will form it anew, so as to give it added strength.

If he were the only one, on the earth or in his Community, to practice poverty, he would not alter his decision, or change his plans in any way; sure of being right in spite of everyone, sure that he has chosen the better part.

~

The interior virtue of poverty does not make its abode in a soul, without immediately driving out those vain and dangerous sentiments called regrets for the past, dissatisfaction with the present, and longings for the future. "Detachment from ourselves," says Saint Basil, "is complete forgetfulness of the past and the banishment of our desires."

What regrets could a religious have, who has set out to

walk in the footsteps of Jesus? Now that he understands the splendor of a poverty he loves and that he wants to practice, of what importance can be the things he has to lay aside? Since he has left the lesser for the greater, he can rejoice over the exchange, and indeed, does rejoice. If the memories from the past ever cross his mind, of a past when he lived in lavish style, in comfort and plenty, if not in luxury, these memories have not a trace of bitterness. He has entered the promised land, flowing with milk and honey, and he would deem it strange, even absurd, to weep for the fleshpots of Egypt. His freedom from captivity dates from his profession: on that day, one of the finest of his life, of which he cannot think without joy and an immense gratitude to God, the net was broken and the bird flew away. With what generosity he stripped himself in days gone by. Now, he repeats the gesture with greater love and greater generosity.

His only regret is that he waited too long perhaps, before divesting himself of his worldly goods; that he was unable to do as he desired and actually give up all things, possess nothing, and cry "Deus meus et omnia"!

The poor soul feels no distress in face of the daily deprivations that are part and parcel of the religious life. How can he grumble and complain about a sacrifice that he has long foreseen, loved and sought? The religious who is truly poor is content with little; and if he lacks even the little, the awkward situation is just another excellent opportunity of practicing poverty. Rightly or wrongly, is he refused a permission? He does without it, and remains unruffled, unlike those half-hearted religious, who are annoyed and irritated by the slightest refusal. They consider that they should be granted everything they ask. The religious who is truly poor is not upset, if the superior takes from him the objects he has for his personal use, and exchanges them for others, or gives them away. He knows nothing of those wretched little ties, the last outbreak of the instinct of ownership, so frequent in convents. It is clearly understood that one does not own one's suitcase, watch, wallet, or pen, but one clings to them: and the proof lies in the resentment one would feel, if the superiors were to remove them. Some would make of it a real storm in a teacup.

"A sister who is afflicted at being deprived of anything by the Superior, shows that she did not retain it with the true spirit of poverty, or at least that she had some attachment to it. . . . What are we to think of the nun who throws the whole convent into confusion whenever the Sisters, with the permission of the Superior, use what she possesses."[9] We read in the Autobiography of St. Thérèse of Lisieux that a Sister had been asked for a pin that she found very useful, and she missed it. Saint Thérèse of the Child Jesus said to her: "Oh! how rich you are! You cannot be happy!" The poor in spirit are always happy, precisely because they have no attachments. Deprivation causes them no pain. One day, the Curé d'Ars accidentally lit his candle with a bank note; he showed neither surprise nor vexation. To a sympathizer, he replied, "Oh, it matters much less than if I had committed the smallest venial sin!"

Finally, interior poverty lops off all vain longings, and teaches the soul to be content with mere food and clothing. There is no desire to go beyond what is granted by the Rule and traditions, no itch to have a little more, and to stock up with superfluities. "Those who have nothing and wish to have, are ranked with the damned. God indeed looks not on what one possesses, but on the greed with which one covets."[10] When one has the cult of poverty, it is so easy to be satisfied. "A little is enough for the wise; still less, for the holy."[11]

[9] Saint Alphonsus, *op. cit.*
[10] Saint Augustine.
[11] Baunard, Life of Mme. Barat.

Chapter XI

THE LIFE OF POVERTY

As THE FLOWER develops into the fruit, interior poverty naturally develops into exterior and actual poverty. How could one believe in the value of evangelical poverty, love and desire it, and at the same time, dismiss it from one's life? Père Chevrier, when he was a curate, was getting rid of all his furniture, and when one of his colleagues told him that interior poverty and the spirit of detachment were quite enough, he replied: "Effective poverty helps in the practice of interior poverty. Those who restrict themselves to interior poverty run the risk of not having it at all!"[1] From the union—which is indissoluble in the religious state—of these two forms of poverty, perfect poverty is brought into being.

To what degree should this actual poverty be practiced? There is little reason to fear excess in the practice of interior poverty—can this admirable virtue ever be loved and esteemed enough?—but there must be limits to actual despoliation: Limits that are fixed, firstly by Canon Law, the Rules and Constitutions; but everyone is free, within the bounds of discretion, to go beyond what is enforced and obligatory. Thus, there are three forms of poverty; the first rigorous and universal, common to all Orders and religious Congregations; the second, more or less severe according to the spirit, object and works peculiar to each Institute; finally a third, optional, consisting of works of supererogation, inspired by the fervor of the individual.

~

[1] Regamey, La Pauvereté.

Community life,[2] enforced by canon legislation, is one of the finest and most necessary forms of religious poverty. "In every organization the community life shall be followed faithfully by all, even in those things pertaining to food, clothing and furniture."[3] "Let everything be common to all," says Saint Benedict, in his concise way. All the goods of the convent form a common capital, administered to the advantage of the whole. Thereafter, each will receive, as the Rule allows, what is necessary or useful.

Thus, in a Community, the aggregate of property belongs to all the religious in general, and nothing to each one in particular. No one is an owner, all are merely users. "Mine and thine" has no meaning. None is the absolute lord of his cell, his furniture, his clothes, not even of a book or pen; he has the use of it; he does not own it. The use itself is not exclusive, and is always dependent upon the good will of the superiors, who can take back tomorrow, what they have granted today. This has given rise to the custom in certain Congregations, which derives from the desert Fathers, and does not deserve the amusement it sometimes causes—of only using the possessive "our"—our cassock, our veil, our missal, our watch; and the custom is as true as it is religious. It is a delicacy of language which at every moment reminds the religious of what, in practice, he is in danger of forgetting, i.e., his state of absolute destitution. An example will make this clear.

A young professed nun, lately arrived in her Community, was sent, in very bad weather, to do some shopping in town. She had not yet been given an umbrella, though it was a compulsory article of her trousseau. Having obtained permission

---

[2] Community Life, in its broadest sense—comprises the whole of the collective exercises and individual acts which form the web of daily life, as it is appointed in the Constitutions. Indeed, it would be most perfectly expressed by perfect observance of the Rule. Here we deal with Community life under its connections with poverty.

[3] Canon 594.

to borrow one, she accosted one of her Sisters. "Would you be so kind as to lend me your umbrella?"—"What! haven't you got one?"—"No, Sister."—"But you ought to have one!"—"Maybe, Sister, but I haven't one."—"Well, try to get one as soon as you can. You understand, I can't pass mine round to everybody." As it was very windy, that happened which was bound to happen to a fledgling of the Novitiate—she returned with the umbrella insideout. There ensued a little family squabble. "Well! that's the last time I'll lend you *my* umbrella!" Fortunately the victim had not yet forgotten her training in asceticism. "Dear Sister, I am very sorry, but I assure you that I did not know it was *your* umbrella; I thought it belonged to the Community." If the religious owns nothing in his own right, he can at least receive from his superiors, and within the limits of the Rule, all that he needs. But in this respect— and here we have a second element of community life—all taint of privilege of favoritism must be avoided. A Community is a family of which all the members must be equal with regard to poverty, and all subject to the same regime. Similar cells, furniture, clothing, food, and treatment, in case of illness. It would be odd, if not shocking, that some should live in plenty and others in want. A holy equality in a strict poverty: such is the law.

Contrary to the idea of community life then, are all dispensations, exceptions, unjustified distinctions, that run counter to or are outside the general rules of poverty. "Unjustified," for there are cases in which uniformity and equality must give way to prudence and charity. Saint Benedict, who was a model of discretion, recommends that the delicate, the sick and the old should be shown special attention and receive special care. Another danger is the use of the peculium.[4] If

---

[4] By peculium is understood any temporal object of monetary value that a religious receives for his personal, habitual use, and of which he can dispose more or less independently of his superior. If the latter cannot revoke the permission once it has been granted, it is independent peculium, otherwise, dependent peculium.

it does not always comprise an infringement of the vow, at least it paves the way for numerous faults against the virtue and spirit of poverty. It is not consistent with the spirit of the Church, and most Rules forbid it absolutely.

The importance of community life is emphasized by the gravity of the sanctions applied to those who offend against it. Those religious, who interfere with it seriously, "shall be seriously admonished, and if they do not amend, they shall be punished, even with deprivation of active and passive vote, and, if they are superiors, also with deprivation of office."[5] Saint Alphonsus called it the "jewel of his Congregation." It is certain that "all the holy founders of religious Orders had in view the establishment of community life; and as long as community life has been maintained, fervor has reigned in the Communities."[6] The source of humility, mortification, charity, and peace, it is also one of the strongest bastions of poverty.

~

Besides respecting community life, the religious will be faithful to his Rule. Where poverty is concerned, every Institute has its own legislation, which is more or less severe. The Constitutions, Customary, and Directory contain, with an abundance of details covering even the smallest point, numerous prescripts and prohibitions. Every religious must know them and observe them scrupulously. On this particular point, it is most important to be a traditionalist and conservative, and to avoid all kinds of dangerous innovation, which could open the door to abuses and laxity.

With regard to the cell "full of the perfumes of poverty,"[7] its furnishing: chairs, bed, toilet articles, pictures, books, the religious must be content with what is allowed. It is far better to have less than more. Likewise, for all that concerns

[5] Canon 2389.
[6] Saint Alphonsus, *op. cit.*
[7] Saint Catherine of Siena, Dialogue.

clothing and linen: let both quality and quantity conform to the Rule and tradition. Let all be simple, unpretentious, ordinary. Let the habit be worn, patched, but clean, not unworthy of one of Jesus' poor. Saint Thomas asks if religious may wear poor, cheap habits, and replies that they may, for two reasons; in a spirit of penance, and as a sign of contempt for worldly riches and luxury.

At table, a true religious is neither dainty nor over fastidious, he gladly contents himself with the daily menu, though it lack seasoning and variety, and will accept his modest portion as an alms, in a spirit of poverty.

It is rare that the Constitutions do not caution against superfluity, luxury and comfort. By superfluity, we must understand all that is not necessary or useful, all that one could easily do without, even if one has a use for it. Why have half a dozen pens or pencils, if one is enough? Why keep five or six pairs of glasses—even if most of them are broken? Why keep a whole collection of books, covered with dust and cobwebs?

What good are all these trifles, knick-knacks, trinkets and trash, that people feel they must collect? There was a religious who, every time he went to a new house dragged with him an enormous trunk, filled with the most incongruous objects—material for a stall in the rag market.

In certain convents, the superiors used regularly to inspect the cells in order to take away or burn what they called "the idols of the religious," everything that was mere "fancy." Let us not wait for this visitation of justice: let us do it ourselves, from time to time; after the example of the saints, let us make the inventory of our cell, and remove what is useless and superfluous. "One evening Saint Thérèse of the Child Jesus was seen putting down outside her cell door a penknife she had used during the day. 'I could not put it back in its place,' she said, 'and, as it is not an object attached to the cell, I did not want to have it during the night.' Like Saint John of the Cross, she would have broken her sleep, rather than keep in her habit one more pin than the regulation three."[8] According to Bourdaloue, "a distinction must be made between what is necessary, convenient, and superfluous; the necessary, that reason requires, the convenient, that sensuality seeks, the superfluous, with which pride decks itself and makes a show. Now, what is the difference between what is worldly and what is religious? It is this—that whereas the man of the world, without restricting himself to what is merely sufficient, which he considers to be less than nothing, wants to have all his comforts, and to live in plenty and luxury; the religious, faithfully practicing the poverty he has vowed, is content with bare necessities."[9]

The religious who has a feeling for poverty will flee luxury with still greater zeal. How wide is the gulf between these two words—luxury and poverty. What a disgrace, what a mockery it would be to have made a vow of poverty and to live in pomp. Perfumed letter paper, stamped with one's initials, solid gold watches, chased silver propelling pencils, the smartest dressing cases, the last word in travel cases; silk stockings, etc.; four-star hotels when traveling, first-class and dining cars—what would the workman or peasant, who lives hard and meanly, think if he saw the poor of Jesus Christ live in such a fashion? The virtue of poverty cannot live in amity with the pursuit of ease. How many times one has said, "Now, isn't that convenient! Much more practical!" and if one did not add "We must get it!" at least one thought it. Not that the convenient must at all times and in all places be eschewed, but one must avoid letting the quest of the convenient become a habitual line of conduct. Convenience is not a synonym of mortification or poverty. Love of comfort has never been recommended as a Christian virtue, still less a religious one. Our Lord revealed to Saint Veronica de Juliani that three things caused Him great displeasure in monasteries: (1) lack of respect for superiors; (2) rancor and spite; (3) a way of

[8] L'Esprit de Sainte Thérèse de l'Enfant Jesus.
[9] Bourdaloue, Pensées Diverses sur l'Etat Religieux.

living that was too comfortable and not in line with holy poverty.[10]

~

Besides the practices, which are in common use in fervent Communities, there is nothing to prevent the use of others, which are not formally commanded, but are none the less excellent.

First, the spirit of economy, which is rare enough in our century, with its high standard of living, and the habit of thoughtless expenditure. This must not be confused with avarice, a vice that would be doubly hateful in a soul dedicated to perfect detachment. Economy is a virtue of the poor, and consists in taking care that nothing is allowed to be broken, damaged, wasted, or lost. Saint Benedict says "Let (the monk) look upon all the vessels and goods of the Monastery as though they were the consecrated vessels of the altar."[11] Contrary to some, who on the pretext of being broadminded, are easy-going and seem to live like the rich, the economical religious takes great care of all that is at his disposal, and tries to make it last as long as possible; he is careful of light, paper, clothes, is moderate in his use of buses and, especially, of taxis; restricts his correspondence, and his use of the telephone and telegraph; uses for jotting down notes, old envelopes turned inside out, and carefully picks up the last crumbs of his bread. It is reported of Père Pouget, a Lazarist, that during the holidays the novices used to go to Gentilly once a week. Père Pouget always returned on foot and came running back after lunch to take his class. "Why didn't you take the bus?" he was asked—"Well, it costs three sous. And three sous would buy quite a lot of bread for a poor man. So many die of starvation!" And he would give the three sous to a beggar.

Another form of evangelical poverty is manual or intel-

[10] Sandreau, Les Divines Paroles.
[11] Rule, Ch. XXXI.

lectual labor. "Then they are truly monks, when they live by the labor of their hands."[12] The poor work to earn their daily bread. Jesus, Mary and Joseph, the most illustrious poor that the earth has ever known, were simple working folk. The religious state is not a sinecure, nor is profession the right to a life annuity. To live idle, doing nothing at all, or nothing worth while, is to be a parasite. We are poor, so let us live like the poor and work like the poor, and not be a burden to our Congregation. Founders and saints have all, without exception, been great toilers. We can read in the life of Mère Véronique: "Our revered Mother used to recommend that we turn back our sleeves as soon as we came out of chapel, so that when we got to the community room we had only to put on our aprons before setting to work. When we went to see her, even for a short message, we had to take some sewing with us, in case there were another Sister with her, and we had to wait. During recreation, we also had to be occupied with some useful work; indeed, it was the same everywhere it was possible."[13]

When faced with the sacrifices of poverty, and these are light enough, the religious will never complain. Silence is his rule. If an involuntary movement of repulsion escapes him, he reacts promptly and courageously. Why should he offer a chill and grudging welcome to a virtue that he loves and esteems? Like Saint Paul, he will say: "I have learned in whatsoever state I am, to be content, therewith. I know both how to be brought low, and I know how to abound: everywhere and in all things I am instructed both to be full, and to be hungry; both to abound, and to suffer need."[14]

Saint Alphonsus names patience in hardship as the third degree of poverty. It consists in "making no complaints, even when one lacks what is necessary." The Mother of God said one day to a Franciscan nun, who was very devoted to her:

[12] Rule of Saint Benedict, Ch. XLVII.
[13] Life.
[14] Phil. IV, 11, 12.

"My daughter, if you had all you need, you would not be truly poor; true poverty consists in having less than what is necessary." To complain of poverty, according to Saint Jeanne de Chantal, displeases God and men. "I am never so happy, as when I have some mark of poverty."[15] When platters were empty, Saint John of the Cross would say: "Children, what else does being poor mean, if not to lack something? Have we not made a vow of poverty? Well then, let us embrace it!"[16]

But most of all we must practice patience and detachment in sickness and suffering. If superiors are bound in conscience to watch with care and tenderness over the health of their subjects, and to give them all the treatment that is compatible with the religious spirit, the religious on their side must not forget that they have made a vow of poverty, and that they must be treated as poor; they must be content with the doctors and treatments they are given, and not launch forth into bitter recriminations. "If you had remained in the world, I do not know if you could have had all those medicines and doctors that the convent procures for you now. Ah! be content, not only to live like a pauper, but to die like one; and when death comes to take you out of this world, rejoice if it finds you treated like a pauper!"[17]

Père Chevrier has drawn up a brief, yet complete program of the life of poverty, and every religious could profitably meditate upon it at any time:

"He is content with little ...

He wastes nothing ...

He accepts everything gratefully ...

He always thinks that he is given more than his deserts.

He is pleased with all that is done for him.

He complains of nothing, for he loves the poverty
    which makes him like Jesus Christ.

He works to earn his living ...

[15] Saint Alphonsus, Ascetical Works.
[16] F. Bruno, Life of Saint John of the Cross.
[17] Saint Alphonsus, *op. cit.*

He is not afraid to do the humblest and lowest things.

He has a horror of all that smacks of luxury and vanity, comfort and ease.

He is ready to help everybody.

He takes great care of all that he has.

He avoids abundance and extravagance.

He makes no unnecessary expenditure for lodging, clothing, food, building and decoration.

He is economical without being avaricious."[18]

[18] Père Chevrier, quoted by Valensin.

Chapter XII

THE CROSS OF THE POOR

A SHORT WHILE before her death, Bernadette, in religion, Sister Mary Bernard, wanted to divest herself of all that remained to her—a few little pictures. Then turning her limpid, deep eyes to the Crucifix, she said: "I no longer have need of anything but Him. He is enough." And thus the confidante of the Immaculate Mother reached the summit of evangelical detachment.

The good religious keeps his vow of poverty; the practice of the virtue stamps the fervent; as for the spirit of poverty, it is one of the characteristic marks of holiness.

To this supreme degree of poverty, we could aptly apply the commentary of Saint John Chrysostom on the words of Jesus " 'If you would be perfect.' . . . Our Lord does not command, He suggests. . . . Even when it is indirect, an invitation has sometimes more effect than an order. Certain souls who rebel against force, only need to be enlightened, and they will make up their own minds and act." They do not like being pushed or dragged; spontaneity is one of the marks of their generosity.

Though the spirit of poverty is not rigorously enforced, it remains none the less an ideal for all candidates to perfection, and so for every religious fully aware of his vocation. The word "spirit" here means the virtue of poverty in its perfect flowering and full maturity.

This chapter will deal with effective poverty, raised to the point where sacrifice in destitution is loved and sought out.

The next chapter will treat of affective poverty resulting in interior and total detachment from all creatures.

~

The first characteristic of the spirit of poverty is the joyful acceptance of grievous poverty. Joy and grief: two sentiments which at first sight are incompatible, and which none the less mix very easily in fervent souls. In most convents, we only find a moderate poverty, which does not impose any great sacrifice.

Easy and amiable poverty: many religious know and want to know none other. Poor—oh yes! since they have made a vow of poverty—but on condition that they have little or nothing to suffer. "Many are they who are proud to be called poor, but often on what conditions? That they lack nothing. They call themselves the friends of poverty, and when they come face to face with the true friends of poverty: hunger, thirst, penury, humiliation, they run away from them as fast as they can."[1]

If a poverty that resembles to some degree that of the Master "abject, set as naught, despised and most necessitous" can repel those who are weak, it does not discourage the true imitators of Jesus Christ. Far from dreading it, they welcome it with love and joy. This joy is spiritual, indeed, for suffering, whatever may be its form and origin, is ever hateful to human nature. Interior joy over privation can only be the effect of lively faith and burning love. Once it is realized that real destitution is a blessing, a grace of graces, when Jesus is loved with that deep love, which tends naturally to perfect likeness in the soul and the life, then grievous poverty becomes a source of joy, and the evangelical beatitude is proved. "Blessed are the poor!"

There are three different attitudes to this grievous poverty, that of disgust and revolt, accompanied by criticism of superiors, who are taxed with harshness or stinginess. For

[1] Saint Vincent Ferrier, Tractatus de Vita et Instruct, Spirit.

two pins one would demand from them—Rule in hand—the respect of one's rights. The case, thanks be to God, is exceptional. Not so rare, perhaps, is the passive attitude. No recrimination, but a resigned silence. One puts up with this unfortunate state of affairs, with the secret hope that it will not last long. Quite different is the attitude of the religious inspired by the spirit of poverty. Does he lack what is useful or even necessary? He rejoices.

He rejoices at being ill-housed; he is glad of a hard bed; an inconvenient cell; of paper and ink of the worst quality. He rejoices if they forget to serve him at table; if the food, besides being far from plentiful, is badly cooked; when the bread is stale and the water brackish. He rejoices if he has to wear a patched habit, a threadbare coat, roughly cobbled shoes—so much so that he is in no hurry to have them replaced. He rejoices when he is refused a permission; if he is not given every necessary treatment, when he is sick; if he is given the hardest and roughest work to do. He is happy to suffer from his poverty and indeed gives thanks to God for so great a grace.

Saint Alphonsus of Liguori did not consider that, as far as his own religious were concerned, such a program was excessive. "Be piously envious of those who are poorer than you, and go so far as to rejoice, when you lack what is necessary, considering that one cannot appreciate poverty, while lacking nothing. Thus, those are the true servants of the Saviour, who not only are not saddened by the inconvenience of poverty, but who carry their imitation of the Divine Master to the point of rejoicing, when they lack what they need."

However, it must be noted that this eminent degree of poverty is not usually attained at the first attempt. Persevering efforts are required, together with special graces of enlightenment and fortitude. With her charming simplicity, Saint Thérèse of the Child Jesus admits that she did not, at first, understand, and only later, practiced this crucifying degree of poverty. "When I was a postulant, I was pleased to have for my use objects in good condition, and I liked to have all that I needed. Jesus put up with this patiently, for He does not like to reveal everything to souls at once, and He usually only gives His light, a little at a time. One evening, after Compline, I searched in vain for our lamp on the shelves where they are kept, and as it was the time of the "Great Silence," I could not recover it. I guessed rightly that a Sister, thinking it was her own, had taken it; but just on that evening I had counted much on doing some work, and was I to spend a whole hour in the dark on account of this mistake? Without the interior light of grace I should undoubtedly have pitied myself but, with light I felt happy instead of aggrieved, and reflected that poverty consists in being deprived not only of what is convenient, but of what is necessary. And in this exterior darkness, I found my soul illuminated by a brightness that was divine."[2] It is related in the life of the Curé d'Ars: "He was told that his bed had been burnt, and could not be used. 'I have been asking God for this grace for a long time,' he replied, 'and He has heard me at last.' I think that this time, I really must be the poorest man in my parish—they all have beds, and I, thank God have not!"[3]

~

But there are souls who are not satisfied with giving a glad welcome to the painful manifestations of poverty. Under the inspiration of the Holy Ghost, "Father of the Poor," they set off enthusiastically to the conquest of a poverty that shall be supreme, abject. It is another and no less admirable form of the "Folly of the Cross." Eager for deprivations and poverty as others covet riches and pleasure, determined to follow step by step their Redeemer, saints have carried their cult

[2] Autobiography.
[3] M. Convert, Le Bienheureux Curé d'Ars et les Dons du Saint-Esprit.

of poverty to excesses which, if they do not condemn our cowardice, do at least confound our weakness, and offend modern rationalism. Such a one is Saint Benedict Labre, ragged, verminous, who begged his bread from door to door, when he did not look for it in the dustbins. While he was still a young man, he was gripped by a passion for poverty. For a time, he was the guest of his uncle, a parish priest, and they vied with one another in deeds of charity and poverty. They gave away all their furniture to the needy, chairs and all, they dug a hole in the beaten earth which formed their flooring, and took their meals sitting on the edge with their legs dangling in the excavation, and praised God.

Such is Père de Foucauld, a viscount, who at Nazareth became the servant and gardener of the Poor Clares. "I cannot imagine love without a need, an imperious need to conform, to resemble and above all to share all the sufferings, difficulties and hardships of life. To be rich, well off, to live comfortably on my possessions, when you have been poor, in straitened circumstances, living arduously by hard work—I can't do it, my God . . . I can't love like that."[4] He joined the Trappists, an Order of great austerity, but left, because in it, he could not carry out his ideal of absolute poverty. He returned to Our Lady of the Snows to prepare for the priesthood, and received, on the night of his arrival, a welcome that delighted him. Darkness was falling, and the Brother doorkeeper did not recognize, among the beggars, the former Trappist novice, who took no steps to enlighten him. "Come in, friends, we'll give you some soup, and a nice corner to doss down in." He took his bowl of hot soup like the others, slept with them in the barn, and only disclosed his identity next morning, when the monastery bell rang for the first Mass. He settled down in the attics, above the old chapel, in a narrow cell, which could be reached by a steep and narrow ladder—provided one stooped. In this pigeon loft he received his few visitors, relatives and friends, who were so amazed

[4] Ecrits Spirituels.

that one of them, as he came down from this roost, muttered to himself: "It's all very odd—yet he isn't quite mad yet!" He did his own cooking which was not complicated—a dish of beans or boiled cabbage. He had to go to Viviers for his ordination, and Abbot Dom Martin who accompanied him, had told him to see to the provisions for their journey. At lunchtime, Charles de Foucauld took a little parcel from his pocket, removed the wrapping, and deposited on the Abbot's knees three figs each, two nuts and a bottle of water.[5] When he said his first Mass he went up to the altar, in honor of the poverty of Nazareth, wearing the oldest and shabbiest alb, which he had discovered at the bottom of a drawer and which he had saved for the occasion.

Such is Saint Vianney, who seems to have beaten all the records. Those who visit the presbytery at Ars, that glorious reliquary of his heroic poverty, can see his old down-at-heel shoes, his hat that has lost shape and color, his cassock that is a mass of patches, his rickety table, his cooking pot that still seems to reek of musty potatoes. How he loved his poverty! How he could defend it when the need arose! Old Catherine thought she had done well in replacing by a delft cup the old earthenware bowl that the servant of God had long used. He took fright at this luxury, and rid himself of it as soon as he could, saying: "Is it impossible to achieve poverty in this household?" He even went so far as to defend those who stole from him. A woman, wanted by the police, had stolen 900 francs from him. He ran to her house, "Keep the money you took from me, and tell the police I have given it to you."[6]

Such was Alphonsus of Liguori; Founder, Superior General, Bishop, yet insisting upon wearing a wretched cassock; no one could make him change it. One night, while he was asleep, a new one was substituted. . . . In the morning, he got up and dressed, and being short-sighted, did not, at first,

[5] Bazin, Charles de Foucauld.
[6] Trochu-Monnin.

notice anything . . . Yet, the sleeves . . . "Brother, have you put new sleeves on this cassock?" "Yes, My Lord, the old ones were too torn!" . . . Then, looking more closely, he saw that the cassock was completely new!" "Ah!" he cried, "I have been tricked!" "It is true, my Lord, but frankly, the other cassock was a disgrace." "Never mind, go and fetch it, and bring it to me!" "It cannot be done, My Lord, it has been given to the poor." And the saint murmured softly: "Ah! God forgive you! You will always go your own way!" One day they were joking about the value of his episcopal ring, and he said, "This ring is the one I wore in Rome, and all those who saw it then, took it for a valuable one, but I said to myself, "They don't know that I broke my best decanter to make a stone for this ring!"—when he left his diocese "all his luggage was contained in a basket which was roped on to the back of the carriage; there was, in this basket, only a candlestick, a brass lamp, a coffeepot and a stove. A donkey trotted behind the carriage and bore his wretched bed."[7]

The pursuit and practice of such destitution constitutes, according to Saint Alphonsus, the fourth and last degree of poverty. One must "not only be content with what is poor, but choose what is poorest; the poorest cell, the poorest bed, the poorest clothes, the poorest food . . ." It is perhaps the opportune moment to quote an excellent instruction in poverty, given by Father Anthony Torrès to a nun who was his penitent: "Love poverty like a treasure, since your Divine Spouse deemed it to be so. Practice it in everything, and wear it as your finest adornment. Do not be at peace, if you see in the convent a choir nun or lay sister, who is poorer than you. . . . Do not possess, or seek to obtain anything, even though you think it necessary, without first meditating upon your Spouse, naked on the Cross, and asking Him, if it is His Will."[8] However, we must not forget that this heroic,

[7] Villecourt. Vie et Institut de Saint Alphonse Marie de Liguori.
[8] Saint Alphonsus, *op. cit.*

and sometimes unusual poverty which is practiced by the saints, and which is only justified by an extraordinary love of Jesus Poor, is not asked of everybody, and is exacted of only a very few. Unless one is inspired by God, and duly controlled by one's superiors and confessor, it is imprudent to aim at what is out of the ordinary. Many acts of virtue are more admirable than imitable.

In spite of this, could we not, without indiscretion, impose on ourselves some little voluntary and superogatory sacrifices in the practice of poverty? Saint Vincent of Paul was of this opinion, saying one day to his daughters: "It is certain that a good way of being happy is to have poor clothes, and to be vexed when you are given new ones; far from desiring better ones than the others, you should say to Mlle. Le Gras: Madamoiselle, that dress is much too good for me. Do you not know that I am already proud, and that this will make me prouder than ever? Oh, I am too vain and full of envy. So I do not deserve to be dressed so finely. There, my daughters, that is how you should behave!"[9]

To conclude, let us recall the program of poverty laid down by Saint John of the Cross:

"Let the soul ever seek what is more difficult, not what is easier;

Not what is tasty, but what is insipid;

Not what is pleasing, but what offends;

Not what offers consolation, but what offers desolation;

Not rest, but work;

Not to desire more, but less;

Not to aim at what is higher and more valuable, but at what is baser and more contemptible;

Not to wish for anything, but to wish for nothing;

Not to pursue the best in all things, but the worst, desiring to embrace, for the love of Jesus Christ, a state of total destitution, perfect poverty of spirit, and absolute renunciation, with regard to all worldly things. These practices must be

[9] Saint Vincent de Paul, Oeuvres Complètes.

embraced with all the energy of one's soul, and the will must be brought to bear upon them. He who gives himself to them with affection, by intelligent and discreet application will very shortly find in them great delight and ineffable consolation."[10]

[10] Saint John of the Cross.

Chapter XIII

COMPLETE DETACHMENT

COMPLETE DETACHMENT—also called "silence, protection and solitude of the heart"—is the highest peak of poverty. It is important that the word "detachment" be correctly understood, and not confused with its counterfeit: hardness of heart and meanness. There is a certain poverty, which may be one of the most loathsome expressions of egoism: the contempt of a pride that imagines itself above everything, and in need of nothing and nobody.

If we are to understand exactly the nature of detachment, we must briefly recall certain fundamental truths on the place and function in our moral lives, of God and creatures.

In fact, there exists but one Being, whom we may desire, seek and possess absolutely and unalterably; one Being to Whom we should bind ourselves, forever, by unbreakable ties: God . . . and His Will. God, the first beginning and final end of our lives; His Will: the sole, obligatory path that leads us to Him. God alone is the necessary Being. As for creatures, they are in our existence accidental and contingent, and we may only want them and use them "conditionally," i.e., in so far as they lead us to God, in so far as it is His Will. From the moment they become, not a means, but an obstacle to the glory of God and our sanctification, our duty is to give them up cheerfully, to leave them without regret. This detachment consists in loving, seeking and possessing nothing —even in desire—in using and enjoying nothing whatsoever, save in God and for God, within the limits drawn by His Divine Will. As the rays of the sun give light, warmth and fecundity, without being soiled or trapped by anything, so the detached soul is raised aloft, and while avoiding all entanglements and contaminations, can pour itself out on the whole of creation.

The ideal would be to love wholeheartedly all that God wishes us to love, but without becoming the slaves of our affections, and thereby of creatures. It is precisely in this that the little miracle consists: to love without being tied, to possess without being possessed, to use without selfish pleasure; to keep one's independence intact, and finally, to seek in all things, and all places, solely the glory of God.

Detachment presents itself under two aspects:

(a) Detachment from all persons.

(b) Detachment from all things, spiritual or material.

~

The first aspect of detachment, the most painful of all, is the renunciation of one's personality. Saint Benedict required of his novices that they "abandon all things that belong to them." This entails a process of impoverishment, belittlement, a purging of that execrable egoism, known as self-love, self-will, sensuality. One clings to one's "self" more closely than the skin to the body. To be detached from one's self, then, is to renounce absolutely and totally all idea, desire, claim, whim, taste, comfort, from the moment that any of these are opposed to the will of God, and the good pleasure of Jesus Christ. This may well explain the considerable number of imperfect religious, vegetating in the lowest strata of spirituality; too full of themselves, they have not yet succeeded in regarding themselves as a thing well lost, they have not yet learned "to forgo all their interests and satisfactions, all their plans and wishes, and to depend thenceforward only on the good pleasure of God."[1] How rare are those who can say, like a certain nun: "I no longer count!"

A danger that is perhaps more noticeable in our times is attachment to parents. Jesus condemns this in terms so strong, that they seem paradoxical, almost shocking. "If any man

[1] Lallement. Doctrine Spirituelle.

comes to me, and hate not his father, and mother, and wife, and children, and brethren, and sisters, yea, and his own life also, he cannot be my disciple."[2] Not, indeed, that love of one's neighbor is prohibited in the convent! A religious, more than anyone else, is not dispensed from the commandments of God and the law of charity. He will keep for his kin all his affection, though he will purify and elevate it. He will love more and better, because he will love religiously, in God and for God, and his tenderness for his mother and father will be, in reality, but an overflow of his love for Jesus Christ. This love will urge him to pray often, and sacrifice himself daily, for the happiness and salvation of his loved ones. Bodily presence is not essential to love, thank God. Our Lord left His Mother to stay in the Temple; he left her for the whole time of His Public Life; He left her when He returned to Heaven. Yet, how Jesus loved his Mother! Detachment from the family is then neither oblivion nor loss of affection, but simply a reaction against an affection that is too natural in its demonstration, too human in its desires, too anxious in its care, and which, therefore, becomes an obstacle to the interior life, and to the accomplishment of the duties of the religious state, even when it does not go so far as to weaken, and cause the loss of the vocation.

Though it is far from being a hardening of the heart, detachment does entail both a certain withdrawal of the spirit, and diminution of familiar relationship. The religious state involves separation from the world: a separation that is more or less severe according to the austerity of the different Congregations.

If one is free where one's close relations are concerned, it is perhaps still more important to be free with regard to the members of one's spiritual family. In Community, detachment is the rule, whether it is a question of superiors or of one's brethren or sisters. Some subjects are only too detached from authority, in the wrong sense of the word, detached to

[2] Luke XIV, 26.

the point of opposition, division or revolt. Whatever may happen, whatever the cost, a religious must always remain united in heart and will to his superiors. And this union will be the result of a mutual affection, open and supernatural. Those who live cut off from the representatives of God are in a bad state of conscience.

But while cordially loving the superiors, we must watch carefully lest we attach ourselves to them from natural motives. A nun may love with obsession a "Mother" who spoils her, gives way to her whims and grudges her no human consolations. She cannot live without her, or far from her; jealous of the affection she shows others, she complains bitterly that she does not love her any more, and the mere idea of a change or a departure brings tears to her eyes. No less dangerous—even though they are often a subject of ridicule—are those particular friendships, which are but a form of egoism à deux, the ruin of fervor, the plague of convents, of which Saint Teresa has painted a portrait still apt today. "It prevents a nun from loving all the others equally, makes her resent any injury done to her friend, causes her to wish she had something to give her favorite and to seek for opportunities to talk to her often, and tell her how much she loves her, and other nonsense of the sort, rather than of how much she loves God. These close friendships, rarely serve to forward the love of God. . . . Keep free of partialities, for the love of God, however holy they may be, for even among brothers they are like poison. . . . O my Sisters, let us not permit our will to become the slave of any save of Him who purchased it with His Blood, or, without knowing how, we shall find ourselves caught in a trap from which we cannot escape!"[3]

Religious dedicated to education must practice the same indifference of heart. Where the pupils are concerned, be they young or older, there must be no selfish attachment, no sentimental affection, but one that is pure, strong and devoted. To flatter a child, give him special marks of interest

[3] Saint Teresa. Way of Perfection.

and love, because he is more polite, more intelligent, more likable, while neglecting his less attractive companions and showing them only coldness, indifference or harshness; all this would constitute a triple offense: a lack of purity of heart, public scandal, and sterilization of a whole apostolate. Mother Barat, that incomparable educator, said to her daughters: "The mistresses must be kind to the children, but they must not allow flattery, or seek to attract them. The more one loves them rightly, the less one flatters them; the less one caresses them, the better one should care for them. Your hearts, my dear daughters, no longer belong to you. The hearts of these children are not made for you. And what would happen indeed, if you let yourself be caught in these earthly snares? You would, at once, become incapable of all good, because your only guide would be passion. . . . Come now, be Christians, be apostles, be men and give up all these womanly weaknesses!"[4]

To nursing nuns more than others, it is expedient to recommend watchfulness over the heart. Compassion in face of suffering, innate in woman, the instinctive urge to console and encourage—these are legitimate sentiments but they are in danger of altering imperceptibly, until they develop into natural attachments. With regard to the suffering members of Jesus Christ one can never have too much gentleness, patience, kindness, maternal tenderness, on condition, however, that this devotion be inspired solely by faith and divine charity. One must know how to give oneself, without ever being tied.

Prudence, coupled with simplicity, must dominate the necessary relations with the confessor or director. The soul must forget the man, and see only the priest, the representative of Jesus Christ, and avoid all familiarity. Is it necessary to warn a religious soul against all profane love? Her heart was consecrated to God like a living ciborium on the day of her profession; how could she dare to profane it by giving en-

[4] Baunard. Histore de Madame Barat.

trance to the world? This heart is wholly Christ's, for time and eternity. Detachment of the affections is one of the rarest and most heroic of virtues, one of those virtues that few even of the saints have carried the whole way. That does not matter, one must learn to practice it with courage and perseverance. Purification of the heart, by its total despoliation, is a long and exacting labor, that death alone can end.

~

The heart sinks countless roots into the whole of creation. Not content with being unduly attached to persons it will cling to anything, howsoever trifling, like a shrub that will strike root and grow in the cranny of a rock. If it is to be transplanted into God, it must first be uprooted, torn completely away from the earth.

Those who practice total detachment will also preserve themselves from the thousand and one little ties that are so common in the monastery. For one forms an attachment to anything and nothing: a cell, a habit, a travel bag, a watch, a pen, a medal, or a collection of post cards. And the proof that one is "caught" is that one would feel it very much if the article were removed. A ninety-year-old religious, on the eve of his death, insisted upon leaving the infirmary and returning to his cell, for fear—so he said—lest one of his brethren should take advantage of his condition and occupy it.

These little failings are to be found in even great souls. Père Lacordaire said, one day, about one of his habits: "That is a habit which I was weak enough to prize. I did not want it used to patch others. It is the one I wore in Notre Dame when I made the funeral oration of O'Connell, and my discourse on the vocation of the French nation. I will cling to it no more. Take it." A child, saying his prayers at his mother's knee, came to the words: "My God I give You all that I have," stopped and added under his breath: "Except my little rabbit." There are many little rabbits running around the cloisters.

Periodically, let us make an inventory of everything in our use, and if we find that we have developed an attachment, let us break it. Another form of detachment, which is sometimes painful and demands great self-sacrifice is detachment from posts, duties and offices, including that of superior. If it is right that one should like work, and the occupations allotted by obedience, it is not permissible to cling to them desperately and to refuse to give them up. Those in authority must be free to employ a religious in any capacity, and without any resistance to make use of his person or his talents for the benefit of the Community and the Church. Here again, how often we find a sorry state of affairs. Faced with a transfer or a retirement what objections are put forward, what entreaties are made, what complaints both public and private, what discouragement is shown. It has been said that it is easier to overthrow a Minister of the Republic than to change the employment of a religious. Yet, the silent smile of a religious who is poor and who prizes nothing but the will of God, would have been, in such circumstances, so fine and meritorious! To remove certain nuns from their occupation as portress, infirmarian, or sacristan can be distressing, even a tragic occurrence and can sometimes cause temptation against the vocation. An old monk who had been withdrawn from the guest quarters and attached to the library was still speaking bitterly of the change a year later. And a cellarer, given another occupation, harbored a grudge for months!

The superior, who is aware of his responsibilities, should cling to his office even less than his subjects. What could be more true to the spirit of humility, detachment and obedience, than to relinquish it gladly at the first sign from those above him, and to return modestly and joyfully to the place, in the middle of his brethren, that in his own estimation he should never have left. Every morning a mother superior said this prayer: "My God, do not let me grow attached to my office; may I love it, since it is Thy Will, but may I never take pleasure in it." Another woman, outstanding for her virtue and powers of organization, had been for twenty years at the head of a large Community, yet certainly had never taken pleasure in her position. When recalled suddenly to the Mother house, to fulfill there a function of no importance, she greeted her Superior General with the delightfully simple words: "Well, Reverend Mother, here I am! Thank you, first of all, for relieving me of a burden that was too heavy for me, and now, do with me what you can; not much, I expect!" A gesture as rare as it is noble!

To detachment from office must be added indifference as to abode: both convent and country. If, in the Monastic Orders the monk takes root in the place where he has made his vow of stability and, with regard to the Apostolate, is content with static warfare, it is a very different matter for the flying columns formed by most of the modern Congregations. The religious is a campaigning soldier, bivouacking anywhere, and settling nowhere; always ready, on the order of his chiefs, to strike camp, and go and pitch his tent in twenty different places; North, South, East and West, France or Africa. He changes his residence like a garrison officer. The true homeland of an apostle, until he gets to Heaven, is anywhere there are souls to save, and harvests to bring home. Nothing is so opposed to the religious spirit as to build oneself a little mossy nest somewhere, and to decide to settle there, even if it means trying out a thousand stratagems and supplying one's superiors with all sorts of motives of health, influences, connections, even of zeal, when one does not go so far as to enlist the intervention of outsiders. The poor religious will cling to his residence no more than the bird to the branch. When Brother Lucidus, the companion of Saint Francis, had stayed more than a month in a certain place, and had grown attached to it, he fled elsewhere saying: "Our only abode is Heaven!"

Père Tissot, the Superior General, asked an old Father

who had returned to Europe, worn out with long years of apostolate "If you were sent to India, Père Larive, how much time would you need for your preparations?" "Three hours!" Then after a moment's thought, "Or rather, no, Father Superior! I can go at once."[5] As we move from one place to another, let us think of Our Lady, going to Bethlehem, fleeing to Egypt, returning to Nazareth; but let us not forget to take Jesus with us in our arms as she did, or at least in our hearts, and say: "I have with me, here, in my heart, all that I must have, all that I may have. I have my God! My God is my family, my friends, my brethren, my glory, my riches, He is my whole past and all my future. He suffices me . . . My God is truly my inheritance, my share of the chalice. If I possess Him, can I be exiled, can I be alone?"[6]

Finally, the truly poor are detached from life itself. They do not care whether they live or die, since nothing retains them here below, and moreover, they are assured of the hereafter. In patience and resignation they await the hour fixed by Providence, the hour in which God will throw open the gates of Paradise . . . and will gather them to His bosom with poor Lazarus of the Gospel.

Happy are they who are detached from all things, for it is in their royal poverty that they will find, as we have already said, the fullness of all riches and all spiritual gifts; fullness of light, strength, liberty, peace and joy; fullness of virtues and fullness of love; fullness of union with God in purity and comtemplation.

Blessed are the poor, for they belong to the race of saints!

[5] Père Buffet. Vie du Père Tissot.
[6] Perreyve. Méditations sur les Saints Ordres.

PART III

CHASTITY

Chapter XIV

THE PURE OF HEART

WHILE CHASTITY is a human and Christian virtue, it belongs more particularly to the religious state, being one of its characteristic and essential elements, together with poverty and obedience. The religious makes public profession of continence, and binds himself by vow to eternal celibacy. In the garden of the Church, chastity is one of the most beautiful and fragrant flowers. Symbolized by the lily, it has the lily's purity, majesty, and delicacy. It is a virtue so beautiful, that even the pagans, while unable to cultivate it, could not but admire it. As for virginity, that which is inspired by the love of Christ, it is one of the great revelations of the Gospel.

From the very beginnings of Christianity, called by the Master, following the steps of the Virgin Mother, and the example of the Apostles, an immense legion of virgin souls sprang up and has never ceased to grow in numbers throughout the ages. This virginity, which had its countless martyrs— the triumph of spirit over matter, the detachment from all that is earthly of a heart athirst for absolute purity and complete love—has been praised with almost lyrical enthusiasm by Fathers of the Church, Doctors, ascetics and saints. This virtue was so dear to the Blessed Virgin that, had it entailed the loss of her ineffable purity—she would never have accepted the prodigious glory of Divine Motherhood.

Yet chastity is not a mere ornament—beautiful, but a matter of choice. It is one of the main pillars of our spiritual temple: if it gives, the whole structure collapses. Indeed, it is impossible to lead a religious, Christian or even—in the full sense of the word—human life, without this virtue. Its practice constitutes one of the essential articles of the moral code that was engraved in every conscience, before it was ever issued in the Decalogue. Under pain of lamentable decay, all souls must be chaste, and without this nuptial robe, none shall enter the Kingdom of Heaven.

During early childhood, purity consists in instinctive innocence and ignorance. Later, when the passions awake, through contact with the world or through diabolical suggestions, it becomes a conscious and combative virtue. In this daily warfare, fierce and full of ambushes, we must have recourse to the "armor of light" which enables us to walk "honestly, as in the day."[1] If we know the many grave reasons, both natural and supernatural, that encourage us to live immaculate, our virtue will increase in lucidity, beauty, strength and merit.

Chastity rests on a triple foundation, according to the different states of life: human, Christian and religious, and we shall study each of these in turn.[2]

~

Chastity, as a human virtue, finds its justification in the principles of the natural law. It is the "Powerful and constant control of the instincts according to the rules of reason."[3] From a sense of personal dignity as much as out of respect for the rights of God, man owes it to himself to live always, and everywhere, in continence and modesty. In the long run, all forms of morality derive from the authority of God: He has the right, in His Wisdom, to define good and evil, what is lawful and what is not, and to fix the boundaries beyond

---

[1] Romans XII, 12, 13.

[2] It is not within the scope of this book to treat of sacerdotal chastity.

[3] Ernst. La Formation de la Chasteté.

which no conscience may venture without fault. Now, in this matter, the rights and commands of the Most High are manifest. God wishes man to remain chaste, and He requires it in His quality of Creator, Legislator and Sovereign Artificer.

It is an incontrovertible fact that we are, body and soul, the creatures of God. We belong to Him more than to ourselves, and the supposed independence of man, with regard to God—and this is heresy to a believer—is, to the sane mind, nothing but pride and folly. Whether we like it or not, we are born in a state of subjection. God has, over all creatures, a right of ownership that is inalienable, absolute and universal: everything belongs to Him without restriction, unconditionally and forever. This right is based on creation; if the vase belongs to the potter who threw it, why should the human body not belong to God, who fashioned it? It is based again on the preservation of this body, which exists and continues to exist only by an act of the Almighty. Finally, it has been won by the Redeemer; for both soul and body were redeemed by the Blood of Christ; so that, as Saint Paul told the Corinthians: "Non estis vestri: You are not your own."[4]

What conclusion can be drawn from this principle? That this body, which belongs not to us, but to God, must be treated with sovereign respect; that none has the right to lay on this body a predatory or sacrilegious hand. The living Ark must not be touched improperly; and woe betide those who, making use of this flesh without discretion or rule, from passion and sensuality, violate the most sacred rights of the Creator! "For this is the will of God, your sanctification; that you should abstain from fornication; that every one of you should know how to possess his vessel in sanctification and honor: not in the passion of lust like the gentiles that know not God: and that no man overreach, nor circumvent his brother in business, because the Lord is the avenger of all these things as we have told you before, and have testified. For God hath not called us unto uncleanness but unto sanctification. There-

[4] Cor. VI, 19.

fore, he that despiseth these things, despiseth not man, but God, who also hath given His holy Spirit to us."[5] This will of the Supreme Legislator is in no wise arbitrary or tyrannical, since it is the expression and application of a law, as wise as it is holy. Chastity is so closely related to the eternal moral code, that its violation has always been considered an act peculiarly "immoral," one of the most hideous forms of "evil," "vice," par excellence.

While it establishes us in harmony, this virtue enables us to associate ourselves with the views of God, to carry out His plans, and finally, to procure His glory. The moral order demands the domination of the spirit over the body, of mind over matter, the triumph of the will over one of the basest and most passionate forms of egotism. Chastity ensures and maintains this fundamental order, whereas its absence can only result in enslavement of the flesh and the most lamentable degradation. The moral order also demands that man, when associated with the act of creation, should only exercise his power according to the designs of God's Providence, for the propagation of the human species and the peopling of Heaven. Apart from this essential object, all use becomes abuse, and a criminal attack upon the constitution of the family and the extension of society. None has the right, without contravening one of the most fundamental laws of nature, to transform into a vile instrument of pleasure and sterility, one of his most noble faculties, productive of love and life.

Moreover, to be chaste is to respect one of the noblest works of the Divine Artist. With one word, Jehovah called forth out of nothing light, the earth, the sea, the stars in the sky; with one word He produced life in the myriad leaves of the plants and the infinite multitude of animals. When He comes to man, God seems to collect Himself, to meditate on something prodigious and to summon all His genius and Power: "Let us make man to our image and likeness; and let

[5] Thess. IV, 3-8.

him have domination over the fishes of the sea, and the fowls of the air, and the beasts, and the whole earth, and every creeping creature that moveth upon the earth."[6] This time the word is not enough, and with His divine hands He takes earth, kneads it, models it, to make of it the masterpiece of His creation: the human body. Then that nothing shall be wanting to Him, "he breathed into his face the breath of life."[7] A spiritual and immortal soul. And it was only then, that God saw that what He had done was very good.[8]

God wills that the human body be treated with sovereign respect, for it was the abode of the Word, and is a living marvel of His artistry. The artist has his rights and his legitimate sensitiveness about his work. Let people admire or criticize his art, but at least, let them not handle it with barbaric and sacrilegious hands. We are rightly indignant at the sight of masterpieces torn and mutilated by the vandalism of rough soldiers. Now chastity is merely respect for the body, as vice is its profanation. For the complete man, virtue is the source of beauty, strength, harmony, light, love, devotion, and sanctity while impurity is a principle of ugliness, exhaustion, lack of balance, egotism, cowardice, in brief, of total degradation. The man, who has forgotten how to be chaste, debases and degrades himself to the level of the beast. Chastity spiritualizes even the body while sins of the flesh brutalize even the soul.

~

For the Christian, living in God, the child of the Heavenly Father, the brother and member of Christ, the temple of the Holy Ghost, the sin is yet more serious. More than the pagan, the baptized soul owes it to himself and to God, to preserve an incorruptible chastity. His body is no longer merely a beautiful work of art, but a masterpiece of sanctity. Even on

[6] Genesis I, 26.
[7] Genesis II, 7.
[8] Genesis I, 31.

earth, he has a share in the supernatural life, and receives
the sacraments of the Church. Washed by the water of baptism, he is anointed with the oil of confirmation, of the priesthood, of extreme unction. How many times the host has
rested on his lips and tongue, on its way to inflame his heart
and sow in his flesh the seeds of resurrection and immor-
tality! Thus, this wretched human body, withered by the
years, falling into ruin, a prey to death and corruption, will
one day rise again, young, vigorous, spiritual, bright as a
fresh spring morning; like the grain of wheat that rots in the
earth so that it may put forth the strong green blade, and
become the bread of man and the Body of Christ. Our soul
will come and snatch our body from the horror of the tomb,
and carry it away into eternal glory.

From all eternity God has loved this body, for which Christ
became incarnate and shed all His Blood. Then, how much
we should love it ourselves! This is the reason for our instinctive fear of death: "For we also who are in this tabernacle, do groan, being burdened; because we would not be
unclothed, but clothed upon, that that which is mortal may
be swallowed up by life."[9] "For no man ever hated his own
flesh."[10] We must love our body, which is now the companion
of our exile, our toils and struggles, and will, one day, be the
co-heir of our beatitude; we must love it, not with a natural
or carnal love, but with a dilection that is spiritual and divine, love it in charity as we love our Father in Heaven, love
it as Christ Himself loved the Church. Under the sway of
this charity we shall use our body in the service of God, guard
it carefully against the passions, that corrupt and kill, transform it into an instrument, not of iniquity, but of justice,
and, through austerity and chastity make of it "a living sacrifice, Holy, pleasing to God."[11]

In our quality of Christians, we are by right members of

[9] II Cor. V, 4.
[10] Ephes. V, 29.
[11] Rom. XII, 1.

the divine family. "Born of God" we have become "truly His
sons." Sons of the Heavenly Father! What a glory, what a
responsibility, and how important it is that we should not
take it lightly! Noblesse oblige. We must then live "as befits
His servants, be holy as He is Holy," "keep clean of sin." We
no longer have the right to be "mere natural man," for we
are the sons of the light, and may not drag in the mire the
living image of God.[12] At the sight of such a downfall and
such a crime what sorrow and indignation must fill the heart
of God! Chastity is also one of the moral consequences of our
incorporation with Christ, on whom we were grafted at Baptism, and with whom we now form one complete being—a
Mystical Body of which Jesus Christ is the head and we, the
members. "Know you not that your bodies are the members
of Christ?"[13] We are members of his body; and flesh of his
bones.[14]

What conclusion can we draw from this dogma, unless it
be the rigorous obligation for every Christian to be chaste,
to touch the body only with a sovereign respect—as the priest
at the altar touches the host—and never to lay upon it a
sacrilegious hand? Is not the pollution of one's flesh the profanation of that of Christ? This would be a horrible crime,
deserving the chastisement of Oza, who was struck dead for
having dared to touch the Ark of the Covenant. The Apostle
cries in indignation: "Shall I then take the members of Christ
and make them the members of a harlot? God forbid!"[15] On
the other hand, chastity is a glorious homage paid by our
flesh to the ineffable purity of Jesus. A writer expressed the
wish to see the annual celebration in the schools of the feast
of "the Blood of France,"[16] in order to teach young folk to

[12] John I, 13-1. John III. I Col. 1, 10-1.
    John V, 18-1. Cor. II. 14 Ephes. V, 8.
[13] I Cor. VI, 15.
[14] Ephes. V, 30.
[15] I Cor. VI, 15.
[16] Paul Bureau. L'Indiscipline des Moeurs.

purify their hearts and respect their bodies. In the Catholic liturgy, we have the Feast of the Precious Blood of Jesus. May the generations of Christians drink this most pure blood, and draw from it the cult of chastity!

In close connection with the dogma of our incorporation with Christ is the mystery of the Trinity dwelling in our souls, and this is another basis for Christian chastity. "If any one love me, he will keep my word; and my Father will love him and we will come to him, and will make our abode with him."[17] If God is everywhere by His essence, His power and immensity, He is none the less in a special manner with every Christian who is in a state of grace.

This is a real and personal presence, the presence of the Father, the Son and the Holy Ghost, which makes of the conscience a foretaste of Paradise. It is a sanctifying presence, not in the way the host sanctifies the ciborium by simple inoperative contact, but by intimate penetration and fermentation of the supernatural life, by an outpouring of divine graces. The Trinity works in us incessantly; the Father to engender, the Son to "Christify," the Holy Ghost to enlighten, purify, strengthen and inflame.

The Presence is continual, and if we so desire it, eternal. God has not come down within us to make a brief visit, but to make in us His permanent dwelling place, which He will never leave, unless He is driven out. Thus the Christian is the home, or rather the temple of the Trinity, an imposing temple, not constructed by the hand of man, but raised at baptism by the power of the Almighty, consecrated at confirmation by the Spirit, sanctified at Communion by the Host Christ, a temple fragrant with perfume; a temple at the same time spiritual and material of which the soul is the sanctuary and the body the visible architecture. "Know you not that you are the temple of God, and that the Spirit of God dwelleth in you."[18]

[17] John XIV, 23.
[18] I Cor. III, 16.

And from this doctrine Saint Paul draws practical conclusions: "Glorify and bear God in your body,"[19] by keeping it in a state of perfect purity; and woe betide anybody who "violates the temple of God; him shall God destroy."[20] "But you are not in the flesh, but in the spirit, if so be the Spirit of God dwell in you."[21] To violate this noble virtue, is, then, to aim a blow at the majesty of God, at the sanctity of His temple profaned and sacked by the most hideous of passions. He is driven out, and his place it taken by the demon of lust. For God only frequents hearts that are pure. Listen to Saint Augustine conversing with his friends at Cassiacum. Saint Augustine: "Tell me, who is he that has God in him?" Licentius: "I judge that he has God in him, who does good." Trygetius: "He has God in him, who does the will of God." Adeodat: "He has God in him, who has not in him the impure spirit."

And Monica approved.

~

While it is a human and Christian virtue, chastity belongs in a special way to the religious state, being one of its essential elements and a fundamental obligation.

On entering religion, the candidate undertakes to follow, for the rest of his life, a path of chastity that will lead him to the highest summits of sacrifice and love. The priesthood may be contemplated apart from celibacy, but there is no such thing as a religious life without perfect chastity. Poverty, chastity and obedience form the framework of the edifice —all the rest is furnishing and adornment. Chastity transforms the religious into an unspotted victim; freeing him from the flesh, it makes his strength "as the strength of ten" in the service of God and souls, while it lends him wings that bear him aloft toward sanctity. In order that this virtue

[19] I Cor. VI, 20.
[20] I Cor. III, 17.
[21] Romans VIII, 9.

may take root in the very depths of his being, he makes an austere and splendid vow: the vow by which he gives up the founding of a family,[22] and the joys of parenthood; a vow that he will keep his body and soul in a state of virginal purity until death. In virtue of this vow, the religious denies himself, under pain of sacrilege, every act, both exterior and interior, forbidden by the sixth and ninth commandments. Made with exact knowledge and full consent, this act always involves a double mortal sin, one against chastity, the other against religion. As for the other acts, exterior or interior, which are of the province rather of modesty: immodest looks, readings, conversations, touches, recollections, imaginings, too tender affections, these, like the others involve a double sin: mortal or venial according to their gravity and the more or less proximate danger they create. The religious will keep this public and sacred promise made to God, in the hands of the Church and in the presence of his brethren, jealously, heroically if need be, from a spirit of religion and fidelity in love.

The temple, the altar and the chalice are consecrated and reserved exclusively for the divine cult: he who uses them for any other purpose is guilty of profanation. The religious, too, is consecrated by his vow of chastity: a mystical consecration, which sets upon him a seal that is eminently supernatural, and dedicates him officially and definitively to the service of God. Separated from the mass of humanity, raised to a superior state of life and perfection, he appears, in the eyes of the world, as the herald of the Most High, and the monstrance of His Sanctity. If Saint Benedict requires that the monastery tools be treated like sacred vessels, what can we say of the religious himself? Thus he who violates his vow of chastity commits a real profanation. Every serious sin—interior or exterior—against the sixth or ninth commandments,

---

[22] The marriage of a person having simple vows would not be invalid, but illicit, whereas the marriage of a person having solemn vows would be null and void.

always involves a horrible sacrilege.[23] This is all the more so, in that the religious soul, who has now a further claim to the title of Spouse of Christ, belongs to Him entirely and is one with Him "two in one flesh." This mystical marriage is in one respect superior to Christian marriage, and requires that the virgin be "holy both in body and spirit"[24] and keep incorruptible faith with Jesus Christ. Faith of mind, heart, will and body, faith that cannot be violated without the committal of a kind of spiritual adultery.

A famous surgeon one day asked a nursing sister, who assisted him in the operating theater: "Do you know, Sister, what I admire most in consecrated souls?"—"No, Professor" —"Well!" and what he had to say sounded particularly striking on the lips of a man of the world, "it is their fidelity to their divine Spouse." For fidelity is so rare in the world! On the day before she died Gemma Galgani asked that her body, even after her death, should not to be touched by profane hands, "because it belongs to Jesus."

[23] If the fault against the virtue of purity is only venial, through inadvertance or lack of full consent, it is evident that the sin against the vow is only light.

[24] I Cor. VII, 34.

Chapter XV

AS THE LILY

Now THAT we are acquainted with the natural and supernatural, human, Christian and religious foundations of chastity, we must study its nature, its enemies and its privileges.

What is chastity? If one gathers certain delicate flowers, one runs the risk of crushing them. Could one not be content with enjoying their perfume? So it is for the angelic virtue. Scruples and anxieties, however, sometimes find their way into the conscience, and the sole origin of these is ignorance or error. The remedy is in the truth, even though it be veiled. May we, with the grace of Jesus Christ and the help of the Immaculate Virgin, speak with enough clarity to enlighten all minds, and enough tact not to shock or give scandal.

Of all the virtues, chastity is perhaps the most fragile and exposed. The dangers that threaten it are almost innumerable. They are exterior and interior, and we shall point them out, for a foe unmasked is half defeated.

Lastly, for our encouragement in this austere struggle we shall recall the incomparable privileges of chastity.

~

The first characteristic of chastity is its power of radiation, interior and exterior, moral and physical. "Souls and bodies, these are opposite extremes; virginity is the middle point which partakes of the one and the other. It is in the flesh, says Saint Augustine, and in this it belongs to men, but it has in the flesh something that is not of the flesh; in this, it approaches the angels, so that it is the connecting link between souls and bodies. . . . This noble principle having been established, I do not wonder, Christians, that holy virginity

176

intervened to unite, in the mystery of the Incarnation, the Divinity and the flesh."[1]

At the same time spiritual and material, chastity is primarily rooted in the will, and extends to all our faculties. Like any moral virtue, it is essentially a perfection of the soul. Let us beware, lest we warp or unduly trouble consciences, lest we give it too material a sense, or attach too great importance to its carnal side. If it means corporal integrity, it means still more, in its fundamentals, the incorruptibility of a will, habitually and firmly resolved to renounce crude pleasures and all sensual enjoyment. Thus chastity is first and foremost a matter of will and of a determination to cling to God. As long as the will does not give under the pressure of the passions, the virtue remains intact, and holds by its roots like the oak battered by the storm. Through weakness, cowardice, or a moment's aberration, one may trample this priceless jewel underfoot, but no power, human or diabolic, can snatch it from us without our consent. With the grace of God, we are chaste if we wish and in so far as we wish, and it is important to remember the distinction drawn by Saint Francis of Sales between "sentiment" and "consent." Let us, therefore, be untroubled and undiscouraged by temptation, though it be frequent and horrible enough. Illustrious saints, incomparably innocent, have endured this terrible trial which had the effect of intensifying their humility, exalting their trust, purifying and fortifying their virtue. "I am going to make a statement full of philosophy and experience. Those who have the most violent, desperate temptations, if they desire, will receive from God more precious graces, a mission much greater than others. The violence of temptations against purity, when they have been overcome, makes of those who have suffered them, veritable miracle workers. Listen to me carefully: what I say is the truth. Every difficult victory, once it is won, gives God in abundance, and precisely because of the vio-

[1] Bossuet. Sermon pour une Profession, le Jour de L'Epiphanie.

lent temptations that have been endured, graces in far greater number and far more precious are given to the soul we
have to direct. If a certain soul is violently tempted, study it
carefully, and try to sustain it. God calls this soul to the performance of incomparable deeds; He destines it to a mission
that He will never give to another. This is a law of nature
and grace."[2]

From the will, where it takes its source, chastity spreads
through the other interior powers. It shines in the intellect,
which is flooded with the spendors of faith, enlightened by
prayer and meditation, ever in quest of God, and in pursuit
of its ideal of perfection. In the soul of a religious there is
no place for a thought that is bad or coarse, for unhealthy
curiosity, for dangerous studies or readings: its home is in
Heaven, and it has the spotless wings of a dove.

There is also the purity of the memory; there must be no
looking back on a past that has vanished, on a world that
has been renounced once and for always. The religious will
recollect his past weakness and sins only with abhorrence
and tears of compunction. The imagination, too, must be
chaste, and no longer indulge in seductive dreams, sentimental reveries or sensual representations.

Most important of all is the chastity of the heart. "Blessed
are the clean of heart."[3] Whatever the world may think, this
purity must not be confused with indifference, harshness or
egotism. A pure heart is not a cold heart; on the contrary, it
is ardent and passionate, with an immense virginal power
of loving. Think of the Saints! Think of the Hearts of Jesus
and Mary! The pure of heart loves all that is lovable, tem-
perately and within bounds, like God and for God. Even his
human affections are, in reality, but the overflow of his charity. A religious keeps his family affections, his ties of friendship, but he purifies them and raises them to the supernatural
level. A pure heart is attached to nothing and nobody save

[2] Père Brisson. Conference.
[3] Matth. V, 8.

God. Where creatures are concerned, he is free; he is bound to Jesus Christ alone. How admirable is the solitude and total detachment of a soul that belongs entirely to God. How wonderful to be in a position to say with Saint Francis of Sales: "If I knew of one fiber in my heart which was not for God, I would tear it out at once even with red hot pincers!" Chastity of the heart excludes all natural ties, all unbridled affections, all sentimental friendships, and above all that sensual love that Saint Teresa called "criminal" because it makes of the heart an adulterer and an apostate. In a religious, all must be chaste; tongue, ears, eyes, touch and most of all, soul.

Chastity of the eyes, which should usually be downcast or ready to turn away from any sight able to trouble the innocence of the soul.

Chastity of the ears, that are deaf to worldly tittle-tattle, frivolous confidences, idle or indecent talk.

Chastity of the lips, so often purified by the Body and Blood of the Saviour. They are innocent of any conversation unworthy of a Spouse of Christ or contrary to the rules of the strictest modesty.

Chastity of the feet: let there be prudence in our dealings and relations. As we pass through the world, let us remain "immaculati in via."

Chastity of the hands, innocens manibus, that will always keep their moral whiteness.

The countenance itself, the bearing and carriage should bear the mark of this divine modesty, the fruit of the Holy Ghost, recommended by Saint Paul to the Philippians: "Let your modesty be known to all men," and which is the visible radiance of a soul that is perfectly pure—the halo, as it were, of its intimate chastity.

~

Chastity is a radiant virtue: it is also extremely delicate and terribly exposed. Brother Giles, the companion of Saint Francis of Assisi, compared it to a mirror tarnished by the slight-est breath. Attacked from all sides by enemies as treacherous as they are violent, i.e., nature, the world and the devil, it demands both strength and prudence. It is only won at the point of the sword: it is the prerogative of great and heroic souls.

Its first enemy—the most dangerous, for it is within the fort—is our fallen nature "the concupiscence of the flesh." We bear within us an abscess, ever on the point of breaking, a consuming fire that smolders, but will burst into flame at a breath.

If a rigorous enclosure protects certain contemplative Orders, it is not the same for most contemporary Congregations, devoted to all forms and works of apostolate, and for that reason, in enforced contact with a pagan and corrupt society. While living in the world, they must not be of the world, and must seek to immunize themselves, by the use of the prophylactic measures, that we shall suggest later. The apostolate of today, which has the praiseworthy aim of going everywhere, of operating at every level of society, and of succoring every kind of physical and moral distress, is not undertaken without risk, and how many, alas! have fallen victim to their intemperate and imprudent zeal!

To crown all, the devil takes a hand. How many obsessions, humiliating and painful revolts are due to him. He counts among his greatest triumphs, the downfall of a consecrated soul. He attacks us with strong temptations, which God allows, sometimes to punish presumption and pride, sometimes, as purifying trials for souls, whom He calls to mystical union and a high degree of sanctity. Saint Benedict Labre and Saint Frances Romaine had great temptations against chastity. Saint Alphonsus Rodriguez endured them for seven years, and the venerable Cesar de Bus for twenty-five.

Who can measure the joy, at once childlike and virile, of those souls that no foul breath has tainted, or of those illustrious penitents who, in penance and tears, have recovered a moral virginity? Bodies enslaved and polluted souls do not know what joy is—a true joy, complete, without remorse or vicissitude. In the world, laughter too often has a note of bitterness. How many unbelievers have succumbed to the charm of the peace and joy that reign in the cloister! Some, even, have gone so far as to enter the convent, simply to find a happiness they had not discovered elsewhere. "I saw Chastity; she was radiant with a pure, serene joy; as a friend or sister might have done, she invited me to come, and ready to embrace me, she held out to me her hands full of encouraging examples: children, adolescents, innumerable young men and women, venerable widows, women grown old in virginity—all these souls were chaste, and this chastity had remained sterile in none; she was fruitful and brought forth a host of true joys, like so many fruits she owed to Thy love, O God Who art her Spouse!"[4]

There is the joy of keeping one's heart pure, and of seeing it filled to overflowing with love; for the pure heart holds love, as the ciborium holds the host. . . . My God! how well one can love with a heart ever young and never shared, all of whose affections and desires are concentrated upon God. Is it not, moreover, for this very purpose, that one has made a vow of chastity? "Virginity of the body is only good in so far as it effects the virginity of the soul. To be content with the former is to reduce religion to physical privation, a Judaic practice. The utility of conquering the flesh is to free the spirit and render it more fervent in the love of God."[5]

Finally, in Heaven, chastity will find its supreme reward: a special crown of glory, like that of the doctors and martyrs; the unique privilege of singing the new song and of attending the Lamb wherever He goes. He who feedeth among the lilies.

[4] Saint Augustine. Confessions.
[5] Bossuet. Sermon sur l'Etat Religieux.

Chapter XVI

AMONG THORNS

RELIGIOUS CHASTITY is a warlike and conquering
virtue. Attacked on all sides by astute or ferocious enemies,
it can only be, especially in its perfect integrity, the result of
a daily triumph of grace and the will over all the combined
forces of nature, the world and Hell. . . . A fortress besieged
will resist all attacks and remain inviolate only if its defend-
ers protect it with a triple rampart: humility, love of Christ
and prudence; and if they can use two priceless weapons:
austerity and prayer.[1]

~

The first defense-work to raise is humility, a real, deep humility. Chastity, humility: these two virtues have so many
points of resemblance, and are calculated to agree with and
support each other. Pride and vice, on the contrary "united
in the first betrayal, have contrived to have an intimate
affinity which means that the one unceasingly calls to the
other, that they attract, support and exalt each other. Pride
is the impurity of the spirit, as impurity is the pride of the
flesh. They form a double revolt of which man is victim: the
revolt of the spirit against God, and the revolt of the flesh
against the spirit. Abelard wrote to one of his friends: "the

[1] We do not mention here the general and indirect means of preserving chastity. Sources of grace which tend to intensify the spiritual life
in the soul, and thereby to reinforce its power of resistance to evil: such
are prayer, recollection, the presence of God, confession and above all,
Holy Communion. Everyone knows the conquering and pacifying virtue
of the virginal flesh of Jesus over the carnal passions; and there can be
nothing better than to recommend, to young people especially, frequent
and even daily Communion.

enthusiasm aroused by my lessons, having amazingly multiplied the number of my pupils, I had abundance of money and fame. But prosperity always puffs up the weak; security in this world enfeebles the vigor of the soul; and the lures of the flesh soften its resistance. Thus I considered myself to be the only philosopher on earth, and having no fears for the future, I began to give free rein to my passions, I, who had ever lived in the strictest continence, and the further I advanced in the path of philosophy and of sacred science, the further I wandered, by the impurity of my life, from both philosophers and saints; for it is certain that the philosophers, and all the more, the saints, that is to say, those who apply their hearts to the exhortations of Scripture, have been admired above all, because of their chastity."[2]

For the proud man is often presumptuous, full of himself, sure of his own strength, scornful of danger, impatient of every yoke, silent in times of temptation or when faced with a dangerous occasion of sin, and for that reason, terribly exposed. None can be chaste without divine grace, and God refuses it to the proud, whom He rejects and casts down. The Chastisement of pride is downfall. Qui se exaltat, humiliabitur. After his conversion, Saint Augustine admitted as much, with tears. "Deaf to the clanking of the chain that my flesh dragged round, as a punishment for the pride of my soul, I wandered far from Thee and Thou didst let me go. I threw myself, and overflowed like a foaming river, on Thy profaned creatures, and Thou didst not speak! O my Joy too long delayed, Thou wert then silent, and I went my way far from Thee, sowing on my path the seed of sterile griefs, proud in my baseness, uneasy in my weariness."[3]

If pride corrupts twice over, humility, on the other hand, is an admirable preservative for chastity. It gives back to men, along with the simplicity of childhood, its candid innocence: If one is humble, one is conscious of one's weakness

[2] Abelard.

[3] Saint Augustine. Confessions.

and failings, and the feeling is a safeguard and a strength: cum enim infirmor, tunc potens sum.[4] If one is humble one keeps away from danger and mortifies oneself; if one is humble, one confides in the representatives of God, superiors or confessors, and one obtains from them light and comfort; if one is humble, one raises toward God a desperate cry in the hour of temptation: "Lord, save us, we perish!"[5] And such a prayer is ever answered. Bourdaloue wrote that if chastity is to be preserved, there must be watchfulness, obedience, penance and, above all "a sincere humility, without which we can have neither safety, nor a sure footing."[6]

The second rampart of chastity is a special love of Jesus Christ. We say "special," for it is obvious, and daily experience proves it only too well, that a waning, tepid love cannot suffice. We must have total love, ardent and generous, a deep affection, the divine passion of a spouse. The soul who can love tenderly, knows nothing of adultery. Now, in the consecrated soul, every fault against purity takes on the character of a spiritual adultery. When one has given oneself completely and forever to Jesus Christ, when one thinks only of Him, lives only for Him, how can betrayal be possible? "While it is fidelity to a promise, chastity is perhaps still more, fidelity of heart. Strong as death, true love always triumphs over all the solicitations of the world and all the assaults of the passions." "With the love of God, the soul is strong against the flesh, its enemy, for where true love of God reigns, neither self-love nor personal interest can gain entrance."[7]

Once one has contemplated the splendors and charms of God-made Man, how can one be caught by the passing beauty of a human creature? "Since I have known Jesus Christ, nothing has seemed beautiful enough for me to look

---

[4] II Cor. XII, 10.
[5] Matth. VIII, 25.
[6] Ve Sermon sur l'Etat Religieux.
[7] Saint John of the Cross. Counsels and Maxims.

at it with desire. All the rest is so little for a soul who has once seen God and felt Him."[8]

In a heart which has given itself to Christ irrevocably and wholly, there is no more room for fraudulent affections. The "house to let" board has been finally removed. As for gross and impure pleasures, how can they have any weight, when compared to the divine joy of loving God? What man would choose to drink from a stagnant, slimy pool rather than a limpid spring? God ever suffices, for those who love Him ardently.

If we are tempted let us fall on our knees. Let us take our heart for a shield and prayer for a weapon. By frequent and ardent acts of love, let us throw ourselves at the feet of God, or rather take refuge in the Heart of Jesus and the Saviour will say to us, as He said to Saint Teresa, "Fear not, my daughter, no one shall tear you from My Hands."[9] If anyone tries to tear a child away from his mother, the harder he pulls, the more desperately the child clings to his mother's neck. . . . Let us cling to Jesus, always, and say like the spouse in the canticle: "I hold him, and I will not let him go," and like Saint Paul: "For I am sure that, neither death nor life, nor angels nor principalities nor powers, nor things present nor things to come, nor might, nor height, nor depth, nor any other creature shall be able to separate us from the love of God, which is in Christ Jesus Our Lord."[10] At the tragic hour when our whole being, obsessed, tottering, thrown into confusion seems to be all flesh, let us love and pray. At such a moment is not the act of love itself a call for help?— and we shall experience the truth of these words of blessed Idiota: "The man armed with Thy love, O most sweet Jesus, stands firm, unshakable, invincible and fearless in the combat of temptation, and would do so even if he had to fight against all the armies of Hell. . . . For thou art, O good Jesus,

[8] Lacordaire, quoted by P. Noble.
[9] Office of Saint Teresa.
[10] Rom. VIII, 38, 39.

a strong support and the powerful defender of all those who love Thee; Thou art love, and he who lives in love, lives in Thee: the Lord guards all those who love Him."[11]

To complete the defenses of the stronghold, there remains prudence. The field of chastity is, indeed, sown with ambushes and surprises, and it is more than ever important to meditate upon the words of Christ: "Watch ye and pray, that you enter not into temptation."[12] How many have been the victims of their ignorance, naïveté and presumption! Therefore, while avoiding scrupulous fears, we must, as far as in us lies, avoid all dangerous occasions. "I know my weakness, and that is why I flee, lest I be vanquished."[13]

Where one's self is concerned, prudence demands constant vigilance over the imagination, heart and senses, supernatural respect for a body that is consecrated to God, the temple of the Trinity and a living member of Jesus Christ. Without despising the prescriptions of hygiene, we must not overlook the laws of modesty, and must beware of rousing passion, that sleeping wild beast.

Relations between members of a same Community must also be very discreet, though cordial. Inspired by faith, perfectly courteous, kindly, patient, obliging and edifying, they must never be allowed to degenerate into too natural affections, sentimental attachments, particular friendships and familiarities more suited to the world; for all such are defects or weaknesses that trouble the heart, and endanger virtue.

But we must be particularly circumspect in our relations with the world. "Be ye, therefore, wise, as serpents, and simple as doves."[14] The carrying out of this evangelical advice is a marvel, if it is not a little miracle. Journeys, errands, letters, visits made or received, spiritual direction, the confessional or the parlor, all involve frequent contacts with all kinds of

[11] Idiota. Contemplation.
[12] Matth. XXVI, 41.
[13] Liber contra Vigil.
[14] Matth. X, 16.

lay persons, and form part of the duties of our state: on all these points, Constitutions and Directories for the most part contain many details of positive and negative legislation, which have been inspired by the experience or wisdom of the Founder, and from which it would be unsafe to deviate habitually, and without good reason.

Though modern apostolate may demand, in certain circumstances, a more free and easy manner, it would nevertheless be quite false to imagine that one can throw overboard all restraint. "I press on regardless," said a young modern apostle. While pressing on, would it not be sensible to look around and see where one was putting one's feet? Neither the ardor of zeal—which is sometimes intemperate—nor a right intention are sufficient reasons for discarding the most elementary rules of reserve and prudence.

This same prudence must be yet more in evidence in the relations between persons of different sex, even though these relations be necessary and spiritual. They must always be conducted with dignity and gravity, albeit with kindness. There must be no free-and-easiness, no unsuitable familiarity, for that would be playing with fire. The approaches to our religious soul must not be too pleasant and flowery, let its surroundings be austere, let it be encircled by a moat and guarded by watchdogs, if need be. Let us play the hedgehog toward those whose manner would be too familiar, or who offer a friendship that is too human. Gather thistles, expect prickles! We are not angels, and original sin, age-old thought it be, has lost none of its virulence. Even the saints, in spite of their virtue, or rather, because of it, took precautions, that frivolous minds would denounce, as being excessive or scrupulous.

To these measures of individual prudence, the Church, concerned about the virtue and reputation of her religious, has thought it prudent to add an official precaution, the enclosure.

"The enclosure, in its final interpretation, indicates the ecclesiastical law itself, prohibiting the entrance of certain persons into the religious houses and forbidding the religious to leave their houses without permission.

"In the material sense, the enclosure indicates that part of the house set apart and affected by the law, i.e., the part of the house, access to which is reserved to the religious, and from which religious may not leave without permission."[15]

The law of enclosure, though it may be more or less severe,[16] is universal and concerns all Orders, Congregations and Institutes, without exception. It contains two kinds of prohibition, the violation of which entails sin, either mortal or venial, according to the gravity of the matter.

The admission or entrance of all lay persons to the interior of the monastery or house is forbidden, especially of persons of the opposite sex, except for legitimate reasons, and with the permission of the superiors.

All religious are forbidden to go out and stay out of their convents, without reasonable cause, and without permission. It is the duty of the competent authorities to keep strict watch over the observance of a law that has the aim of preserving religious spirit from the contagion of the world, of promoting the life of prayer, study, silence and recollection, and especially of safeguarding chastity. "It is very certain that it is for the sake of the chastity professed by religious persons, and to shelter them from the dangers to which they would be exposed, that the law of enclosure has been intro-

[15] Choupin, *op. cit.*

[16] Canon Law makes distinction between three kinds of enclosure: papal, episcopal and statutory. The first and strictest, is established by the Sovereign Pontiffs, protected by penalties reserved to the Pope, concerning all religious Orders with solemn vows. Episcopal enclosure concerns enclosed nuns with simple vows and the members of all Congregations, pontifical or diocesan.

Statutory enclosure is imposed and determined by the Rules and constitutions of the different Institutes.

duced."[17] How many abuses and even scandals arose in former times from the neglect of these wise regulations!

~

The Jews rebuilt the walls of Jerusalem, with a trowel in one hand and a sword in the other. When the ramparts of chastity have been firmly built, active defense must be organized with the help of two weapons: Mortification and prayer.

Mortification is not a fashionable word, and might with advantage be found more often in the mouths of preachers, and in the writings of spiritual authors. The age we live in has no use for it and readily treats it as a "luxury" virtue. Yet without its help, no chastity can preserve its virginal freshness.

What salt does for meat, mortification does for the soul; it is an element of preservation and incorruptibility. A religious who loves ease, comfort, who has no spirit of sacrifice or abnegation, is always in danger, often at fault. Pleasure, even when it is legitimate—and notice that the word appears nowhere in the Gospels—is a poison. Doled out drop by drop, it can momentarily stimulate fervor and invigorate; but a heavy dose softens the body, weakens the will and prepares for surrender. Without equaling the heroism of the saints—a heroism which sometimes shocks our pusillanimity and offends our cowardliness—none the less a certain austerity is required of those who would avoid danger or triumph over it. The soul must always dominate the body to which it gives life. A "padded" religious life, from which all suffering, privation, and discomfort are removed, would be an anomaly. In every Institute, the Rule and Constitutions contain many prescripts of varying severity concerning fasting, abstinence, discipline and active poverty. This is a minimum and obligatory program, with which many generous souls will not be

[17] Choupin, *op. cit.*

content. Another excellent penance, that covers every moment, is exact and scrupulous observance of the Rule.

Another safeguard or antidote to temptation is a passion for intellectual, artistic or manual work. The industrious have scarcely time to be tempted. "Idleness is an enemy to the soul," says Saint Benedict, and sloth is the mother of all vices. The devil ever finds work for idle hands to do. A venerable religious, who through his whole life was subjected to difficult and terrible temptations, admitted to his intimates that he only found safety near the Tabernacle, and in study. One must also refrain from any abuse of rest and sleep. When the body is too well treated, it becomes an insolent and recalcitrant servant.

This austerity of life will be strengthened by control of our faculties and exterior senses, with mortification of the mind, imagination and memory. We must banish all dangerous studies and readings, disturbing reveries, unhealthy curiosity. Where purity is concerned, let us be content with the knowledge required by the duties of our state. Most of all the heart must be protected from error and aberration, cutting it off from all sentimental affection and doubtful friendship. We must "strip off the old husk of the heart," that is, every self-seeking love. Saint Thérèse of Lisieux was well aware of this, when she wrote: "How can a heart that is given over to a human affection be closely united to God? I feel that it is impossible. I have seen so many souls, seduced by this false light, dashing into it like poor moths, burning their wings, and returning wounded to Jesus, the divine fire that burns, but does not consume."[18]

Modesty of the eyes is not a virtue for novices only. While it is necessary, even in the solitude of the cloister, modesty of the eyes is yet more essential for religious whose charitable works or apostolate bring them into frequent, or even permanent contact with the world. In our times, when evil is placarded everywhere, when many, Christians included, have

[18] Esprit de Sainte Thérèse de l'Enfant Jesus.

lost the sense of shame, it is often best to see nothing, or at least to look at nothing, if one would not be forced one day to say with deep regret, "My eyes have lost my soul!"

Temperance in food and drink must not be overlooked. While a widespread lowering of health or exhausting work may, to a certain extent, justify exemption from fasting and abstinence, let us not imagine that we are ipso facto dispensed from the rules of sobriety, so strongly recommended by Scripture and the Fathers. Any excess is dangerous, sometimes gravely so, particularly for young people; and the danger has been pointed out by the traditional writers in the very strongest terms. Greed is a particularly repulsive vice in spiritual persons. It is an excellent habit to deprive oneself of some small thing at every meal, and never to rise from table completely satisfied.

Of all human passions, lust is indeed the most violent and widespread. It clouds the mind, disorders the heart, crazes the senses, and dethrones the will. It is a consuming flame that penetrates to the very marrow of the bones.

Chastity, like humility, charity and perseverance, is one of the fundamental graces that we must ask daily, of the goodness of God. It is a slice of that daily, substantial bread we ask for in the Pater Noster.

Let us implore the Virgin of Virgins, and put our virtue under her powerful and maternal protection. Let us ask of her the great grace of dying, rather than fall into sin. When the tempest rises, let us adopt the cry of the apostles, "Save us, we perish!" With childlike confidence, let us throw ourselves in her arms and cling to her, as long as the temptation lasts. If we are to believe Saint Alphonsus, whoever continues to pray to Mary with all his soul, even in the midst of the vilest suggestions, can be sure that he has committed at least no mortal sin.

If we ever happened to succumb—we are so weak and so hardly tempted!—let prayer again be our salvation. No sooner down, than up again, let us with Magdalen at the feet of

Crucified Jesus, cry, "Pity!" so that we may obtain from His infinitely merciful Heart the grace to forge anew for ourselves a moral virginity in His Blood; and in tears of repentance, shame, trust and love. Then, all things considered, we may say "Felix culpa!" For we shall find, in the constant bitter reminder of this sin, due to surprise and weakness, a new and powerful motive for increasing our watchfulness, prayer, love and fidelity.

PART IV

OBEDIENCE

Chapter XVII

THE KEYSTONE

OBEDIENCE IS THE CENTER of the religious state, and so to speak, the essential structure of the edifice. Why has one left the world, if it be not in order to obey, and thereby glorify God supremely, to sanctify oneself and to save souls?

Like poverty, obedience has degrees: the vow, the virtue and the spirit.

The vow is a sacred promise made to God, and imposes submission to all superiors, every time they command in the name of obedience, i.e., in virtue of the vow.

Of wider range, and related to justice, the virtue inclines the will to accept and carry out all the legitimate commands of those who have authority.

The spirit of obedience is but the intensification, refinement and extension of the virtues. What trust is to hope, the spirit is to the virtue. To his submission, the religious brings the whole of his will, promptness of execution, and a joyful heart. To obey is a pleasure. Far from being annoyed or irritated by the number of commands he receives, he is delighted. He is not content to wait until they are given, he foresees and anticipates them. Contrary to some, he can never have too many superiors. Bringing prudence and humility to bear upon love of dependence, he takes for commands the simple direction, advice and requests of those in authority. Still further, in his eagerness to mortify his self-will, he goes so far, according to the advice of Saint Benedict, as to conform to the wishes, desires and even whims of his brethren.

Again Saint Thomas makes a distinction between two kinds of obedience, one general, and the other particular.

The first consists in carrying out, no matter what be the motive for our submission, everything that is prescribed, individually or collectively, by those in authority. This is our common obedience, to be found in the practice of the commandments of God and the Church, respect for canonical and liturgical laws, briefly, in the fulfillment of all our duties. On the other hand, "special obedience, in so far as it is a distinct virtue, consists in the performance of the precept, from the motive of obedience, i.e., because the command obliges and justice imposes on us the obligation of subjecting ourselves to the command of a superior."[1] The latter, which is the only one with which we are concerned, assumes, in the religious state, two forms in general: obedience to the Rule,[2] of which we do not intend to speak, and obedience to superiors.

In a preliminary chapter, we should like to indicate the place of this virtue in the religious state, recall its social role in different Institutes, and finally emphasize its influence in the life of every religious.

~

Ascetics and theologians have always given a sort of priority to obedience, in the religious state. Is it not, indeed, its end, condition, essence and, to a certain extent, its plenitude?

In the prologue to his Rule, with admirable conciseness, Saint Benedict reminds the monk that he belongs to the race of the seekers after God, and that he has entered the monastery solely in order to find, possess and enjoy Him. And

[1] Choupin, *op. cit.*

[2] We have already dealt with this in a special work entitled "Obedience to Rule."

the only path that leads to God is that of obedience. Man strayed from his Creator through disobedience, and his obedience is the only path by which he can return. Indeed, if Saint Bonaventure is to be believed, "the whole perfection of religious life consists in the renouncement of self-will."

Of the three vows which form an integral part of the religious life, the most important, "the most essential, is incontestably the vow of obedience. For if someone, apart from obedience, practices poverty and chastity, even by vow, he is not for that a religious."[3] This is because, of all the virtues, obedience is the one that expresses, with the greatest purity and force, the nature and fundamental characteristics of the religious state. Profession enlists us in the service of God. By vocation, every religious is a servant. And what is required of a servant, if not that he obey? To obey is his function, his raison d'être, the first and the sum of his duties. Again, the monk is a soldier, enrolled under the standard of Christ, for the extension of His Kingdom. What is the prime virtue of the soldier, if not obedience, even unto death? And the shining armor and flashing sword of this soldier of Christ are again obedience. Another essential aspect of the religious state is that it is the complete and irrevocable oblation of oneself, one's being and life to God, the souls of men and the Institute. But in this universal dedication, not everything is of the same value. It is good to give up one's possessions to follow Christ; it is better to dedicate one's body as an inviolable sanctuary of purity; it is best to renounce what man clings to most closely, what constitutes the core of his personality, i.e., the independent use of his liberty.

After the Mass and martyrdom, no sacrifice can surpass or equal that of religious profession. Now, what is most sacrificial in a monastic life—and daily experience confirms the teaching of the Doctors—is neither poverty, nor chastity, but obedience. How great is the cost, amounting sometimes to heroism, of ceaselessly giving up one's wishes, initiative, plans

[3] Saint Thomas Aquinas.

and tastes, even one's whims, in order humbly and silently to wear the yoke of the Rule and the orders of those who have authority!

The exceptional importance of obedience, also arises from its power of sanctification. The vows are but excellent means of achieving the first and essential aim of the religious state, i.e., moral perfection. More than either poverty or chastity, obedience is the tool of holiness. Of all the roads that lead to the heights, it is both the safest and the most direct.

In brief, the vow of obedience is so essential to the religious state, that it seems to contain it and express it fully, embracing implicitly, as it does in effect in the ancient Orders, the other two vows of poverty and chastity.

~

The privileged position occupied by obedience in the religious state allows us to appreciate its important role in the life of Communities and Institutes. Nevertheless, this role can only be understood in its relation to authority. Authority, obedience, are two correlative ideas that are mutually explanatory. Authority is the core of all human or divine, political, social or religious society; it is its principal constituent element, the active principle of its life, development and influence. Unless there be this power presiding, governing and directing, there exists nothing but an amorphous conglomeration, without either unity, cohesion or common aim. Lack of authority leads fatally to disorder, revolution, anarchy. This doctrine is particularly true when it applies to those spiritual societies, the religious Institutes. Of these, the authority is truly the head, the heart and the soul. On it, indeed, depend, to a great extent, the vitality or decline, the sterility or fecundity, the life or death of the Congregations. The captain makes his company, the superior makes his community. Who can tell the deep, all-embracing influence of a superior, who is aware of his duties and rights, and who knows how to govern with prudence, firmness and kindness?

On the other hand, how many abuses, disorders and scandals arise, through the lack of wisdom and strength in those who govern. It is incumbent on those in authority, to obviate any danger threatening the existence or fervor of the Order; to remind their subjects of the Rule; to rectify any false interpretation of it; to oppose any harmful customs or laxity of observance; to cut short rash undertakings, and untimely innovations; to restrain certain manifestations of a zeal that is too natural; in short, to rectify anything that could corrupt the life of the Congregation, falsify its end and adulterate its spirit.

Besides warding off all harm from his religious family, the superior must promote good in all its forms, both individual and collective, have an eye to the formation and sanctification of each one of his subjects; spur on the nonchalant; rouse the lazy; support the weak; raise up the discouraged, and stimulate the zeal of one and all. Where general government is concerned, he must assign to each religious, according to his health, and his intellectual and moral qualities, the place and charge that he is suited for; put talents to the best possible use; obtain the maximum yield from all, for the glory of God, the prosperity of the Institute, and the salvation of souls, create new works and supplement old ones; in short, exercise over all, within the limits of his jurisdiction, a profound and durable influence.

But it is evident that all this governmental activity is largely dependent, in its exercise and results, on the docility of the religious. The Superior does not act alone, but on and with his subjects. His government is a collaboration; how can there be close and effective collaboration without harmony or union, and therefore, without dependence? "To govern," says Saint Thomas, "is to move." But this movement must be accepted and obeyed. Whatever may be his own military qualities, a leader must have complete control over his men, if he is going to win. Is not discipline the great strength of armies? It is also the strength of those picked troops, the religious Institutes, because it is a principle of unity in cohesion and peace. How are those in authority to govern if they are forever coming into conflict with different points of view, opposition and resistance; if everybody wants to go his own way and do as he pleases; if instead of having at their disposition a solid block of supple wills, they find themselves with a handful of slippery eels that slither through their fingers? How is one to govern the ungovernable? It is not enough to command, one must also be obeyed. Of what use is an excellent spring in a watch, if the wheels are all twisted and blocked? A Community in which obedience is no longer observed, where authority is judged, criticized and resisted, is the Kingdom divided against itself.

It has been proved by experience that laxity is generally introduced into religious Orders by deficiency, or misunderstanding of the principle of authority; deficiency in superiors, who either cannot, or dare not command boldly; misunderstanding on the part of subjects who have refused to submit and obey. This explains the exceptional gravity of disobedience, which, unlike violations of poverty and chastity, is not a strictly personal fault, but constitutes a sort of attack upon the good and the very life of the Institute. He who disobeys becomes the enemy of the brethren, and a danger to the Community. It also explains the insistence with which Founders have recommended obedience to their sons, as being the keystone of the edifice they had raised.

~

Besides, being a social virtue, obedience is also an individual virtue, closely connected with the personal life of the religious.

If it is the chief virtue for men and Christians, it is even more so for the religious, and the noblest, the most necessary and the most excellent of the moral virtues, the best tool with which to fashion his perfection. It is the only path that leads to holiness; to leave it is to lose one's way.

What is the source of its tremendous power of sanctification? Firstly, as we have already stated, the vow of obedience implicitly includes those of poverty and chastity, and we know the important part played by these three vows, in the pursuit and conquest of sanctity. The practice of perfect obedience also involves the practice of many other virtues, such as faith, humility, mortification, renunciation and above all, charity. Finally, is it not the obligatory setting for all our spiritual activity? No act can be truly virtuous, agreeable to God and meritorious, unless it conform to obedience.

It is the most characteristic trait of religious holiness. Christian, sacerdotal, monastic holiness, though identical in their essential elements, purity and charity, nonetheless, each preserves its own particular character. And what distinguishes religious perfection, one of its most distinctive traits, is the exceptional quality of obedience. There are many souls in the world, who are admirably humble, poor, chaste, recollected, pious, but not obedient as the religious is. Obedience constitutes his special vocation, the great duty of his state, and his religious spirit is judged by his obedience. It is not faith, or trust, or austerity, or a spirit of prayer, or the office or zeal that makes the religious, but obedience. Half obedience means a half religious. Saint Teresa says: "I should have insisted especially on obedience, for, in my opinion, as soon as it is lacking, the nun ceases to exist. One word only on a matter that is so well known and so important, a word that I beg you not to forget. If a person, who is subject to obedience by vow, fails in it, and does not bring every possible care to the perfect observance of her vow, I declare I do not know why she is in a monastery."[4]

To sum up, let us say that perfection in the religious life consists in the imitation of Christ: "If you would be perfect, come, follow me." Now what strikes us most about Jesus—the first religious of the Father—is precisely His heroic submission usque ad mortem. Thus, whoever strays from obedience, strays from Our Lord. And let such a one beware, lest

[4] Saint Teresa. The Way of Perfection.

he incur the effects of the terrible threats the Sacred Heart spoke to Saint Margaret Mary: "All religious separated and disunited from their Superiors must regard themselves as vessels of reprobation, in which all good liquors are changed into corruption, on which the Divine Sun of Justice, when it shines upon them, has the same effect as the sun shining on mire. These souls are so rejected by my Heart, that the more they try to approach It, by the means of the Sacraments, prayer and other exercises, the more I remove Myself from them; such is the horror I have for them. They will go from one Hell to another, for it is this disunion that has lost so many and will lose still more, since every superior holds my place, whether he be good or bad. That is why the inferior who strikes out against it, inflicts as many wounds on his own soul; and after all, he will cry out in vain at the gates of mercy, he will not be heard, unless he hear the voice of the Superior."[5]

[5] Gauthey. Vie et Oeuvres de Ste. Marguerite–Marie Alacoque.

Chapter XVIII

THE TRIPLE FOUNDATION

Since it is the center of the religious state, the soul of the Congregations, and the source of sanctity, it would appear that perfect obedience must be common, if not universal. Yet is it not far too rare? How many deviations, corruptions and falsifications there are! Without going so far as formal disobedience—the spirit of revolution, thank God, has not yet invaded the convents—how many are too often content with negative obedience, or a half obedience, without life or savor.

For this laxity in the practice of an essential virtue, there are many causes, interior and exterior, individual and general. Among the latter we may include a lack of understanding and the absence of solid convictions concerning the very foundation of obedience. Why should one obey? On the clarity of the reply depends the quality of the submission; for in this above all, the more enlightened one is the greater is one's obligation to practice the virtue. A blind obedience, in the lowest sense of the word, can only be a matter of routine, a rickety affair indeed. From the moment that we clearly see that our dependence is a necessity, a sacred duty—in attacking obedience do we not attack God Himself?—that any revolt, whether open or veiled, is in reality nothing but weakness and cowardice, perhaps then we shall no longer be tempted to evade the orders of our superiors. Even if, in spite of everything, we are attacked by temptation, we shall find, in the strength of our convictions, the means of triumphing, reacting and obeying.

Religious obedience rests on a triple foundation which is

indestructible: authority, fidelity, religion. Authority of superiors, fidelity to the profession, religion of the vow.

~

The superior is the authority and he possesses authority; this is the first foundation of all reasonable aand supernatural obedience. By reason of his office he is the authentic representative of God, His official delegate. "For he is really believed to hold the place of Christ in the monastery," says Saint Benedict of the Abbot. This belief can alone insure a solid basis for obedience. Whosoever forgets it, must needs sink into automatism or servility.

God is present in every creature by His Essence, His Immensity, and His power; and in some men especially by His Sovereignty. God is in every superior, and if my faith reveals to me Jesus Christ under the consecrated species, it must also allow me to discover Him, under the human guise of authority. When a superior speaks, commands or forbids, he does it in the name of God, of whom he is the representative and "vicar." It is the Lord who speaks, commands and forbids through his mouth, and his orders are not, as one might think, the expression of his own wishes, still less of his whims, but are the faithful reproduction of the Divine Will. "He that heareth you, heareth me; he that despiseth you, despiseth me," me, Jesus Christ.

But perhaps you may ask why God did not reserve to Himself alone, without any intermediary, the government of souls? Why entrust to poor men, who are as weak and sinful as others, so splendid and redoubtable a ministry? This is a mystery of wisdom, power and goodness. It is the effect of His Wisdom that He has established, in both physical and moral spheres, an admirable hierarchy of great and little, of authority and obedience. It is the work of His power to achieve this collaboration of humanity with the designs of Providence and the sanctification of souls; for superiors exist only for the good and salvation of their subjects. And what generosity He showed in giving us a hundred times a day, the opportunity of submitting to a man, of practicing fervently faith, humility, patience, self-sacrifice, love, and thus of acquiring an immense treasure of merits and eternal glory. Obedience is one of the most priceless gifts of God. The superior is an authority, and he holds authority, that is, the right to govern in the name of Christ. The right—not that material and brutal force which bends or snaps any resistance —but that moral power, before which the will should freely incline. For, while he is a wise counselor, a guide and consoler, the superior is first a leader, and the essential function of a leader is to command and obtain obedience. Though this jurisdiction is not absolute or universal, since it is deputed, it has none the less a sacred character, even in its lesser forms —such as a bursar, or the head of a department—and this is the participation in the power of God, the Master and Law Giver. "Let every soul be subject to higher powers; for there is no power but from God; and those that are ordained of God. Therefore, he that resisteth the power resisteth the ordinance of God. And they that resist, purchase to themselves damnation."[1]

In the Congregations, authority is found under three forms: power of jurisdiction, dominative power and domestic power.

In its fullness, it resides in the Sovereign Pontiff who delegates a part of it to bishops, and to exempt clerical superiors belonging to a clerical Congregation.[2]

Due allowance being made for dignity and extent of rights, a superior should govern his community as a bishop governs his diocese. He has charge of souls; he is the good shepherd of a flock, small in numbers, but chosen. He must lead it into fat pastures, and protect it from robbers and wolves. He must watch over the formation, perseverance and salvation of all

[1] Romans 13, 1, 2.
[2] "In exempt clerical organizations the superiors and Chapters have ecclesiastical jurisdiction for the internal as well as the external forum." Canon 501, 11.

those souls whom Jesus Christ has entrusted to him, and whom he must account for one day at the judgment seat.

In default of this special jurisdiction, the other superiors, to whatever Institute they belong, have at least the power of domination, which devolves from the vow of obedience[3] and consists in commanding the subjects in the name of God and in virtue of their vow. Once a religious binds himself by his profession to submit to the legitimate orders of authority, that authority acquires the right of commanding him. There remains the domestic power, the power of the leader over the organization that he is commissioned to direct. Every Congregation is a society, every monastery a family. Now, is it possible to imagine a durable society, a united and peaceful family, without a presiding and governing authority, and consequently, without the obedience of the children and subjects? Therefore, whoever enters religion, by the sole fact of his admission, falls under the jurisdiction of superiors. Though he may be merely a postulant or novice, he must submit to the orders of authority and keep regular discipline.

What should be the feelings and the attitude of the religious to this divine authority of which the superiors are the representatives and trustees? Feelings of respect and affection, an attitude of submission. In this age which is set upon equalitarianism, and in which the notion of authority has been lost, it is an excellent thing that the religious Congregations endure as great schools of respect. It is better to be unsparing with respect, like the saints, than to show too little.

To respect must be added love, which is enjoined as much by gratitude, as by filial piety. The superior is a father or mother whose kindness, patience and obligingness are, alas, too often misunderstood. Apart from certain natural advantages, which are negligible, but which the subjects are tempted to esteem too highly and sometimes to envy, how many worries are involved in the government of persons and

[3] The Superiors and Chapters have dominative power over their subjects according to the Constitutions and Common law. Canon 501.

things! How much anxiety, opposition, failure, heartbreak, and above all, what heavy moral responsibilities! Would it be too much to repay all this unobtrusive devotedness with a little cordial affection.

More than respect and love, authority requires obedience; that is, the interior and free submission of the will. Revolt is always a fault, when it is not a crime. If the superior has the sacred right of commanding, the subject has a no less sacred duty to obey. Thus none, without mortal or venial sin according to the gravity of the matter, can violate an order given in virtue of holy obedience, or with the intention, on the part of the superior, of binding the conscience. It is true that this intention is rare; and in the government of the Institute or of Communities, the authorities—as a general rule—only command within the limits of the Constitutions, which do not bind under pain of sin. None the less, it would be difficult, in practice, openly to disobey a command, or wilfully and without good reason, to fail in a point of rule, without committing a moral fault. When obedience is in question, both prudence and charity call for a great delicacy of conscience. Between one extreme and the other, it is better to be overcareful.

~

Obedience is the logical consequence of profession, and becomes, for every religious, a matter of justice and loyalty. Saint Benedict reminds his monks that they must obey "on account of the holy servitude which they have taken upon them." We have already said that profession is a bilateral contract made between the Institute and the novice. One of its clauses seems to sum up all the obligations of the newly professed: complete submission to the superiors and rules. By establishing oneself in the religious state, one gives up one's independence and sets aside one's liberty. The authorities, within the limits of the Constitutions and in accordance with the demands of wise government, can dispose of our person, our talents and our activities. It would obviously be unjust subsequently to revoke this complete and irrevocable surrender, to quibble about its range, to make clandestine attempts to take back, bit by bit, what one has renounced. Before the altar, in the presence of our brethren or our sisters, we have freely, after mature consideration, given our solemn promise to submit to every lawful command: it only remains for us to keep this promise until death, for a Christian's word is his bond.

When we signed the register of professions, did we think that we were putting our names at the foot of a blank page; that the superiors have the right of filling it as they please, without concerning themselves overmuch with our tastes and wishes? The result may indeed hold some surprises that we find disagreeable enough. Is that a reason for repudiating our signature? In this lies the difference in gravity between the disobedience of a Christian and that of a religious.

As the Congregations are picked troops in the service of Christ, could not religious profession be justly compared to a military enlistment? When the soldier has signed his enlistment, he is no longer master of his person, his life or his time. The voluntary slave of an iron discipline, he has but to obey in silence, and that is what he does. Progressive training, unending fatigues, night marches, mobilization exercises, routine inspections, tactical exercises, change of station and sometimes actual campaigns—all is part of his job, with its inconveniences and risks. Nobody thinks of protesting or making a fuss. There are always inconveniences and risks in the religious state, and they too, are part of the "job." There is the risk of receiving annoying, difficult or painful commands. The risk of being put under the jurisdiction of uncongenial superiors, or in the company of disagreeable colleagues. The risk of being misunderstood, pushed around, set on one side; how many have experienced this trial! The risk of being allocated to a difficult post, that does not correspond to our tastes or aptitudes. The risk of being transplanted from the north to the south, perhaps from Europe to Asia. And when the risk becomes a reality, what are we to say? Nothing! What are we to do? Obey. Act like a good soldier of Christ. The man who is perfectly obedient must needs live dangerously and often painfully.

In a certain Mother-house, after the general retreat, the superior goes up into the pulpit, with the list of changes in her hand. At each name, a nun rises, listens, bows, and returns to her rank. There is not a complaint, no recrimination; a little surprise, perhaps, or a discreet tear that is quickly dried. When the list has been read, a railway ticket is given to each nun concerned, who, without returning to her former residence, must set out that same day for her new post. This is magnificent and austere obedience, sometimes tempered by the kindness of superiors, reminiscent of military obedience, but graced with deep faith and ardent charity. One day there was present at this "general post" a venerable nun, 65 years old, a former superior, worn out by labor. She had returned to a little Community, and there was humbly waiting for the Great Departure. The list was being read. "Sister Margaret!" Goodness, that was she! Somewhat startled, she rose. "Dear Sister, will you go to Buenos Aires, to start a new foundation?" A deep bow. A smile. And she left to catch her boat. Did she ever reach her destination? We do not know. But she, at least, honored her signature, and took back nothing that she had given.

~

By his profession, the religious enters upon an obligation toward his Institute to obey at all times and in all places the legitimate authority. Will he keep this promise faithfully? His will is so weak, so inconstant in face of the difficulties and sacrifices that are part of a whole life of submission. So, to strengthen his decision, he makes a special vow, the vow of obedience. This is a sacred promise, made to God, that he will carry out precisely what he has promised to his superiors. This is another foundation of obedience, which henceforward binds the conscience under pain of sin. Religion has come to the rescue in order to raise and fortify the virtue, and in this case, the subject is doubly bound to obey. The authority may then, in its government, refer to this vow in order to exact from all the accomplishment of its commands. But the superior must make it clear to his subject that he intends to command him in virtue of the vow. To this end, he will use some formula such as "in virtue of holy obedience, or in the name of Jesus Christ." It would even be advisable that in this case the formal precept be given in writing, or at least in the presence of two witnesses.

It must be remembered, too, that not every superior can command in virtue of the vow, when fulfilling his office. This right is reserved to the Sovereign Pontiff, to the Sacred Congregation of religious, the General Chapters, major and provincial Superiors. As for local Superiors, differences occur in the various Institutes: and the point is decided by the Rule or Constitutions. But it is beyond doubt, that none of the subaltern officers—assistants, counselors, sub-priors, cellarers, bursars, heads of departments—can wield this power. Is it necessary to add that a superior should have recourse to this power, only with great discretion, very rarely, and for truly important motives? What is the point of running the risk of alarming and troubling timid souls by having frequent recourse to "extraordinary means," when one can secure obedience by appealing to their good will and fervor?

Again, it is important that the authorities when commanding, should not go beyond their rights, i.e., enforce nothing that is contrary to the letter or spirit of the Rule, nothing that is not necessary to the good order of the Community or the Society. "A superior may not command anything that goes beyond the Constitutions, such as heroic acts, excessive penances, nor anything that is less than the Constitutions, i.e., anything useless, absurd, or indifferent in every respect, unless the superior's aim is to humiliate or perfect in virtue. Neither may he command anything that would be contrary to the Constitutions; therefore nothing that would be less perfect; nothing contrary to the Constitutions or their spirit; nothing bad. Yet, if the superior had power to dispense from certain points of the Constitutions, the religious would be bound to obey. As for interior acts, we think that the superior cannot command them directly, but can do so indirectly; for example, he can order examination of conscience, mental prayer, etc., etc. In such a case, the law of religious respect requires one to act in accordance with the will of the superior."[4]

When all is said and done, the religious has few occasions for practicing his vow. But it would be quite wrong to think that for that reason, he loses all the merit of the vow. The vow dominates our whole life, which is full of its sap and its spirit. The vow has placed us in a state of complete submission to authority; and our virtue is in reality, but its extension and expansion. All our acts of obedience are then truly religious acts. Moreover, nothing prevents the religious from obeying every order he receives, from the explicit motive of religion.

There are many violations of the vow of obedience; and the principal are: to flee the authority of the superiors; to oblige them to pronounce exclusion from the Order; to resist a formal command of obedience; formally to despise authority by refusing to obey absolutely. Though it is a sacrilege against the virtue of religion, every violation of the vow is not necessarily a mortal sin; for in certain cases, there may be lightness of matter, inadvertence or lack of full consent.

[4] Bastien. Directoire Canonique.

Chapter XIX

A VIRTUE IN DANGER

IF WE ARE TO BELIEVE certain ascetical writings, religious life is nothing more than a charming and rapid sail on the yacht of obedience. The authority holds the tiller firmly, and grace swells the sails, so the fortunate passenger has only to let himself be borne peacefully into port. The picture may not be false, and is certainly agreeable, but could easily be misleading. Indeed, we have already said that obedience facilitates the voyage and makes it safe, but the sail does not do away with the oar, and the religious, who is a sailor rather than a tourist, must often row, in storm or dead calm, with aching muscles and sweating brow. And that does not include such factors as groundswell and reefs. Yes, the voyage is surer and faster, but it is none the less arduous and full of peril. According to Saint Benedict, the practice of obedience is a labor, and even more a combat. We are now going to point out these difficulties and dangers. The practice of perfect obedience cannot be conceived without abnegation, without reaction; for there are enemies within and without. Within, there is nature to be tamed: rationalism, pride, self-will, bad habits. Without, there are certain obstacles or pernicious influences, which originate either in the authority itself, or from the entourage, or the environment.

~

The first enemy of obedience, which shakes it to the foundations and corrupts it to the very roots, is the lack of supernatural light: absence of convictions, too human an attitude toward superiors, false maxims.

In her "Dialogue," Saint Catherine of Siena insists on the primary importance of the part played by faith in the practice of perfect obedience: "This unfortunate who does not obey is deceived by self-love. The eyes of his intelligence, no longer enlightened by faith, delight in his own pleasure and in worldly objects." Our submission can only be complete if it is based on solid convictions: conviction as to its necessity and nobility, its power of apostolate and sanctification. Not to comprehend its exceptional place in a religious life is always to expose oneself to the danger of shirking it, or enduring it with ill will. Still graver is the danger of yielding to a spirit of rationalism in one's relations with authority, of seeing in the superiors only the man or the woman, with their qualities and defects; the colleague exalted today by chance or intrigue, but tomorrow, back in the ranks like everybody else. It does not even enter one's head that he is the representative of God, the delegate of Christ, armed with sacred authority. Hence, his commands appear to be nothing more than the expression of a human will, more or less wise, but often intolerable. In such a case, what becomes of religious obedience? Certain questionable maxims, also, go the round, true in the literal sense, but made extremely pernicious by false interpretation. The fragment of truth is thrown aside, and the dross gathered up. "Superiors have not a monopoly of common sense. Authority is not infallible; it can be deceived. Personal initiative should be respected and centralization is a pest. Why treat us like children? One should know how to interpret the orders that are given. The use of power needs to be controlled. Nobody has the right to order what is contrary to the Rule." It would be a strange illusion to parody these aphorisms and use them as an authority to shake off the yoke of obedience, or only to wear it sullenly.

Another enemy, just as formidable, is pride. Obedience is the daughter of humility. Saint Benedict makes prompt obedience the first degree of humility. It is, moreover, a matter proved by everyday experience that the difficulties and oppositions encountered in the government of Communities rarely have their source in subjects who are modest and self-effacing, but nearly always in those who are headstrong, proud, self-satisfied, full of themselves and wedded to their own opinions and judgment. Pride is an upthrust of self-exaltation. Now, he who commands is termed "superior," just as he who obeys is acknowledged to be "inferior." Whence the proud man's instinctive desire to command, his natural reluctance to submit. He considers that he lowers himself by obeying, and it is of such as he that Bossuet said: "Who commands me annoys me." Satan's "Non serviam," was but the cry of pride in revolt. Gifted and successful men are also tempted to masked insubordination—more indeed perhaps than others, for pride is not the exclusive privilege of the stupid. Too aware of their personal worth, they may easily bring to authority, especially if it is nondescript, an attitude that is distant or irreverent, and behavior that is contrary to religious obedience. Vainglory can turn heads and stiffen wills, unless humility keep watch. Initiative is not the same thing as independence.

Age can be another real obstacle, though this is rare. As the religious state is of its nature a constant progression in holiness, it would appear that as one advances in years, all the virtues, including obedience, must take deeper root and flourish more vigorously in the soul. It is none the less true that, with time, the personality, while developing its qualities, also accentuates its demands and susceptibilities. What can be more natural than that a novice should obey blindly, in silence, and with a smile? But it is a different matter when one is forty or sixty. That colleagues, even superiors, should show consideration and charity to these older men who have grown gray in the service, is well and good; but they should not use their services as an excuse for relinquishing the respect and submission they owe to the authority. Like the old monk, who would have plenty of variety in his fare, and used

when asking permission the formula, more succinct than ob-
sequious, "Reverend Father, I give you notice that I am
changing my diet." To which the Abbot replied with a generous blessing. And another, who doubtless forgot that leadership as well as obedience has no age limit, grumbled "Ah,
these young Rectors! The way they order you about!"

And what of the former superiors, who have been removed
from that office? While a long, and maybe arduous period of
rule can be an excellent introduction to obedience, some may
even be more apt to command than to submit. If one can
obey simply, humbly and joyfully a superior who was formerly a pupil or subject, it proves that one has a great spirit
of faith and eminent virtue. And it occurs more often than
we may think. When a young Father was made superior of
a Community, in which there were six former superiors, one
a provincial, a venerable nun—a superior herself—came to
congratulate him, and said with a smile: "We shall pray very
hard for you, Father!" Her prayers were doubtless answered,
for the young superior could congratulate himself on the
simplicity and docility of his veteran subjects.

But of all the enemies of obedience, the most common is
self-will: that inborn tendency which, contrary to the commands of God or the provisions of authority, puts us under
the sway of our tastes, whims and little passions. Self-will,
obstinacy; these are two cancers that eat away the hearts
of religious.

It is the effect of this self-will to make every order we
receive a burden, every forbidden thing desirable—Quanto
minus licet, tanto magis libet—and to make us prefer those
superiors who give us a free hand.

Self-will is that spirit of opposition, veiled revolt and criticism; that pretension to obey only as we see fit, that art of
persuading the authorities to reconsider decisions we do not
like; that persistence in obtaining or avoiding certain offices
or tasks; that attitude which leads us to go our own way in
the spiritual life, without direction. Nothing can be more

agreeable than to do what we like always and everywhere, but nothing is more dangerous. Self-will is the ruin of obedience. And how many religious fall victims to it! Hence the obligation for those who enter the service of God to renounce their own will and "to leave their self-will at the door of the monastery, and to have God's alone," and to repeat after Saint Thérèse of Lisieux, "I do not want to be a saint by halves. I am not afraid of suffering for You, O my God! I fear one thing alone, and that is to keep my own will; take it, for I choose all that You wish."

Other stumbling blocks in the path of perfect obedience are certain defects of character or temperament, such as the spirit of independence, contradiction or stubbornness, quick-wittedness, or a weak will. The spirit of independence, which is common nowadays, and has found its way into the convents, consists in an instinctive tendency, often strengthened by habit, to exclude the intervention of superiors in the organization of our life, works and occupations, to the point where we carry what we imagine to be our rights to such an extreme, that we live as we please, not in flagrant opposition to authority, it is true, but apart from it. Few orders, no control, free and easy ways—these are supposed to be the ideal conditions. The spirit of contradiction, the mania of "ego contra," which is merely annoying in ordinary or family relationships, can become most dangerous when it concerns one's relations with superiors. No sooner is an order given, an arrangement made, than we discover a thousand difficulties and propound a host of objections. But, in this case, what becomes of blind obedience?

Others are inclined to stubbornness. These religious cling to their own ideas and personal views, and Saint Vincent de Paul has sketched their portrait when describing one of his spiritual daughters: "She will stand firm in her own opinion. The advice of her Sister, confessor, director, or superior will not make her yield, because she is established in her own judgment. It is rooted in her mind she cannot be forced to change her opinion. This is a mark of hidden pride and a diabolical characteristic, for it is peculiar to devils to persist in their obstinacy. Sometimes, this person feels remorse, but she has not the strength to respond; she would like to, but she cannot."

The obedience of the apathetic is also unsatisfactory. Here there is no ill will, no systematic opposition. The word of command finds them ready and submissive. But they lack a spirit of decisiveness, and while they wait for their will to make a move, the order is forgotten. "What's the hurry?" is their watchword, and theirs is an obedience deferred.

Finally, there are some who, the victims of their own quick wits, are prompt to seize upon the weak or funny side of persons or things. Though they revere their superiors, it does sometimes occur that, without malice, they make cutting remarks and disrespectful judgments about the authorities and their arrangements. The quip is regretted as soon as it is uttered, but too late, the damage is done.

To the above may be added bad habits, acquired in contact with the world, or through a bad education. The spirit of equalitarianism and insubordination is one of the characteristics of our century. In the name of equality, the principle of authority is undermined and under the guise of liberty, everybody assumes the right to judge, control and criticize everything. The influence of the press is particularly baneful. Open any newspaper or magazine, and you will see how little store they set by the representatives of authority, if not of the authority itself. Disparagement and caricature in some of them are a tradition or institution.

How is one to live in this atmosphere of revolution and free thought without absorbing some of its pestilential miasma? For it is an historical law that the clergy, both secular and regular, has always come under the influence of its times. During the Renaissance, how many priests and monks dabbled in pagan humanism! The spirit of the world has tainted the religious soul. Parliamentary government has come to stay, and one is ready to argue with those in authority, when one should simply obey in silence.

This danger of contamination is even graver for those who have to do their military service. The army may be a school of discipline, but it is not a novitiate of obedience, and the malaria of disrespect is endemic. It would be a catastrophe for the religious spirit if time-serving, criticism and mockery, the "couldn't care less," the "take it or leave it" attitude, were brought into the convent. Modern education may also have to shoulder some of the responsibility in the present crisis of authority. In many families, and those Christian ones, parents have laid aside a part of their powers and rights. The result is fatal. Children no longer have that religious respect and filial obedience which is the basis of all serious formation. Brought up to be independent, trained for leadership in the Catholic action groups, how many bring to the convent, principles and tendencies that are not in alignment with a vocation that is composed of unselfishness, renunciation and self-denial? Here again, masters of novices and directors of scholasticates are unanimous in deploring in their young disciples a more or less serious absence of humility and pliability.

~

The difficulties, inherent in the practice of obedience, which devolve from our nature, vitiated by original sin, and from the individual defects of the religious, are not the only ones. There are others that derive from the authority itself and from the influence of environment.

In principle, the authority causes the practice of obedience; in fact, it happens incidentally, that it corrupts and weakens it. Complete submission, as exacted by the religious state is already, in itself, a heavy yoke to bear. If a hard or clumsy hand should make it yet heavier, the inferior is tempted to shake it off, or to bear it with reluctance.

A superior tries the obedience of his subjects by the very

exercise of his authority, by the defects of his government, or by his lack of virtue.

Commandment is the first right and the natural function of the leader. Now, the use of this right, even within the just limits of prudence and kindness, sometimes imposes painful sacrifices. Orders are given, arrangements made, penalties are inflicted which, it would seem, must tarnish a reputation for science and virtue, sterilize a whole apostolate, convulse or break a whole life. Such was the case of Saint Alphonsus of Liguori, condemned by the Sovereign Pontiff and expelled from his Congregation; such was Père Didon, Prior in Paris, a famous preacher, summoned to Rome by his Superior General, and exiled in Corsica, for many long years. In such a predicament, there is a choice between two attitudes: Heroic obedience or scandalous revolt. When he was fifty years old, a religious unexpectedly received the order to join a mission in Uganda. His family, and particularly his old mother, were in despair. When his superiors were begged to reconsider their decision, they replied "He that loveth the father or mother more than me, is not worthy of me. . . . For woe is unto me if I preach not the gospel . . . follow me, and let the dead to bury their dead." Blessed are those generous souls who can "embrace hard, contrary things patiently with a quiet conscience," and who, using the obstacle as a springboard, make strides in self-denial and the sacrifice of their selves.

But what a danger it constitutes for weak or common virtue! What a downfall it sometimes causes! Some have lost their vocation through it. It was rumored that the works of Desvallieres, tortured and passionate in tone, but full of profound religious inspiration, were severely judged in Rome, and that sanctions might be applied against him. When a friend asked him: "Well, if you were condemned, what would you do?" he replied without hesitation: "What would I do? why I should submit with enthusiasm!" In certain cases the command is apparently impossible to carry out: gravia aut impossibilia. This eventuality arises often enough in the distribution of offices and the nomination of superiors. The burden seems crushing. The authority has obviously overestimated our abilities, both intellectual and moral, and underestimated our deficiencies. Would it not be mad, even sinful, to accept such a post, to the detriment of the common good? And we are assailed by the temptation to object, protest and resist. In fact, many are unawares the victims of cowardice and want of trust in God, or else, in all good faith, they surrender to dread of responsibility and selfish concern for their own peace of mind. This is false humility, the corrupter of obedience and of abandonment to Providence. In such a case, the best course to take, is to leave the whole matter to the wisdom of the superiors. When the first shock has passed, after reflection and prayer, we may simply and loyally put to the superiors, who, after all, are not angels, one's difficulties and reluctance, and thus give them very valuable information—there is nothing contrary to religious spirit in that. But it must be on the condition that one is in a state of holy indifference, prepared to submit joyfully and generously to the final decision.

"Do not imagine that this refusal of office, through fear of committing faults in the discharge of its duties, will be excusable before God; but be persuaded that by becoming a religious, you bound yourself to serve the convent. Could the fear of committing faults justify you in declining a charge, the same fear would exempt all the sisters from the obligation of accepting office. Should they give way to such fears, who would serve the monastery or support the Community? Have a pure intention of pleasing God; fear not: He will assist you."[1] If even a wise authority gives to the religious many a cause for struggle, how much more does this apply to imperfect or bad government. Certain defects in the handling of souls and the government of a Community make

[1] Saint Alphonsus. The True Spouse.

obedience both distressing and dangerous, though very meritorious.

One of these defects is centralization: the excess of an authority which is determined to absorb everything, even to the most insignificant details. Nothing escapes its eagle eye and clutching hand. The subjects are deprived of all personal initiative and transformed into a living conveyor belt, with the result that they are in danger of practicing a submission that is spiritless, dull and automatic. At the opposite pole to this force that compresses all individual energy, we find that good-natured weakness which from human respect, fear of opposition, love of popularity, desire for peace at any price, lets the reins lie slack, and dares not command. The independence of the few may turn it to account, but it is not for the common good. What is the fate of an obedience that is never exerted? No less dangerous is authoritarianism or autocracy, before which all must bend or break, which knows nothing of discretion and patience, with its peremptory orders, demands, whims, outbursts, persistency, brutal repression—sic volo, sic jubeo—and which only succeeds, too often, in making subjects that are bitter, revolted or deceitful.

Is it necessary to mention the very rare case of a subject being the victim of the prejudice, antipathy, envy or spite of a superior? More than one saint has experienced this fearful trial, and has triumphed, thanks to humility and heroic submission. "The imperfection of a superior does no harm to him who obeys; it is even profitable to him sometimes, for the persecutions and indiscreet hardships of over-severe orders help in the acquisition of obedience and of its sister, patience."[2] But what a stumbling block it proves for fragile virtue! Every religious is not like Père Rabussier, who, having much to put up with from certain decisions of authority, wrote: "A good religious can never say that he is persecuted by his superiors. Why? Because all he asks of them is that

[2] Saint Catherine of Siena. Dialogue.

they will ever give him the bread of the Will of God. The only thing that could cause him real suffering would be to be left to his own will; that would be to snatch the bread from his mouth. My food is to do the will of my Father."[3]

Apart from the faults and failings of his government, a superior cannot be free from personal defects; for superiority of office does not necessarily imply eminent virtue. He may be narrow-minded, insensitive, ill-mannered, sharp-tempered, cold, distant, impatient and irritable; a wet blanket, self-seeking, irregular in observance and in no way edifying: in short, he may be a collection of imperfections and defects which make him unlikeable, and thereby threaten to weaken the respect, affection and submission to which, in spite of everything, he has a right by virtue of his authority.

An imperfect subject will find in this, another rock, on which his obedience will be dashed and may founder. But for the fervent religious, such a superior can be a providential piece of good fortune, if he turns it to account and uses it to strengthen his virtue and make it more supernatural. When saint Gertrude besought Our Lord to remove certain defects from a superior, He replied, "Do you not know that not only this person, but all who are in charge of this beloved Congregation, have some defects? None in this life is altogether free from imperfection. This is an effect of My goodness, and I allow it in order that the merit of all may be increased. There is far more virtue in submitting to a person whose faults are evident, than to one who appears perfect."

The climate of the convent is, in general, favorable to the growth of the virtue of obedience. But there may be found organized resistance to authority, and this, without any doubt, is one of the most virulent forms of bad spirit. "Grievances are pooled; sometimes a special code is created by which they are exchanged. The acts of authority are criticized and the victims are pitied." In the convents there are "trouble makers, unconscious agitators, diplomatists by de-

[3] Louis Étienne Rabussier.

sign, nature or passion. They gather together the malcontents, and pour poison into the wounds of their self-love. All their barbs are wrapped in implications, hypocritical understatements, protestations of obedience in spite of everything, punctuated by sighs, etc. And, naturally, there is always, in these condolences, a pretext of charity, pity, independence of character, even piety. How easily one can be deluded, even on this ground!"[4] Some have even been known to boast that they had forced superiors to give way, or that they had been the cause of their removal.

This undermining of authority, for which there is no excuse and still less justification, constitutes a real attack upon the union of subjects and the peace of souls. It is the source of a multitude of faults and must inevitably draw down upon the whole Community, the wrath and punishments of God. It is the Kingdom, divided against itself. So each must take care to guard against this disease, and even if it means persecution, keep aloof from any clique, while maintaining a respectful and loyal obedience.

The spirit of criticism, of murmuring, of insubordination can exist in single members of a Community. This is less grave, but the danger of an epidemic is not absent, especially if the afflicted religious are aged or influential. Let the young avoid them, and the old, kindly, and prudently have recourse to fraternal correction. If need be, these public malefactors must be denounced.

[4] Père Delattre. Commentaire sur la Règle de Saint Benoit.

Chapter XX

COUNTERFEITS AND MALPRACTICES

"O MY BELOVED DAUGHTER, how many voyage thus in the ship of obedience, and yet how rare are those who obey perfectly."[1]

These words, spoken by God to Saint Catherine of Siena are justified by the very complexity and delicacy of the virtue of obedience, which, that it may be perfect, according to Saint Thomas, must be adorned with seven qualities: spontaneity, simplicity, joy, promptness, virility, humility, perseverance. Who, in actual fact, possesses all these?

The religious owes to authority total submission: submission of judgment, will, heart, even of body, when it is a matter of exterior works. Is one of these elements missing or weak? At once, obedience disintegrates or becomes corrupt. The worm is at the fruit. Howbeit, "virginty of obedience"[2] is a marvel. Hence, there exists a collection of quasi or false obediences, "waste products" that must be pointed out, that they may be avoided.

~

In the first place, perfect obedience demands complete submission of the intellect. To weigh the rights of an order, to seek to get to the bottom of it, for the pleasure of condemning or approving it, is a fantasy of pride, or intellectual pedantry, which has a deleterious effect on the docility of the heart and the acquiescence of the will. A true religious

[1] Saint Catherine of Siena. Dialogue.
[2] Saint Bernard. De Statu Virtutum.

is sparing of his criticism and lavish with his faith. He has a blind eye and a seeing one; the blind eye judges neither the person nor the orders of his superior; the seeing one only perceives God in the authority, and the divine Will in that authority's decisions. Too much reasoning or lack of supernatural spirit leads to an obedience that is a mere matter of routine, and is critical.

A routine of obedience turns into automatism. One acts without a thought. It is the obedience of the factory worker, of the soldier in his barracks, of the clock as it strikes the hours. It is a matter of habit and custom. The order, as it is given, presses the button of the will which at once begins to move, with no other motive than the vague idea of respecting discipline, and avoiding any clash with the powers that be. What store does God set by obedience such as this? It is obedience without soul or merit, for the value of a virtue depends on the faith that inspires it, and the charity that gives it life. Is it quite unknown in the convents? We should like to think so.

Where the supernatural spirit is wanting, the human spirit flaunts its pretensions. There exists an informed obedience— or rather informed religious, or religious who think they are informed. Such a one has made it his business to supervise and control the exercise of authority, so as to lay down its limits, and point out its abuses. Learnedly informed on the rights of the superior and the duties of inferiors, he fully intends that neither shall be exceeded. When occasion arises, he will prove peremptorily, with the Codex in one hand and the Rule in the other, that the authority is in the wrong, that either it is ignorant, or that it exceeds its jurisdiction, and that, all in all, the subject is not bound to obey. If he does obey, it is really an act of condescension, so that worse may be avoided.

Does this learned doctor not know that the superiors have the graces of their state, to interpret the Constitutions and power to dispense? Could he have forgotten that the holy Founders require him, except in the clear case of sin, to obey every order? It is a fine thing to get out of obeying one's superiors, under the terms of the Rule, like the Protestant rebelling against the Pope, while quoting the Scriptures! To this bookish and often doubtful learning, to this spirit of complaint, to this abuse of appeal, the perfect religious prefers modesty and silence, for he would rather obey in all humility and simplicity, than find fault with the authority.

Critical obedience is allied to informed obedience. While it does not contest the authority of the superior, and the legitimacy of his orders, it assumes the right to appraise the latter, and judge the former. The superior is superior, of course. Nonetheless, he is not very likable; he is narrow-minded, curt, impulsive, tactless and unkind. Of course, one must bow to his wishes, though they are often untimely, lacking in common sense, prudence, and charity. God grant that we be soon delivered from such a leader!

The critical spirit is widespread nowadays, and is proved to be a plague both for individuals and communities. Nothing is more contrary to the religious spirit. How many of these judgments, which are, moreover, inspired by passion, pride, envy and bitterness, are proved to be exaggerated or false! We all know that authority is neither infallible nor impeccable in its government. It is nonetheless true that superiors have special lights, secret reasons, broader views, that escape us, and amply justify their decisions. We must trust their wisdom. From his post of command, the leader has higher, longer and clearer vision, and is less likely to be mistaken than his inferiors.

The critical spirit is often unreasonable, and always dangerous. By attacking the person of the superiors, it undermines their authority and destroys the respect and affection which are their due. By disparaging their orders, it makes prompt, total and loving submission of the will difficult, if not impossible. This is all the more so, as open and public criticism is always accompanied by scandal, sometimes grave scandal.

~

Obedience is essentially the submission of the will, and everything that tends to weaken this compliance is the cause of different forms of deformation and degeneration; we find an obedience that is mummified, pseudo-mystical, camouflaged, paradoxical and pharisaical.

Obedience is mummified, when it is rarely if ever practiced. Any virtue is an operative process, that is maintained and developed by its own activity. If it ceases to act, it grows stiff and atrophied. "I have revealed to you the good and salutary means that the religious takes, every day, to increase within him, the virtue of obedience, by the light of faith. . . . So that obedience and its sister patience, grow not weak, nor ever fail him, when he needs to practice them, he continually utters the cries of this desire, and he ever makes use of the time, for he is hungry for these virtues. Obedience is a zealous spouse, who would never remain idle."[3]

Now, there exist religious, who though they do not disobey, no longer know how to obey. Their obedience is completely negative, for it no longer comes into play, either because the superior, for fear of giving displeasure or arousing irritation, no longer dares to command, or because the subjects neatly evade his orders. Keeping themselves to themselves, invisible and silent, while about their business, avoiding the presence of authority as far as in them lies, they live, not in opposition to, but withdrawn from obedience. To their mind, a superior's worth is in inverse proportion to his use of authority. Provided that he is silent, gives no orders, forbids nothing, they will prove themselves the most respectful and docile of sons. Unfortunately, it can be said of this obedience, as of faith: "Can a faith that is inactive be sincere?" A lazy virtue is only half a virtue.

[3] Saint Catherine of Siena. Dialogue.

"For certain souls, one danger is to feel urged to arrange their own little existence apart, so as to be disturbed as little as possible, and practically to live, as if the superior did not exist. This outlook may sometimes be concealed under the pretext of safeguarding the soul's union with God. But this is only a fallacious pretext, hiding a singular illusion full of perils."[4]

The remark of a certain Brother Thomas, a gardener, and, what is more, a pious and devoted religious, deserves not to be forgotten. When he was reproached, in fun, with cultivating his garden according to his own ideas, and only admitting his superior on Rogation Days, he replied with charming frankness. "What do you expect? I am perfectly willing to obey. But what does Father Superior know about gardening? As for Father Bursar, it is still worse! he doesn't know the difference between a pumpkin and a melon! But I don't want to lose the merit of obedience, so do you know what I do?"—"No"—"Well, I obey myself!"

And what can be said of that pseudo-mystical obedience that resists the superiors, on the pretext of obeying the Holy Ghost? It is a lamentable illusion, to take indiscriminately one's pious musings and empty desires for perfection, for so many supernatural inspirations. The orders of superiors are the authentic expression of the divine will, and none, without falling a prey to illuminism, can appeal to God against legitimate authority. Besides "when God sends inspirations into a heart, the first is that of obedience." To leave the path of obedience to one's superiors is to get hopelessly lost.

The Sacred Heart would never allow Saint Margaret Mary to disobey the decisions of her superiors, even when these decisions were not in accordance with His own. One day, He said to her; "You must know that I am in no way offended by the way you have to oppose Me, out of obedience, for which I gave my life; but I want you to know that I am the absolute Lord of My gifts and My creatures, and that nothing can

[4] Don Marmion. Christ, the Ideal of the Monk.

prevent the fulfillment of My plans. That is why I want you, not only to do what your superiors tell you, but also to do nothing I tell you, without their consent. I love obedience; without it, is is impossible to please me."

Another counterfeit is camouflaged obedience, or the art of cunningly inducing the superior, by excuses and objections, to withdraw or modify his command. When an unpleasant order is given . . . one has not time, one is already overworked . . . one is tired . . . one is not fitted . . . another would do it better. . . . It amounts to a real assault, before which, in the end, to the great satisfaction of the subject, the authority, exhausted, capitulates.

Another form of camouflaged obedience is to obey only formal and explicit orders. A religious knows perfectly well the wishes or desires of the authority; but he ignores them, on the pretext that he has been neither told nor forbidden.

Yet more dangerous, because more widespread, is paradoxical obedience. It is, indeed, a paradox, to pretend to obey, while doing one's own will, or even while imposing one's will on the authority.

Such are excesses of initiative, amounting to independence. Without advice or permission, one throws oneself headlong into a thousand occupations, works and charities. For fear of causing resistance and scandal, the superiors are silent, sigh and leave well enough alone. In this way, intelligent and active religious, with the best of intentions can spend their whole lives doing their own will, asking nothing of the authority, save to be left to their own devices. And this, unfortunately, is granted them. Others, skilled in maneuvers, lay seige to their superiors. Turning their personal influence to advantage, counting on services rendered, on former friendship, even taking advantage of the superior's defects, they succeed, by dint of prayers, entreaties, even intrigues and threats, in obtaining occupations, offices and residences that are to their taste. A contemptible diplomacy which, in the eyes of some, passes for the height of competence.

Finally, of all the deformations of obedience, the most lamentable is pharisaical obedience, which surrenders a will that is defeated, but not submissive. This is the obedience of the slave, and is composed of cowardice and hypocrisy. On the whole, in the eyes of God, there is no virtue in those religious "who should also be guilty of pride by stiffening their will. Every time they had to obey, if it was not humility but force that bowed their heads, that will would be broken by violence, and such obedience could not be pleasing to their superiors and their order."[5] To this rebellious obedience is allied the spirit of opposition, either veiled or open; a truly satanic spirit, which consists in wanting just the opposite of what the superior wants, just because he wants it. If parliamentary terms could be applied to the convent, one would say that these religious always form "the opposition."

~

If a want of simplicity and supernatural spirit, of docility and loyalty of will corrupt obedience, the same applies to a want of love in the heart. Charity plays a major part in the spiritual life in general, and particularly, in the practice of obedience. We must obey ex animo, with all our hearts. Without love, submission is a flower without scent, and can only lead to selfish and surly obedience.

That obedience is egotistical which, caring little for the divine will and pleasure, is inspired by selfish motives and tortuous intentions. To submit to authority, because its orders comply with our human views, because the work or charge imposed is in harmony with our need to act, or our self-love—can this be called obedience? Null or mediocre obedience, asserts Saint Thomas, commenting on a passage of Saint Gregory. In the practice of obedience, perhaps more than in that of the other virtues, the purity of intention often leaves much to be desired. To obey because one likes the

[5] Saint Catherine of Siena. Dialogue.

superior, or to get into his good books or win his favor; this is venal submission, and is, alas! not unknown.

Grumbling is one of the clearest signs of this want of love. We must beware of confusing complaint with grumbling. In the Garden of Olives, faced with the horrors of the Passion, Jesus was dismayed, and besought His Father to remove the chalice from His lips; on the Cross, He uttered the filial complaint: "Father, why hast thou forsaken me?" But Our Lord never grumbled. The cry of dismay rises from a broken heart, that begs for mercy and calls for help, whereas grumbling is the protest of a soul that has not learned to say "Fiat." To submit unwillingly, querulously, with a long face and sour look, making it quite clear to our superior that he annoys and crosses us, must multiply the difficulties of obedience and diminish in proportion its merits. Saint Benedict seems to have been obsessed with a horror of this vice. He orders, in the most downright terms, that any manifestation of it whatever, either by word, gesture or murmur, be absolutely banished from the monastery.

The habit of open murmuring is a permanent scandal, and nothing, perhaps, does more to banish interior peace, and to foment disgust with the vocation. Core, Dathan and Abiron, because they murmured against Moses, were plunged living into hell, and Mary, his sister, was afflicted with leprosy. Judas began by murmuring against Jesus, and this fact moved Saint Vincent de Paul to say: "Sisters, you must know that when one of you spreads complaints against the superiors or the Rules among her sisters, it is the beginning of the work of Judas. But when these complaints are spread abroad, Sisters, one is a complete Judas."

~

A final deformation lies in the treatment of the order that has been received. Whereas Jesus "did all things well," the quasi religious is content with an obedience that is but a shadow of itself. The order is carried out indeed, but with a difference; it is a disagreeable task that must be got rid of. It is done, but badly, or half done. There is no attention to detail, to finish, to polish. The result is botched. How many, nowadays, overlook the finer nuances of the virtue. The teacher skimps his marking, to pursue his own studies; the supervisor at study or recreation is absorbed in an interesting book; a cook declares that a cordon bleu is wasted in a convent, and that it is a charity to give one's Sisters the chance of practicing mortification. Sweeping consists in pushing the dust from one spot to another; meditation, in having a nap. Five or ten minutes suffice to prepare a theological thesis or an ascetical case. An aged nun, full of rheumatism, and in danger of falling at every step, had often been advised in vain, and was finally ordered, to use a stick. In order not to disobey, and yet, at the same time, to keep an appearance of youthfulness, she carefully carried it about under her arm. . . . The least that can be said of such obedience is that it is trivial and scamped.

In Saint Bernard's opinion, the truly obedient will brook no delay. With ears pricked, hand outstretched, foot raised, scarcely has he received an order than he is off to carry it out. But the semi-obedient, the blasé, makes a slow start and suffers many a breakdown. His virtue is an "also ran," so the superior must use whip and spur, repeating the same orders, three or four times over. If he is asked the reason for his delay, he replies, "But I hadn't time . . . I was busy . . . I was going to do it . . . I didn't think it was so urgent . . . I forgot." Poor excuses! Perfect obedience cannot compromise with such apathy and negligence.

This quasi obedience, in its many forms, constitutes one of the gravest dangers of our times. Let those lax and independent religious meditate upon these words of Saint Catherine of Siena: "In every way it is hard for them to live under a common rule; for tepidity makes observance difficult: these listless hearts find the lightest burden heavy, and they exhaust themselves to little purpose; they sin against the state of perfection, that they have embraced, and to which they are bound to tend. If they do less wrong than those of whom I was speaking, they yet do wrong."

Chapter XXI

ROYAL SERVITUDE

WE HAVE PASSED THROUGH the picture gallery of
quasi obediences, so let us now pause a little, before the portrait of perfect obedience. A certain Trappist monk, in the
world, a cavalry officer, had been seriously disabled. He had
entered religion, as much from horror of the world, as from
love of Jesus Christ. His Abbot would say of him: "He has
been seven years in the monastery and during that time, I
have led him a dance more than anyone. Well! I have to
admit that I have never seen a sign of protest, never seen
a shadow of displeasure on his face. Unfailingly, he greets
every command with a deep bow, a smile, and immediate
execution. He obeys here in the monastery, as he commanded
in the army. It's simply amazing." Perfect obedience, is, indeed, a marvel, unless it be authentic sanctity.

From the first instant of his Incarnation, Jesus had the
vision of God: from this contemplation sprang His immense
charity, which, in turn, was the source of His incomparable
submission to His Father. Luminous, universal and loving;
such is the obedience of Our Lord in its origin and its com-
pleteness, and His obedience is the model of ours.

~

The first characteristic of perfect obedience is a supernatural principle. As we have already said, one can submit for
many natural motives: from necessity, habit and routine;
from love of peace, or fear of conflict with the authority; out
of natural liking, policy or secret ambition; from human reasoning, the superior being wise, and the order, convenient.

The religious has higher motives. If he obeys, it is exclusively because he sees God in him who commands, and in his orders, the unquestionable expression of the Divine Will. "Servants, be obedient to them that are your lords according to the flesh, with fear and trembling in the simplicity of your heart, as to Christ: not serving to the eye, as it were pleasing men, but, as the servants of Christ doing the will of God from the heart, with a good will serving, as to the Lord, and not to men."[1]

A venerable religious who was blind and crippled with rheumatism that had twisted his limbs, was visited every morning by his rector. As soon as he entered, and in spite of his cries: "Father, I beg you, don't move! I forbid you to move!" the poor cripple made heroic efforts to rise from his chair saying: "Ah, Reverend Father, I must at least make the gesture." Saint Francis Xavier always wrote to Saint Ignatius on his knees, out of respect.

To deference, the man of faith will add submission of judgment. How can one presume to criticize and blame an order, that one considers has been issued by God? But it is important to understand the meaning and scope of the voluntary blindness. Blind obedience is not an act of faith in the infallibility of the authority: any superior can make a mistake, and his orders are not necessarily the wisest or most timely. Nor does it prevent us, far from it, from offering information of which the authority is in ignorance, and which could be useful, provided that we do so with simplicity and charity. In case of obvious error—I repeat, obvious—it does not oblige us to distort the truth, and say that black is white. But it does absolutely forbid the detestable mania for preferring our own judgment or opinion, for weighing in the balance of our own intellect, all the orders we receive, in order to estimate their worth. It does demand—in all cases where there is doubt, if our point of view differs from that of the authority—that, by a free act of our will we immediately bring our

[1] Ephes. VI, 5, 7.

intellect into subjection, and our judgment into line with that of our superior, convinced that—in this case—both the safest and the most meritorious course is to obey.

"If anyone proposes to make an entire and perfect oblation of himself, he must sacrifice his understanding, as well as his will. It is the supreme and third degree of obedience, to have with the superior, not only one same will, but one same thought, by submitting one's own judgment to his, in so far as a will, already in submission, can subject the understanding to it. Although the intellect is not free like the will, and naturally gives its approval to what it considers true, nonetheless, in many cases, where the mind is not constrained by the evidence of truth, the will can sway it to one opinion or another, and it is in such a case, that the truly obedient must bow to the opinion of his superior."[2]

The best is to imitate Saint Thérèse of the Child Jesus, who had made it a habit "never to wonder if what was ordered were useful or not."

~

The fact that the obedience is supernatural implies that it is also universal, in the sense that every religious must obey all legitimate authority, whatever the orders may be.

In religion, nobody is completely free from the law of dependence, because nobody possesses absolute power. Local and provincial superiors depend on the General, who again, is dependent, in his government, upon the General Chapter, the Roman Congregations and the Sovereign Pontiff. From top to bottom, at every rung of the hierarchical ladders, obedience is imposed on all, within the limits fixed by the Codex and the Constitutions. Would it not be a peculiarly shocking thing, to find leaders who were undisciplined or rebellious? With what right—or rather, since the right remains intact—

[2] Spiritual Letters of Saint Ignatius.

how could they have the face to demand from their subordinates, what they themselves refuse to a higher authority? In this matter more than any other, on pain of joining the ranks of those Pharisees, whom Our Lord anathematized, the superior owes it to himself and to others, that he should set the example.

At first sight, it would appear superfluous to recall that the Pope is the first of all superiors. "All religious are subject to the Roman Pontiff as their highest superior, whom they are bound to obey also in virtue of the vow of obedience."[3] And yet it does happen that certain religious, without formally disobeying, do at least indulge in open criticism and censure of the Head of the Church. Have they forgotten that by their profession and the very privilege of exemption, that subjects them directly to pontifical jurisdiction, they, more than others, are bound to absolute, filial obedience? "Let us speak frankly; it cannot be denied that there are religious, and even sometimes, chaplains or superiors, who prefer their own personal views, conveniences or the capricious use of their authority, to the most formal pronouncement of the Holy See. Results follow quickly: troubled souls, a drop in recruitment, disaffection toward the vocation, development of the spirit of criticism, etc. Fortunately, such cases are extremely rare."[4]

Diocesan Congregations owe the same obedience, due allowance being made, to the Bishop or his delegate.

With equal respect and the same promptness, the perfectly obedient submit to any holder of authority, whatever his rank, talents, virtue or age, from the superior general to the simple head of office. And who knows but that, in the latter case, their obedience is not more virtuous and meritorious, since it is inspired by a more lively faith and more supernatural love? "Among all the graces I have received from the goodness of God," Saint Francis of Assisi would say,

[3] Canon 499 l.
[4] Revue des Communautès Religieuses–Janvier 1931.

"this is one; that if I were given as guardian a newly-clothed novice, I would obey him as punctiliously as the oldest and gravest of the Brothers."[5] The lesser the authority of the superior, the less this authority is enhanced by the prestige of personal qualities, the greater is the merit of our obedience; for then, it is inspired by the sole desire of pleasing God. By superiors, must be understood "all that hold office in the convent: such as the Infirmarian, the Sacristan, or the Sister who is charged with the care of the refectory. In obeying the Abbess, a religious may be easily influenced by human respect; but in obeying sisters entrusted with inferior offices, she shows that she possesses the true spirit of obedience."[6]

This eagerness to obey orders, this inward satisfaction at being able to submit, everywhere and always, is one of the most striking characteristics of perfect obedience. Saint Anselm of Canterbury asked the Sovereign Pontiff to give one of his chaplains authority over him, only too happy, Archbishop as he was, to be in a position to submit and practice obedience.

This passion for obedience is displayed in that virtue of urbanity, which makes us ready to bow to the views, desires and wishes of our brethren. What is the point of contradicting, quarreling, asserting oneself? Is it not better to yield in a spirit of humility, kindliness and peace, and always, when it is not a matter of conscience, to accede to the most trivial requests and fancies of our neighbor, making ourselves "everybody's slave"? Is it not what is meant by the passage in the Benedictine rule: "Let them vie with one another in obedience"?

Obedience is universal also in the sense that we carry out any order, whether it falls in with our tastes and ideas or not, even though it entails a painful sacrifice. After the example of Saint Thérèse of the Child Jesus, the perfect religious chooses everything and rejects nothing. There is one

[5] Saint Bonaventure. Legenda St. Francisci.
[6] Saint Alphonsus. The True Spouse.

sole exception, that very rarely arises. Should the authority
command what is obviously a sin, it is better to obey God
than a man who betrays his trust. We say "obviously a sin"
for when there is doubt as to whether an order is good and
valid, one must submit. In this case, "the generality of theologians and masters of supernatural life teach that a religious
is bound to obey, and that in obeying, she is certain of not
sinning, and of even pleasing God.

He who is perfected in obedience goes still further. Divin-
ing the secret thought and tacit will of the authority, he fore-
stalls his orders and executes them before they are uttered.
A mere wish or word of advice has for him all the weight
of a command. Convinced that dependence is an infinitely
precious good, he sets upon all his acts the seal of obedience.
Mortifications, prayers, literary or theological works, diverse
occupations: all are submitted to the approval of the superiors. In this way, he is sure of not yielding to the fantasies of
his self-will, but of ever acting within the bounds of the
divine good pleasure. Saint Francis of Sales recommended
this practice very strongly to his daughters of the Visitation.
Saint Benedict bade his monks to make known to the Abbot
their supplementary mortifications in Lent. Father Long-
haye, a Jesuit, never began one of his works without having
it approved by his superiors, who were sometimes his former
pupils. When obedience is practiced in this way, to its fullest
extent, with regard to every authority, it becomes the very
tissue of religious life; it makes that life noble and fruitful,
on the condition that it is inspired by a great sentiment of
charity.

~

Love is the beginning and end of perfect obedience. Obedience without love is a rose without scent, an empty ear of
corn. "Let a man for the love of God submit himself to his
superior in all obedience," so as to accomplish his will and
imitate Jesus Christ who obeyed his Father in an ecstasy of

love. Then obedience is but the living expression of charity. It is love in action, and thus a religious life, which is exclusively devoted to obedience, becomes a life of pure love and eminent sanctity. When obedience is rooted in love, it will find in this love the secret of its strength, energy, delicacy and joy. "All that is done for love, is done strongly, promptly, joyfully." In Saint Bernard's opinion, perfect obedience is only to be found in monks who have nothing dearer to them on earth than Christ. Without love, none would willingly accept the renunciations and sacrifices, sometimes heroic, that are inherent in the practice of obedience. Faith is not enough; charity, stronger than death, must come to the rescue. Religious servitude is a slow martyrdom; now martyrdom, the supreme act of the virtue of fortitude, is always commanded by love. To persevere for forty or fifty years in total subjection is a crushing yoke, that the heart alone can bear with valor and joy. Whoever sees Christ in the authority and loves Him passionately, will brook no delay, suffer no beating about the bush. The will then resembles a high-pressure engine; it starts both smoothly and promptly.

The rapidity of loving obedience will ever be accompanied by care in execution. This virtue has the cult of work well done, polished, perfected. "The best possible" is its watchword and it follows it faithfully. Charity also gives to obedience its last characteristic, that of joyousness. What a joy it is to be in the service of those one loves, to accede to their smallest wish, to devote oneself to the point of sacrifice! It is a deep and stable joy that nothing can devalue or tarnish, even when the authority weighs upon us to breaking point; a truly divine joy, the fruit of love, the joy of doing the will of the Father, of rejoicing the Heart of Jesus, by walking in His steps. Blessed are those who in obedience, can always keep a smile! And such is the privilege of all the great friends of Christ.

The greatest help in gaining a better understanding and

acquiring a better practice of this great virtue is the assiduous meditation of Jesus, the great model of obedience. "For Jesus, everything came down to obedience. . . . In Him the beatific vision was like a sap; adoration was like a living root; obedience was to be the trunk which would divide into innumerable branches, bearing countless thousands of fruits. . . . To be made Flesh is His constitution, to be made obedient, His condition; the one issues from the other, and the latter is founded on the former, so that it is so to speak essential, and incapable of change."[7]

The clear-sighted and universal obedience of the Son of God caused Him to be subject, not only to Joseph and Mary, et erat subditus illis, but also to the most iniquitous judges and savage executioners. In His whole life, from the Crib to the Cross, every decision, word, act, prayer, journey and suffering was made in response to the will of the Father and the desire of the Spirit. "For I do always the things that please Him." His obedience sprang from His immense love, and its one aim was the glory of God and the salvation of the world. "But that the world may know that I love the Father, and as the Father hath given me commandment, so do I."

Many will become just, through one man's obedience, just as many through one man's disobedience, became guilty. It was a mute, heroic obedience, that led Him to His death, and the death of the Cross. In the soul of Jesus, as in His Gospel, love is indissolubly united to obedience. "You are my friends if you do the things that I command you." "If you love me, keep my commandments." This spirit of living obedience, which is an eminent virtue and a priceless grace, we must implore of God's goodness, and must practice with the greatest care. Everyday, at Mass and Communion especially, let us ask Jesus that we may imitate Him, that for us too, the will of the Father may be our daily bread, that we may be "one with Him" in the Unity of the Father and the Holy Ghost.

[7] Mgr. Gay of Christian Life and Virtues.

At morning meditation, let us loyally dispose ourselves to submit, at every moment, to the law of obedience, even though this submission were to impose on us acts of bitter renunciation and painful sacrifices. When we gaze on Christ crucified, the victim of obedience, how could we complain or draw back? "Let us also go that we may die with him."

Chapter XXII

FRUITFUL LABOR

SAINT BENEDICT calls obedience now a labor, *labor,* now an excellence, *bonum.* In fact it is both; a labor that is fruitful in all sorts of results. At first sight, religious obedience appears to be austere. Does it not seem to repress, if not to stifle, the human personality, put a curb on all our powers: intellect, heart and will, and exact some painful act of renunciation at every step? In fact, all these restrictions and sacrifices, like the Cross, of which they are but variations, are seeds of virtue and sources of powerful vitality. To them can be applied the paradoxes of the Gospel: "He that loveth his life shall lose it; he that hateth his life in this world, keepeth it unto life eternal." "For you are dead; and your life is hid with Christ in God." Unless the grain of wheat falling into the ground die, itself remaineth alone. But if it die, it bringeth forth much fruit." "Every branch in me that beareth not fruit, he will take away: and every one that beareth fruit, he will purge it, that it may bring forth more fruit."

Would it not be ungracious of the shrub to complain of the stake that supports it, or the knife that prunes it? The benefits conferred upon the soul by obedience are innumerable, and it was the realization of this fact that decided the monastic vocation of Dom Marmion.

"I had all I needed for my sanctification, except for one good, that of obedience. That is why I left my country, giving up my freedom and all else. I can say . . . that I become a monk, in order to obey. I had while I was still very young, what is called a good position, success, and friends who were very dear to me, but I had not the opportunity to obey. I become a monk, because God revealed to me the beauty and greatness of obedience."[1] It is a rich mine for those who know how to work it and extract from it assurance and certainty of intellect, freedom and strength of will, peace and joy of heart. What is more, obedience constitutes the true nobility and all the merit of the religious life.

The first advantage of obedience belongs to the intellectual order: the certainty of being on the right road; infallible expectation of divine grace; and the assurance, whatever happens, of always doing an excellent work. For those who subject themselves, in all simplicity and loyalty, there can be no fear of error, no motive for discouragement, no possibility of failure. Are they under obedience? Then all is well, and could not be better.

It should be the constant preoccupation of the religious soul, to know God's will where he is concerned: for this will is the only path of salvation, and the one instrument of his sanctification. Every spiritual life is summed up and condensed in the words "Fiat voluntas tua."

Now this precisely is one of the privileges of obedience. The orders of the authority reveal to us, without the shadow of doubt, the will of God. He who submits cannot go astray; obedience is an infallible line of conduct. The superior may be mistaken, but not the subject.

Many fervent souls in the world anxiously wonder where their duty lies, and what exactly God expects or requires of them. How many are the victims, albeit unconscious ones, of their own ignorance, self-will, false inspirations and diabolical illusions! For it is not enough to do what is good, we must do only the good that is willed by God. Who will tell us where this good lies? The Rule and superiors. Has the authority spoken? We know exactly where we are. "One of the greatest sufferings of the servants of God on earth is not to be able to decide clearly and surely, what is the will of the divine Master, and to endure, often in the noblest actions,

[1] Dom Raymond Thibaut. "A Master of the Spiritual Life, Dom Columba Marmion."

the fear, more or less justified, of seeking themselves rather than the glory of God, and of doing their own will, while persuading themselves that they are obeying the divine Will.

The certainty that one is doing right by obeying, has the corollary, that one is assured of divine assistance. Since God commands us, we have the right to count on His powerful and efficacious collaboration. The overflowing store of His grace is always at the disposal of those who serve Him generously. Thus, there is no room for fear or discouragement. Though the authority, in its government, may lack benevolence or prudence, may impose on us orders that are extremely hard to obey, may place us in situations that are awkward and unpleasant, it is of no account: we may rest assured that the support of God will never fail us. In the designs of Providence, the order of a superior cannot be a trap set for the weak or inexperienced, though it may prove to be a formidable test of virtue. Yet, with the help of God it is always possible to come through the trial unscathed, ennobled. When Moses, aghast at his Mission, asked: "Who am I that I should go to Pharaoh, and should bring forth the children of Israel out of Egypt?" Jehovah replied: "I will be with thee." Our Lord has often repeated the same words to His saints, when He gave them orders. He repeats them to every soul that trembles before the sacrifices imposed by obedience: "Fear not, for I am with thee: Noli timere, quia ego tecum sum."

The assurance of doing the will of God and of obtaining His aid if we obey, involves another surety: that of success; not indeed of apparent or human success, but of real and supernatural success. A religious who obeys, must succeed, at least, in the sense that his submission—and this is the essential—always contributes to the glory of God, to his own sanctification and the redemption of souls. From ignorance or illusion, a superior can impose on one of his subjects labors, an office, a charge, that clearly form a burden too heavy for his physical strength, his intellectual capacity or his moral qualities. It is sometimes said that obedience works miracles. Sometimes. But it would be rash to presume that God is going to make an extraordinary intervention, in order to make good our weakness, or the mistakes of authority. So it may happen that, in spite of his good will, the obedient man may find his efforts result in a resounding failure. But in fact, the failure is only apparent. For the perfect religious will turn his mortification to account, and find, in his very humiliation, a wonderful opportunity of rising to the heights of abnegation, spirit of sacrifice and perfect love of Jesus Christ. There are defeats that are as glorious as victories. More than one saint has known these magnificent and immensely fruitful failures. The death of Christ on the Cross, by obedience, appeared to all, even His own apostles, like the failure of His mission and the final ruin of His work. Yet it was at the very hour, when everything apparently collapsed, that Jesus saved humanity, and founded His Kingdom. The same must be said of the case, when the authority, underestimating the worth of its subordinates, or not concerned with making the most of them, keeps a religious in the background and hides his talents under a bushel. Some would call it a life rendered sterile. That remains to be seen! Who can say if this life, stifled and mutilated, has not gained in depth and in intimacy with Christ, in personal sanctity and apostolic power? It is better to suffer than to act. Moreover, Saint Benedict's words are still true in every circumstance, "Obedience always works for good." And Saint Paul's: "To them that love God, all things work together unto good."

~

After fixing the intelligence in a restful state of assurance, obedience becomes for the will a source of freedom and strength. Religious servitude has a bad reputation with unbelieving psychologists. They say that it can only make passive creatures, without initiative or independence. It is both an extinguisher and a strait jacket. The truth is very different. There is nothing perhaps, more capable of forming men and forging characters than obedience. The support and safeguard of true liberty, it has nothing in common with slavery. Moral liberty—which must not be confused with the faculty of each one to do good or evil, to practice at will, vice or virtue, or still less, to follow meekly the lead of the passions—consists in the power and the right to choose, without exterior violence, freely, the path of duty, the path that leads to God. What the world calls "liberty" is too often only a multiple and varied form of slavery. The slaves are not in the cloister, but outside; slaves of pride, of money, of sensuality, slaves of human respect, of a political party, of fashion. "Amen, amen, I say unto you: That whosoever committeth sin, is the servant of sin." Thus the world—not the convent—is a prison, for "the whole world is seated in wickedness."

To make a vow of obedience is not to give up one's liberty —far from it! It is to safeguard it, strengthen it and turn it to excellent account. By raising the rampart of a Rule and sacred authority against the assaults of egotism and the passions, I have but defended my liberty against its worst enemies. By making a sacred and eternal promise never to stray from the will of God, expressed to me by His representatives, I have merely shored up my buckling will and so made good the deficiencies of my liberty. And when, at every hour of the day, gladly, lovingly, I submit to the orders of my superiors, what else do I do, if not make a splendid use of my liberty for the conquest of sanctity and the storming of heaven? Is the motorist, who avoids the roads full of potholes, and who, to prevent accidents, has his steering gear and brakes tested, to be accused of being the slave of his machine? Besides a holy liberty, the obedient man possesses an incomparable strength. Religious belong to the race of the strong, of whom Saint Benedict speaks, "who take up the strong and bright weapons of obedience," and whose characteristic virtue is fortitude. If it is easy enough to let oneself go with the stream, it is a different matter to stem the current. It does not take courage to go one's own way, the plaything of one's passions; it needs courage, heroic courage at times, to obey. Nowadays, more than ever before, there are too few characters of steel or marble, and too many weathercocks and puppets. This may well be explained by the weakening of authority and lack of discipline. One can no longer will, because one has forgotten how to obey.

The convent remains one of the best schools of energy, precisely because it is a school of subjection and renunciation. Here we are inured to obedience, as we speak of being inured to fatigue or work. This breaking in of the will means that it is tempered, strengthened and trained. Like any faculty and virtue, the will develops and hardens through the frequency and energy of its acts. By dint of making acts of will, wholeheartedly, generously and perseveringly, we forge a will of granite. Now it is precisely the obedience of the cloister that provides, and imposes this exercise of moral formation.

A hundred times a day, either through the Rule or his Superiors, the religious has the chance to obey, i.e., to will, and if his submission is what it ought to be, to will fully, promptly and vigorously, so that the whole being, intellect, heart, and the body itself, takes part in the obedience.

These acts are all the more virile, in that they are ever assisted by supernatural grace, which inspires, supports and fructifies them. Every time we obey, God becomes our collaborator, and with His omnipotence as a springboard, everything becomes possible, even miracles. "I can do all things in him who strengtheneth me." Did not Saint Mawrus, at Saint Benedict's command, walk on the waters, and save the young monk, Placidus? Obedience, by canalizing our energies, restrains the field of our activity, but what we lose in scope, we gain in intensity.

Monastic servitude is formative both by the well-ordered and powerful action it requires, and also by the constant reaction it calls for. Until virtue has become second nature, perfect obedience cannot be conceived without bitter daily strife. It demands reaction against our apathy, or sensuality; reaction against our ideas, whims, self-will; reaction against all the enemies, both interior and exterior—and we have already seen how many there are—who try to deflect our progress. Nothing, then, is more formative than this war to the knife. It is in strife, and through strife, that the will hardens, and the character is strengthened. "Everything that irks man, strengthens him. He cannot obey without perfecting himself, and from the very fact that he overcomes himself, he is a better man."[2] Obedience does for the soul, what tempering does for steel. The religious state owes it to obedience, more than to poverty and chastity, that it is a holocaust, a martyrdom, and a true martyrdom, though without executioner and scaffold. What indeed is martyrdom, but the supreme act of the virtue of fortitude? What moral energy is demanded of a soul by that perseverance until death in self-sacrifice, that immovable fixity in the will of God! A half century of total obedience, often difficult, always smiling: what a noble triumph of endurance and virility!

It has been said that discipline is the main strength of armies. For the religious, his strength is in his obedience. How truly Saint Bernard spoke when he said: "He who obeys is clothed in strength." And if obedience has deserved to be called "the mother, nurse and guardian of all the virtues," it is surely thanks to its profound influence over the will, where the moral virtues are rooted and whence they derive their nourishment.

~

Individual and collective peace is another noteworthy boon conferred by obedience. A Community, in which reigns obedience to the Rule and humble submission to the Superiors, must necessarily be a house of peace, domus pacis. A handful of turbulent, undisciplined or critical subjects are

[2] Joseph du Maistre. Du Pape.

enough to throw trouble and unrest into souls. Oh how great is the peace of a religious whose desires are the dictates of obedience! Saint Dositheus having consecrated his whole will to obedience, enjoyed continual peace. Fearing that in this peace, there was some delusion of the enemy, he one day said to his Superior, Saint Dorotheus: "Father, tell me why it is that I experience such tranquility as to be free from every other desire?" "My Son," replied the Father, "this peace is altogether the fruit of obedience."

On the other hand, how sad and restless is the existence conducted apart from obedience, and above all in constant opposition to the authority! "He who does not obey in the religious life is such a burden to himself and others, that he has, even here below, a foretaste of Hell. He ever lives amid sorrow, shame and the remorse of his conscience; he displeases his Superiors and his Order, he becomes intolerable to himself."[3]

Peace consists in the tranquillity of order: tranquillitas ordinis. Obedience is a gushing, perennial spring of this order and tranquillity. The fundamental order of creation is that man abase himself before the divine Majesty, and submit to all His commands. The order of justice: it is the place of the superior to rule and command, of the inferior to bow and obey. The order of humility: each must vie in taking the lowest place, in being the servant of all his brethren, in complying with their slightest wish. These three orders, the generators of peace, will be supremely and universally respected by the obedient; in all places, and at all times, they keep in their place, and stay there. For that very reason, they live in sovereign peace of soul. One of the most striking characteristics of the perfectly obedient is serenity. Why should he be troubled, since he incurs no moral responsibility? Obedience is a completely safe situation. Aware of the obligations, dangers and difficulties of a good government, how many superiors wonder with anguish whether they understand, and

[3] Saint Catherine of Siena. Dialogue.

perform their duty, as they should! If authority, in its orders, can lack prudence, justice, and benevolence, the subject, when he obeys, cannot help but practice all kinds of virtues. Thus, in the day of judgment, religious will be charged with every act of disobedience; but, as Saint Philip Neri used to say, they shall be most certain of not having to render an account of the actions performed through obedience. For these, the Superiors only, who commanded them, shall be held accountable. Speaking particularly of nuns, the Lord once said to Saint Catherine of Siena: "Religious will not be obliged to render an account to me of what they do through obedience; for that, I will demand an account from the superiors." "Obey," says the Apostle, "your prelates, and be subject to them. For they watch as being to render an account of your souls." Freedom from responsibility brings freedom from scruple. The docile religious need not wonder if he has done rightly, whether he could have done better, whether he has sinned. He who obeys never sins and ever does what is most perfect.

An obedient religious also lives at peace, because he has triumphed over the demands of his self-will, and the thousand and one whims of his egotism. An obedient soul is a peaceful soul. On the other hand, how many malcontents, embittered and restless souls exist, who have not had the courage to conquer themselves and obey! "Attachment to self-will is the sole reason why many nuns lead an unhappy existence." "One is troubled, because she cannot have the confessor or superior she would wish. Another, because she would like a certain employment, and it is not given to her. By dint of complaint, she obtains that her superior, for the sake of peace, gives her satisfaction. The unhappy soul does not find peace, for it is not the means of finding it to force one's superior to obey, instead of obeying her oneself."[4]

Yes, it cannot be repeated often enough, the secret of peace and happiness in the convent is in a life of obedience

[4] St. Alphonsus, *op. cit.*

250 THE PRACTICE OF THE VOWS

and love. How easy and sweet life is, when one is always doing the holy will of God! And, yet more, how easy and sweet is death! What must be the joy of a religious, who, at the hour of death, can say like the Abbot John: "I have never done my will."

And what glory shall they attain in Heaven! Perfect obedience, being the constant practice of perfect charity in the accomplishment of the will of God, is the source of an infinity of merits. Saint Dorotheus, whose health was frail, and who could not keep all common observances, only lived for five years in religion. Yet, after his death, it was revealed that his incomparable submission to his Abbot had earned for him a glory equal to that of Saint Anthony, and Saint Paul, the hermits. Thus, far from stifling and abasing the human personality, religious obedience insures for it an admirable development. Obedience enlightens, purifies, strengthens, frees, pacifies, fructifies and ennobles; it raises man to be the associate of God and His collaborator, in the realization of His providential designs; and since it is one of the most authentic forms of humility, we can say of it, qui se humiliat, exaltabitur.

Yes, happy and blessed is the religious, of whom it can be said, as it was said of Jesus, the Son of God: Et erat subditus.

PART V

PERSEVERANCE

Chapter XXIII

FIDELITY

THE RELIGIOUS STATE, of its nature, calls for stability, and those who embrace it, must remain faithful unto death. Indeed, what is the profession, but the definitive rooting of the soul in deep soil, the total and irrevocable gift of one's person to the service of God?

This fidelity to the vocation is at once a mystery, a virtue, and a special grace.

Perseverance is linked with the mystery of our liberty. Poor human will, so fragile and wayward! Yesterday, we were resolute; today, the wind has changed, and with equal tenacity we are determined on the exact opposite. We have only to recall the twelve Apostles, swearing that they would follow their Master, if it cost them their lives, and, only a few hours later, deserting Him like cowards. In every Congregation, some desert, and some have to be weeded out. The remote causes and immediate reasons are hard to disentangle. Why did this religious, who seemed to be exemplary, go back to the world, whereas another, who was very mediocre, stayed on to the end? Impossible to say. These are secrets of the conscience and of the judgment of God. Fidelity in the Institute is also very closely related to the great virtue of fortitude. According to Father Faber, "perseverance is the greatest of trials, the heaviest of burdens, and the most crushing cross." The fidelity of a religious may be

251

subjected to long, severe trials, which he can overcome only with sturdy courage and a vigorous spirit of sacrifice. Further, unless the will be reinforced by a special grace, it will not suffice. This is a precious gift, which is often confused with final perseverance, and which we must ask daily of the goodness of God, and the mercy of the Blessed Virgin. So that we may better grasp the nature, basis, and moral gravity of this duty, we shall consider it, under its positive and negative aspects: fidelity and infidelity.

~

Fidelity! This is a brave and noble word, one of the finest in the Christian vocabulary. Is it not one of the glorious titles of Our Lady: Virgo fidelis?

Like any other virtue, this fidelity consists essentially in a disposition of the soul: the unconquerable and effective resolution of a religious to belong forever to God and his Congregation. What is the value of mere bodily presence in a convent and the proximity of men clad in the same habits, if the heart is not there? Fidelity means primarily, the indissoluble union of souls, in the pursuit of one same ideal, under the same flag.

Whatever may happen, and whatever the cost to myself, I am determined to live among my brethren, and to die in the bosom of my religious family. I am determined that, until my last breath, I will keep my Rule, my vows of poverty, chastity and obedience, devote my energies to the service of Christ, the Institute, and souls. This is an irrevocable decision on which I will not go back. The brutal or insidious temptation to look back, throw everything overboard, and return to the world, may shake or entice me: with the grace of God, I will overcome it like the others. At the Profession ceremony, the superior asks the novice: "Perseverabisne usque ad mortem? Will you persevere until death?" He replies: "Ita, Pater, usque ad mortem. Yes, Father, until death." Will he ever dare to retract? Such fidelity excludes even the slightest voluntary thought, the most transitory yearning to recover our liberty. Whoever dwells on such feelings is already a traitor at heart, as the man who looks on a woman with desire, has already committed adultery. The moral obligation to persevere rests on a fourfold basis: docility to grace, love of Jesus Christ, justice and gratitude to the Order and God, duty of religion.

Right at its source, the vocation is a choice of God and a call to eminent holiness. Surely, such a grace must find in souls perfect docility, and an enthusiastic welcome. From all eternity, Providence has determined the background, and arranged the program of our lives. These plans that God has made for us, which are inspired both by love and wisdom, cannot, without peril, be cast aside or modified. Now that is precisely what the unfaithful religious does. To turn back after several years, to leave the path traced by God, and follow another that we choose for ourselves, is a most imprudent course, which must lead to terrible moral catastrophe, and which, in any case, implies ingratitude, and often cowardice.

Saint Alphonsus tells us that after redemption and baptism, no grace equals the religious vocation; it is a prodigious grace that embraces a multitude of others. How should one dare to reject this royal gift of God, which He only offers to those dearest to His heart, and say to Him: "Lord, that is enough: I have served You as a religious for ten or twenty years, and that will do. I have not found in Your service what I thought I should; I am going to seek it elsewhere." And with that, one would turn one's back on Him! What rank ingratitude! If, in the litanies of His holy Name, we ask Jesus that we may avoid negligence in following His inspirations, what are we to make of those who reject and profane the incomparable grace of their vocation? One is culpable if one resists one's vocation; still more culpable if having followed it, one abandons it, through cowardice. And, indeed, when a religious leaves his convent, it is not usually for very honorable motives. Whether he goes because of sensuality, pride, tepidity or disgust, when all things are taken into account, he goes because he is defeated, because of weakness, or lack of courage. Perseverance also draws its inspiration from, and rests upon, the friendship of Christ, and the love of the Spouse.

Profession seems to have created a new, deep friendship between the Saviour and the soul. To those whom His love has called apart from the world, Jesus can say, as He said to his apostles: "You have not chosen me: but I have chosen you; and have appointed you, that you should go, and should bring forth fruit; and your fruit should remain." "I will not now call you servants . . . but I have called you friends." Although the religious state is of its nature a servitude, it is none the less, in its origin, its development and its end, a divine friendship. Was not Our Lord and Saviour Himself, both the servant and beloved Son of the Father?

It is true that Jesus chose and called us first; but also, on our part, we have put much love into the acceptance of this choice, and the response to the call! Moreover, can one effect the total and irrevocable gift of oneself, without love? Yes, we became religious, so that we might become the close friends of Christ.

What, in a man, is friendship, in a woman, is the love of a spouse. Why should a nun renounce human affection and the glory of founding a family, unless it be to unite herself to Christ and adopt a countless family of souls? Her profession was her wedding, and on that day, with what joy she gave herself to Jesus Christ! "Ecce venio ad Te, quem amavi, quem quaesivi, quem semper optavi! Beloved, I come to Thee, whom I have loved, sought, and always desired!"

But is not fidelity one of the most striking traits of love, in friendship and marriage? Saint Jerome says: "When a friendship can cease to be, it has never been true." If one has given oneself completely, one no longer has the right to take oneself back. There is little to choose between abandoning an old friend and betraying him. As for the nun who, without grave reason, breaks the mystical ring of the profession, she "divorces" Jesus Christ.

To these reasons of sentiment, must be added another, equally weighty: that of equity. We have said that the profession is a bilateral contract, made between the religious and the Institute, and imposing on both parties strict reciprocal obligations. If the Congregation is bound, in justice, to keep the newly professed, unless he prove unworthy or incorrigible, the professed is bound in conscience to remain, until death, in the service of his religious family. Except under extraordinary conditions, the contract of profession cannot be broken, and none may do so, without flagrant injustice.

As a soldier, who has enlisted in the army, is bound whether he likes it or not, to serve his time, so the religious, a voluntary recruit in the picked troop of his Congregation, is also obliged to respect his signature, and remain faithful to his flag, until death. He was free before his profession, afterwards, he is free no more. Besides, religious receive from their Order great graces and innumerable gifts. After being educated for long years with maternal solicitude, freely, would it not be strange, even shocking, if, when they were in a position to repay their debts by their work, they were to leave the Institute, without reason or regret?

The last motive for perseverance is religion. The perpetual vows—the word itself says as much—have irrevocably consecrated the religious to God. He has entered the service of God; he may not leave it, except for reasons, the gravity of which the competent authority, the Sovereign Pontiff, the Superior General—has alone the right to judge. Any dispensation that is granted without motive, is illicit and invalid. When one has sworn fidelity to God publicly at the altar, on the Gospels, one must keep one's promise, whatever happens.

Certain Orders or religious Congregations have strengthened this fidelity by a special vow of stability or perseverance. This is the sacred promise to die a religious, and in the monastery, in which one was professed, stabilitas status et loci; to stay "in the place where one was consecrated, until the great removal." "It is one of the misfortunes of man, that he cannot live within a space of six square feet." This misfortune can be remedied by stability and death.

~

To fidelity is opposed infidelity: the voluntary and unmotivated abandonment of a certain vocation, the culpable snapping of the sacred bonds, that tie the religious to God and his Institute. We must now define the nature of this Infidelity, and then point out its various modalities.

Not every departure from the convent is to be condemned; quite the contrary. The novitiate and the temporary profession are at once a study and a preparation, for entry into religion does not necessarily imply a certain vocation. If, after trial, the religious life appears to the postulant or novice to be incompatible with his temperament, and beyond his physical or moral strength, the solution is clear: he must abandon a career that is not for him, and seek another. One can be mistaken in all good faith, and the rectification of an error is always an act of prudence and honesty.[1]

Neither can the name of infidelity be applied to the transfer to another Order or Institute. The Church sometimes allows this, for just motives. Saint Thomas names two: the desire of a religious for a higher perfection, and the impossibility, owing to chronic infirmity or poor health, of faithful observance. These are not the only ones, and the following could be added: "if experience has proved to the religious that he has clearly been deceived about his capacities, in believing himself to be called to a contemplative life, whereas

[1] After the Perpetual vows have been made, what is to be done in the case of discovery that there has been no vocation? Remain. Such is the opinion of Saint Alphonsus: God cannot refuse this soul the graces necessary to sanctification and salvation. C.f., The True Spouse, ch. XXIV.

a more active life would suit his temperament better, or vice-versa; if (the religious) has fallen away from his first perfection. . . . But, if the transfer is to be licit, it must not be made lightly or from caprice; neither must it give scandal or be prejudicial to the Order, from which the transfer is to be made."[2]

Sometimes it happens that, in the secret designs of His Providence, God grants to a few souls, as it were, a double and successive vocation, the first being a mysterious preparation for the second. However that may be, great prudence must be used in such situations in order to avoid illusions, which can be all the more dangerous, as they are often masked under an appearance of what is better. The right course is to reflect, pray, consult superiors and director, and only come to a decision, when one is sure of the will of God. These transfers are always difficult and rarely successful. At a certain age, after long years in an Institute, it is very difficult to shape oneself to a different mold, to put off one's well-worn habits, to acquire new ones, briefly, to adapt and remake oneself. Often a shrub that has been transplanted too late can only vegetate and wither. How many religious have regretted swapping horses in midstream! "Saint Philip Neri said that one ought not to lose a good state of life for a better one, without being certain of the divine will. Thus in order not to err, you should be more than morally certain that it is the will of God to have you pass to another state; but when does this certainty exist, especially, if your Superiors and your spiritual Father tell you that it is a temptation?"[3] It is a quite frequent temptation nowadays, to pass from an active Congregation to a contemplative Order . . . to one's cost!

"We should not even go from one Order to another without very weighty motives, says Saint Thomas, following the Abbot Nestorius cited by Cassian. . . . A young Portuguese,

[2] Bastien. Directoire Canonique.
[3] Saint Alphonsus. Ascetical Works. Vol. XII.

called Francis Bassus, was admirable, not only in divine elo-
quence, but also in the practice of virtue, under the discipline
of the Blessed (Saint) Philip Neri in the Congregation of the
Oratory at Rome. Now, he persuaded himself that he was
inspired to leave this holy society, to place himself in an Order, strictly so called, and at last he resolved to do so. But
the Blessed Philip, assisting at his reception into the Order
of Saint Dominic, wept bitterly; whereupon being asked by
Francis Marie Tauruse, afterward Archbishop of Siena and
Cardinal, why he shed tears: 'I deplore,' said he, 'the loss
of so many virtues.' And in fact this young man, who was so
excellently good and devout in the Congregation, after he
became a religious was so inconsistent and fickle, that agi-
tated with various desires of novelties and changes, he gave
afterward great and grievous scandal." And Saint Francis of
Sales, who relates the incident, wisely concludes: "Let everyone then, having once found out God's holy will touching his
vocation, keep to it holily and lovingly, practicing therein its
proper exercises, according to the order of discretion, and
with the zeal of perfection."[4]

The reproach of infidelity must not be leveled against the
religious who, for exceptionally grave motives, returns into
the world after the expiry of his temporary profession, or
with the legitimate dispensation from his perpetual vows.
The fact that these motives must be exceptionally grave, implies that they are extremely rare.

Filial piety can provide a reason for leaving religion, in
order to support a father, or a mother, who in their old age
are completely alone and destitute. But if the Institute were
willing to be responsible for them and assist them, it would
appear that the religious could not in conscience ask to be
dispensed from his vows and return to his family.

As for sickness and physical infirmities, they are not, as a
general rule, a sufficient motive for leaving one's Congregation. Did one enter the service of God in order to enjoy flour-

[4] Saint Francis of Sales. Treatise on the love of God. Bk. VIII, ch. II.

ishing health and not to die? Why should one wish to return to the world on the pretext of getting treatment, when one can be sure of finding in one's religious family, along with fraternal charity, the most devoted care? So as to procure medicines for the sick, Saint Alphonsus asked that the library and even the sacred vessels be sold. And he exclaimed: "I am sorry for those who say: My health suffers in the Congregation. Did they want the Congregation to make them immortal, or immune from disease? We must die, and before we die, we must pass through suffering. What else should be the main object of him who joins us, if not to make himself agreeable to God, and make a good death in the Congregation? It is the grace that has already been obtained by many of our brethren, who are now in eternity; and I am sure that all give thanks to God, that they have died in the Congregation. So, my Brethren, when we are attacked by some illness, let us accept it from the hands of God, and let us not hearken to the devil who, when he sees a sick religious, seeks to tempt him about his vocation."

There remains the case, which is truly exceptional, in which the religious life itself, owing to the temperament of the subject, becomes a danger for his physical, intellectual or moral health. A request for secularization is licit, though regrettable, under such conditions.

On the other hand, those religious are unfaithful to their engagements and gravely at fault, who leave their Institute illegitimately; who, by their repeated faults and incorrigibility, secure expulsion or who, without sufficient cause, themselves ask and obtain dispensation from their vows.

Illegitimate egress consists in leaving one's Institute, without permission from the competent authority, either before the expiry of the temporary vows, or after the perpetual profession. A "fugitive" is the religious who leaves his Order ad tempus, for a more or less protracted period, but with the intention of returning some day.[5] If he leaves for good, with-

5 Codex Canon 644.

out any intention of returning, it is apostasy.[6] This desertion cannot be carried out without several grave faults: "sin
against the vow of obedience, since the religious withdraws
himself completely from the authority of his superiors; sin
against justice towards the Institute, to which he is bound
by a bilateral contract: by refusing to remain faithful to the
engagements he has undertaken, the religious violates the
strict right he had given to the Community over himself, and
by withdrawing himself, he is more culpable than a thief
who steals material goods; generally, there is sin against the
vows of poverty and chastity, either because the religious
has decided not to take them into consideration, or because,
through his imprudence, he has made it difficult to practice
them; a sin of scandal, either for the Community, or for people in the world."

Though they have actually thrown off the yoke of the religious life, these fugitives are none the less bound, in the
eyes of God, to keep their vows and the Rule, and to return
to the fold, there to do penance, and suffer the penalties they
have earned.[7]

Meanwhile, the fugitive religious is deprived of all office
in his Congregation.[8] As for the apostate, he immediately incurs excommunication, is deprived of the Sacraments, of all
the privileges and spiritual favors granted to his Institute
and of ecclesiastical burial, if he dies unreconciled. When he
returns to his convent, he is forever deprived of an active and
passive vote.

Again, the religious is guilty of infidelity, who having
made temporary or perpetual vows, forces his Congregation
to expel him for manifest and scandalous offenses, formal
disobedience, open rebellion, grave violation of his vows,
open contempt for all the rules, for his bad spirit, for causing

---

[6] Codex Canon 644. Apostasy from religious life must not be confused with apostasy from the faith.

[7] Codex Canon 645.

[8] Codex Canon 2386.

disturbance and disorders, for resentment of all correction. He is a gangrenous limb, and must be amputated, lest the contagion spread through the whole body. But the most common form of infidelity consists in unjustified request for secularization. Those who, for false or clearly insufficient motives, obtain dispensation from their vows, fail to keep their promises to God and the Institute. The weight of the Rule, the sacrifices and renouncements inherent in a state of poverty and obedience; clashes and misunderstandings with the authority, weariness with common life, disgust of the vocation, failure in the apostolate, sickness and infirmity, change of province or country; dispersal, in time of persecution: none of these can be used, as pretexts for leaving one's Congregation, and returning to the world. Even if the dispensation were valid, none the less, on the part of the subject, it would be illicit and gravely culpable.

Chapter XXIV

THE SECRET OF PERSEVERANCE

STABILITY in the vocation is, with regard to God and the Institute in which one is professed, a duty of obedience and love, loyalty and justice that none can violate, except for grave reasons, without betraying one's conscience and exposing oneself to the worst moral catastrophes.

Therefore, each religious must make use of prudence and fortitude to insure his perseverance. He is planted in the rich earth of the religious state, and he must become so firmly rooted in it that nothing can tear him away.

There are many ex-religious nowadays. Some under the assault of discouragement or diabolical illusions, lose their vocations in the novitiate. Others, young professed, desert during the first years of their religious lives: disconcerted by the difficulties and sacrifices that they had not imagined, the victims of passions that were somnolent, but not tamed; or else recaptured, when about their exterior apostolate, by the corrupting spirit of the world. We even come across veterans who, after thirty years or more of profession, turn back and throw away their habit.

Temptation against perseverance is not an extraordinary phenomenon of the spiritual life. "Son, when thou comest to the service of God, stand in justice and fear: and prepare thy soul for temptation." Many religious undergo this trial at one time or another. Happy are those who are victorious. For this purpose, it is necessary to remove everything that is likely to weaken fidelity, and at the same time, to bring into play all the moral forces that can strengthen it.

~

Passion, some defect, and tepidity: such are the usual causes of infidelity. It is very necessary to be forearmed against these destructive powers.

At the source of certain desertions is to be found the sudden and tempestuous awakening of a passion; a violent outbreak that could not be foreseen, any more than one can see beforehand the branch that will be snapped, and carried away by the tempest. The religious has been the victim of a crisis: a crisis of pride, independence or sensuality.

The religious life sometimes holds in reserve, crushing humiliations: talents unrecognized and hidden under a bushel, a reputation compromised by odious suspicions, even infamous calumnies, the unjust deprivation of a distinguished office. A saint would find here a unique opportunity for rising above himself, after the example of Christ covered with opprobrium, in his self-abasement and humiliation. But it also happens that pride, like the scotched viper, raises its head, bursts out in indignant protest, demands justice, and if rehabilitation is refused, brings about egress from the Order.

The spirit of independence, the habit of imposing one's own views on the authority, of organizing one's apostolate to suit oneself, is another danger to perseverance. Let an unexpected order come, which seems to make nonsense of our plans, and put our life out of joint; let the necessity arise of uprooting oneself from well-loved and fruitful works, to which one had consecrated the best years of one's life and the greater part of one's strength, in order to set off and break new stony ground; it is often enough to cause a revolt and a complete break. "I have always noticed," said Mlle. Legras to St. Vincent de Paul, "that this is very true, and that all those who have left the company have only done so, through attachment to their own will."

Again, sensuality of the flesh or the heart is the explanation of many a lapse: serious faults that dishonor the subject and compromise the reputation of the Order; dangerous, or even sinful relationships, countless acts of imprudence. Friendships are formed that have the head of a dove, but a serpent's tail; caught in the snare, the heart cannot free itself. Less serious, but sometimes more dangerous is exaggerated and too human a love of one's parents. Under the false pretext of consoling and helping them, Christ is sacrificed to the family, and the word of the Gospel is proved: "He that loveth father or mother more than me is not worthy of me."

In order to anticipate these crises and overcome them, the best weapons are prayer, true humility, a great spirit of obedience, prudence toward the world, austerity and watch over the heart. Anemic virtue is ever in peril.

Far from suppressing nature, grace relies upon it, while perfecting it. Certain souls, rich in natural gifts, early prove themselves to be exceptionally apt for a superior vocation, whereas others, affected by congenital vice or moral deformation, offer the religious virtues, a thin and barren soil. Such are defects of temperament or character which form obstacles of fidelity.

"The first natural guarantee of perseverance must be sought in the character of the subjects. Peaceable temperaments, well-balanced, docile and modest intellects, naturally constant wills, which are not obstinate, but are guided by reason, devoted and generous hearts, open and upright souls, people with simple and lowly tastes, indifferent to worldly vanities, are all inclined by nature to perseverance. On the other hand, melancholy and happy-go-lucky temperaments, ambitious and pretentious individuals, intellects without order and judgment, self-satisfied and unruly, light and inconstant men, enslaved by their impressions, always swayed by sentiment or passion, tender or sensitive hearts, egotistical and calculating men, introverts or hyprocrites . . . all bear in them the natural enemy of their vocation, against which they must be on their guard,"[1] from the first years of their religious formation.

But of all the causes of defection, inveterate tepidity is the most usual. Those subjects are almost non-existent, who leave their Institute in full spiritual fervor. He who lives his religious life integrally and generously, carefully observing his vows and rule, humble, pious, recollected, charitable, the true friend of Jesus, he possesses incontestably one of the surest guarantees of fidelity. On the other hand, the commonplace religious, who is without delicacy of conscience and solid virtues, lacking fervor, and interior spirit, the slave of his egotism; he is in grave peril.

There is nothing so gloomy and sad, as a life of tepidity: fatally, divine consolation is unknown, clashes with the authority and disunion with the brethren frequent, common life intolerable; the soul grows embittered, obstinate and irritable, esteem for the vocation and love of the Order turn to disgust, one feels a stranger in the family. . . . Then the idea of a change arises. Repelled at first, the thought returns, takes root, one is haunted by it, grows used to it, toys with it. . . . Is one in the right place; would one not be better in the world? It is a temptation that daily disappointments and the devil's astuteness only aggravate, and which, in the end, one can no longer resist.

Avoid tepidity: such was the advice St. Alphonsus never wearied of giving his Congregation: "I urge you to avoid deliberate faults, especially those for which you have been reproved. When one mends one's ways after correction, no harm is done; but when one neglects to improve, the devil makes use of it to cause the loss of the vocation. By this means he has brought about the loss of so many." Happy in his vocation, in the service of God and of souls, at peace with

[1] Desurmont. Rapports de la Règle.

his conscience, his superiors and brethren, the perfect religious does not entertain the thought, still less the desire of returning to a world he has left, which he has never regretted, and in which he would lose, and well he knows it, his happiness, the hope of sanctification, and the assurance of his salvation.

~

Besides taking these preventive measures against the danger of infidelity, the religious who is concerned for his perseverance will also resort to prayer, frankness, and filial love of his Institute.

Fidelity in the vocation is a capital grace which is very closely linked with the gift of final perseverance. Both are infallibly obtained by prayer. Qui petit, accipit. But we must be wise enough to pray for it, to our last hour, with deep humility and unshakable confidence. The divine power alone can make good the weakness and inconstancy, that are inherent to the human will. A saintly Cistercian nun was slowly dying at the age of 70 of a cancerous condition, a victim of reparation. To the priest who came to hear her confession, her last words, as he took his leave, were always the same: "Ah, Father, pray hard, pray for my perseverance!" Every day, at meditation, at Communion, let us repeat after the Prophet! "One thing I have asked of the Lord, this will I seek after; that I may dwell in the house of the Lord all the days of my life."

St. Alphonsus insisted on this point. "Therefore, I urge each one of you to ask specially, every day, for the grace of perseverance in the vocation; for lack of so doing, many have lost it. Let us ever tremble and pray; he who does not tremble and pray continually, cannot persevere. Do not count on any sensible fervor; for when some ugly tempest rises, all our resolutions flee, and unless God helps us, we are lost. Support yourselves always with prayer, and ask the Lord without ceasing that He grant you to die in the Congregation." A filial devotion to Our Lady and the habit of invoking her in the hour of peril are together one of the best guarantees of perseverance. How many religious owe it to her that they have made a holy death in their vocation! Among others, we have Father de Meo, a disciple of St. Alphonsus, and very devoted to Our Lady. During his Novitiate, overcome by temptation, he was running away secretly, and passed by a painting of the Virgin, in a corridor of the convent of Ciorani. Out of habit, he stopped, knelt, and for a farewell, said his last Ave. He had scarcely finished, when he heard a voice. "Unhappy youth! Where are you going? If you leave the Congregation, you are lost and damned!" Terrified, he turned back, and eventually, became one of the pillars of the Institute. After seeking the help of God, we must rest upon the wisdom and goodness of the representatives of God. Superiors, confessors, director. Openness of heart, the daughter of humility, is of major importance in this respect. Temptation against the vocation; as we have already said, is often accompanied by strange illusions. To rekindle light in the mind, and peace in the heart, it is often enough to hear a word of friendship, sympathy or encouragement. Though the authorities are forbidden to probe the consciences of their subjects, the latter are none the less permitted, and even recommended, to have recourse to the prudence and charity of the superiors. Or else they may speak to their confessor or spiritual director. Spiritual direction, which is useful at all times, is necessary under certain painful circumstances. Nothing is more dangerous than a policy of silence. To refuse to speak is to be lost. "The second remedy, which is equally essential and necessary in similar temptations, is to communicate what one is feeling to one's superiors or one's spiritual Father without delay, before the temptation has got a hold. . . . In these cases, one must do oneself violence and reveal oneself completely to the superiors; for then God will be so pleased with this act of humility and the effort one has made, that immediately, by a ray of light, He

will disperse all the darkness and doubts that filled the soul."[2]
One last strong buttress is the total and never-regretted gift
of oneself to one's religious family, love of the Institute, esteem for its spirit, devotion to its works, reverence for its
founder. Love is a chain, "vinculum," that nothing can break.
How could one abandon a mother, though she be infirm and
sick—and the Congregation, in which one was born to the
religious life, is a Mother—if one loves her dearly? How
could one give the slip to brethren with whom one forms one
heart and one soul, in the service of the same Lord, and for
the conquest of one same ideal?

But as soon as fraternity gives way to individualism and
indifference, when feelings of affection are changed to antipathy and hidden irritation; who can tell if one is not, all
unawares, taking the first steps along the path of infidelity.
It is so difficult to stay for long in a place, whence one's heart
and one's happiness have fled.

A beautiful prayer of St. Alphonsus for perseverance will
provide a fitting close to this chapter.

"My God, how can I ever worthily return thanks to Thee
for having so lovingly called me to the bosom of Thy Family? And what claim had I to such a favor, after all the offenses I had committed against Thee? How many of my
companions have remained in the world, amid so many opportunities and dangers of being lost, whereas I have been
admitted to live in Thy house, among Thy privileged servants, in the abundance of means of sanctification. I hope,
Lord, better to express my gratitude in Heaven, by proclaiming eternally Thy mercies unto me. Meanwhile, I am Thine,
and wish to be Thine forever. I have made to Thee the gift
of myself; I renew it at this moment. I am resolved to be
faithful to Thee, never to abandon Thee, were it to cost me
my life a thousand times over. Here I am; I devote myself
entirely to carrying out Thy Divine Will, without any reserve; do with me what Thou wilt. Make me live as Thou

[2] St. Alphonsus, *op cit.*, Vol. III.

wilt, in desolation, sickness and contumely; treat me according to Thy will; it is enough for me to obey and please Thee. I ask nothing of Thee, but the grace to love Thee with all my heart, and to be faithful to Thee until death."

"O Mary, my tender Mother! Thou hast obtained from God all the graces that I have received, the forgiveness of my sins, my vocation and the strength to follow it; it is for thee to complete thy work, by obtaining for me perseverance until death. This is my hope. Amen."

Chapter XXV

COST WHAT IT MAY

THE RELIGIOUS owes it to himself to persevere in his vocation until death, cost what it may. A duty of religion with regard to God, and of justice with regard to the Institute, fidelity is, moreover, a matter of prudence and personal charity. This is yet another motive for standing by one's promises and never leaving the service of God.

Infidelity is not merely a grave fault that may subsequently be regretted like so many others, and effaced by penance. It is a precipitous fall, with terrible and often irreparable consequences. A whole life can be shaken to its foundations, or even crumble to ruins.

It is always extremely imprudent, even disastrous, to leave one's Order and expose oneself to every danger, perhaps to eternal catastrophe. How wise are they who avoid these dreadful contingencies at any cost!

Fidelity is a great grace and an abundant source of divine blessing. Those who love themselves in the right spirit, and have a proper concern for their temporal and eternal happiness, will beware of turning aside, and losing their way.

If we point out these dangers and blessings, it is in the hope of providing an encouragement to perseverance, upon which it is good to ponder.

~

The Founders of Orders, enlightened by God and taught by experience, have often recalled the lamentable results of lost vocations. But have their convictions on this matter passed into the souls of their subjects, and is this salutary fear of an ever possible defection always to be found in the hearts of religious? It is a question that needs to be asked, nowadays especially, when we see how glibly—and apparently without a shadow of remorse—some demand to be dispensed from their vows and return to the world. Are such people really aware that they are imperiling their life and their eternity?

A wasted life, an uncertain death, a severe judgment, danger of hell: such is the gloomy outlook of a soul that is unfaithful to its vows.

The ex-religious is, in the full force of the term, a fish out of water. Uprooted from rich earth, in which he barely kept alive, how could he bear blossom and fruit in the desert of the world? The life of a fugitive from the cloister is usually full of sorrow and remorse, rendered sterile, in part at least, from the point of view of virtue and apostolate.

Happiness and peace are only to be found within the will of God. Now, the soul that neglects his vocation has deliberately and finally cut himself off from that holy will, and is forced thence forward and forever to remain where he should not be, and to do what he should not be doing. Only to faithful religious can Jesus' words be applied: "Take up my yoke upon you . . . and you shall find rest for your souls. For my yoke is sweet, and my burden light."

"My Daughters," said St. Vincent de Paul one day—and as he spoke, his voice shook and tears filled his eyes—"my daughters, when you hear that a Sister has left, slighting the graces she has received from God, do not be dismayed; weep for her loss, mourn the deplorable state in which she will find herself, and be yourselves strengthened by this example."

A few months after leaving the monastery, a young religious wrote to his former superior: "What am I to do now? I am unhappy and harried by remorse, like all those who leave the religious life. The life, of which I dreamed during my temptations against the vocation, brings me no consolation, and I find it so contemptible! . . . Ah! if you only knew how unhappy I am . . . ! All day long I suffer from my unfaithfulness . . . I don't know where to turn . . . I pray a great deal . . . but prayer brings me no relief . . . May God and Our Blessed Lady forgive my infidelity! That is all I ask: the rest is lost."

How many admissions such as this, all of them infinitely sad, could be brought forward! In such a state of soul, how could one effect a serious work of sanctification? If, while a religious enjoying exceptional graces, encouraged by the example of colleagues and the exhortations of superiors, one has only managed to lead a mediocre and tepid life, it would be a marvel if, on one's return to the world, with fewer graces, more serious temptations and numerous obstacles, one expected to serve God with greater fervor and generosity.

This mediocrity is found again in the apostolate, which also suffers from decay. Indeed God cannot give the same blessing and fruitfulness to an activity, that takes place outside the plans of His Providence: working as a free lance, the apostle can no longer draw upon the store of merits accumulated by his Institute, for he is no longer supported by his brethren and the esprit de corps, which could make up for his own deficiencies and shortcomings. "No man putting his hand to the plow, and looking back, is fit for the kingdom of God." Does not "bankruptcy in the vocation" involve bankruptcy in the spiritual and apostolic field?

What sort of death awaits all these deserters? A bad death? Maybe! In any case, a death full of anguish, when they stand on the brink of eternity! What will they answer to Our Lord, when He bids them render account of the immense gift of their vocation, of the religious duties that they have so often forgotten or violated, of the innumerable, priceless graces that they have profaned, and finally, of their desertion and betrayal? What will be the sentence of the Supreme Judge?

In a circular, St. Alphonsus described to his sons the end of one of his religious, who had left the Institute. "For several years, I have been doing my best to instill some courage into one of these unfortunates, who had lost his head at the thought that he had thrown away his vocation; he was frantic; he said that he despaired of his salvation, because he had willfully renounced his vocation." And the saint added: "The sorry fate of those who are reduced to this dreadful state must give us courage to endure everything, in order not to lose our vocation." And what will be the eternal destiny of these souls? Doubtless many will be saved, but, as St. Paul says "so as by fire." None can say what Purgatory awaits them after death! In any case, more than one will become, in Hell, the victim of his infidelity. The loss of the vocation, in the opinion of the saints, is an immense danger to salvation, and this thought alone should suffice, in time of temptation, to strengthen the religious in his unshakable resolution. Saint Alphonsus wrote to certain troublesome Brothers of the monastery of Illiceto: "If you force me to expel you from the Congregation, I do not know what will become of you; in any case, I shall fear terribly for your eternal salvation." St. Benedict, usually so discreet, issues the same threat: "Let him who is to be received, make before all in the Oratory, a promise of STABILITY, CONVERSION OF LIFE and OBEDIENCE, in the presence of God and His Saints, so that, if he should ever act otherwise, he may know that he will be condemned by Him Whom he mocketh."[1]

Who would be so foolhardy as to risk his eternal salvation? It is surely better to suffer and die in harness.

~

If fear must preserve the religious from infidelity, his sentiments of fidelity should be strengthened by hope. What immense and eternal advantages are reserved by God for perseverance! "These are some of the principal blessings by which the sacrifice of those who persevere faithfully is rewarded:—the special protection of the Most Blessed Virgin in all temptations and dangers, together with her watchful

[1] Rule of St. Benedict, Ch. LVII.

care over us, in all the vicissitudes of this life; preservation from mortal sin; an increase of strength and interior lights; that peace of heart and tranquillity of mind, which surpasses all understanding, which the world cannot give; a happy death; and finally, when the journey through life shall come to its close, that particular glory and aureola, in store for those faithful servants who, beyond the common debt of duty, shall have devoted themselves entirely to the divine service."[2]

Half a century, more perhaps, consecrated exclusively to the service of God, to the pursuit of perfection; to the daily practice of poverty, chastity and obedience, humility and abnegation, fifty years brimming with fervent prayer and meditation; hidden sacrifice, unselfish devotion; overflowing with love of God and our neighbor: what must such a record represent, in terms of virtue, holiness and merits? It is a wonderfully full life, in which every day has been put to the fullest use; in which not an hour has been wasted or marred; in which every fault due to our weakness had been immediately expiated, and compensated by a renewal of fervor. The harvest is great indeed, rippling as far as the eye can see, and every golden ear, heavy with grain, has ripened beneath the vivifying rays of grace. The earth is rich and has yielded a hundredfold.

The yield is no less excellent, from the angle of the apostolate. If it be true that "every soul that rises bears up the world along with it," how fruitful must be the religious life which is nothing else but a striving for perfection, and an ascension toward God! Prayers, sacrifice, the vows, observance of the Rule: what wonderful tools for the apostolate! How many souls have been saved, thanks to those unknown apostles, the lay brothers and sisters! "Going, they went and wept, casting their seeds. But coming, they shall come with joyfulness, carrying their sheaves."

[2] Novices Rule, C.S.S.R.

Wherever he may reside, whatever be his talents, or the obscurity of his office, the religious always shares in the labors and conquests of his Institute, and is, through the radiation of his personal sanctity, one of the best collaborators of Jesus Christ in the work of Redemption. "God has chosen us to be the co-adjutors of his Son and to snatch souls from the clutches of the demon. . . . What a consolation, at the hour of death, for a member of the Congregation, to see beside his bed the countless souls, who will say to him with jubilation: 'Opera tua sumus! We are your work!' "

Yes, what a joy it is to die in one's Institute, surrounded by one's brethren clothed in one's religious habit! And why should one fear death? Has one not desired, sought, and loved Christ, all one's life? Has one not toiled, labored and suffered for Him? Then how can one fear His coming? For a perfect religious, death is a deliverance and a triumph. During his agony, an old Father of the desert said to himself: "Why dost thou fear, my soul, to go forth? For nigh seventy years, thou hast served Christ, and dost thou dread to appear before him?"

Beati mortui qui in Domino moriuntur. "Who are those blessed dead who die in the Lord, if not the religious who, at the end of their lives, are already dead to the world since they cut themselves off from the world, and all its goods, when they made their vows." . . . Honorius II at the point of death, regretted that he had not remained in his monastery, washing the humble crocks of the monks, and that he had been called to the Papacy. Philip II of Spain, on his deathbed, wished that he could have been a simple lay brother, serving God in some religious house, instead of a king. . . . Another religious of the same Company (of Jesus), seeing his last moments at hand, began to laugh with all his heart. When he was asked the cause of his merriment, he replied: "Why should I not laugh? Has not Jesus Christ promised Paradise to those who give up all things for love?

I have abandoned all for God; now, God is faithful, He cannot break His promises. Then how could I not be joyful, how could I not laugh, since I am sure of Paradise?"

Indeed, is not assurance of Heaven the supreme grace granted to fidelity? To die as a religious is one of the surest pledges of predestination: Founders, theologians and ascetics have never wearied of recalling and commenting the promise of Our Lord: et vitam aeternam possidebit.

"Consider firstly, that according to St. Bernard, it is easy for a religious to be saved, and rare that one is damned, if one dies in religion: Facilis via de cella ad coelum, vix unquam aliquis a cella in infernum descendit. The reason given by the Saint in support of this opinion is that it is difficult for a religious to persevere until death, unless he is numbered among the elect. Quia vix unquam nisi coelo praedestinatus in ea usque ad mortem perstitit. This is why St. Lawrence Justinian called the religious state the gate of Paradise: illius coelestis civitatis iste est introitus. And he concluded that it is for religious a great sign of their predestination: Magnum quippe electionis indicium est."

In the words of the Sovereign Pontiff Pius XI: "In the religious life, one progresses so surely and easily on the path of perfection, that one would have seemed already to have dropped anchor in the harbor of salvation."[3] Thus it is to the religious who is faithful to his promises, that the words of the Gospel apply, in a very special manner: "But he that shall persevere unto the end, he shall be saved."

[3] Acta. Ap. S. 1st April, 1924.